CONSUMPTION AND AMERICAN CULTURE

To Eric Mottram

Best wishes

David Nye

Previously published in this series:

* These volumes have been produced for the European Association for American
Studies (E.A.A.S.)
Copies can be ordered from your bookseller or the publisher:
VU University Press, De Boelelaan 1105, 1081 HV Amsterdam, The Netherlands

CONSUMPTION AND AMERICAN CULTURE

edited by

David E. Nye
Carl Pedersen

with contributions from

Niels Thorsen
Roland Marchand
David E. Nye
Stig Hjarvand
Barry Shank
Sharon Thomas
Nina Roth
Lis Møller
William J. Clark
Alan Shima
Eric Sandeen
Richard Thomas
Gertrude Øllgaard
Carl Pedersen
Harvard Sitkoff
Helle Porsdam
Rob Kroes

VU UNIVERSITY PRESS
AMSTERDAM 1991

EUROPEAN CONTRIBUTIONS TO AMERICAN STUDIES

This series is published for the Netherlands American Studies Association - N.A.S.A.,
and the European Association for American Studies - E.A.A.S.

General Editor
Rob Kroes, Amerika Instituut, Jodenbreestraat 9
1011 NG Amsterdam

On behalf of the Scandinavian American Studies Association and the Netherlands American Studies Association, the editors gratefully acknowledge that the
publication of this book has been made possible by the generous support of the
following institutions and organizations:

Danish Research Academy
Danish-American Fulbright Commission
University of Copenhagen
Roskilde University Center

VU University Press is an imprint of:
VU Boekhandel/Uitgeverij bv
De Boelelaan 1105
1081 HV Amsterdam
The Netherlands

tel. (020) - 6 44 43 55
fax (020) - 6 46 27 19

isbn 90-6256-960-9
nugi 651

lay-out by Ansy Jensen
cover design by DP Plus, Amsterdam
printed by offsetdrukkerij Haveka b.v., Alblasserdam

Contents

Introduction:
Consumption and American Culture

A Danish manor house proved to be the ideal site for an international conference on "Consumption and American Culture." Sandbjerg was secluded; its food was excellent; and the location was the antithesis of our theme. For Sandbjerg was built before the American Revolution, before the industrial revolution, before the culture of consumption. While the manor functions within that culture today—as a conference center for the leisure of the theory class—the building and its grounds are a constant reminder of an organization of life quite unlike that we set out to examine. Its architecture and rural setting recalled a rural, agricultural society dominated by local nobility, and it served as a sharp contrast to our scholarly concern with cultural transformations since the 1850s. Sandbjerg is at a comfortable remove, inviting visitors to contemplate the difference between it and our everyday world.

The reader of Washington Irving's "The Legend of Sleepy Hollow" is likewise invited to escape into a pre-capitalist pastoral landscape created by the Dutch. Sleepy Hollow is an idyllic America of self-sufficient farmers, which Irving already 175 years ago described as a lost world that had disappeared before the onslaught of Yankee culture. Icabod Crane, the Connecticut schoolmaster, loves Katrina Van Tassel on these terms: "his heart yearned after the damsel who was to inherit these domains, and his imagination expanded with the idea, how they might be readily turned into cash, and the money invested in immense tracts of wild land, and shingle palaces in the wilderness."[1] In these few lines, Irving suggested the effects of capitalism on the American imagination. Katrina's value to Icabod lies not in her self, but in her equivalence to the "fat meadow-lands" and "rich fields" she will inherit. Her property, in turn, is of no intrinsic value or use to Icabod, who wants to transform it into cash, and then transform that cash into "immense tracts of wild land," that he can later sell at a profit. Irving's Yankee wants to engage in a perpetual game of substitution and reinvestment. He understands the world much as Jean Baudrillard suggests our contemporaries do: "everything. . .is immediately produced as sign and exchange value."[2] Icabod is a precursor to our present culture of consumption, and just as importantly, Irving's ironic distance from this character and his preference for the settled Dutch farmers is a recurrent attitude in American letters. Long before the advent of national markets, world fairs, advertising, public relations, or the mass media, some Americans were skeptical about consumption.

If Irving early charted one literary escape route from Trade into Sleepy Hollow, James Fenimore Cooper found a variant form of withdrawal. Beyond the "shingle palaces" of land speculators lay the realm he imagined as an escape from the marketplace, the West of Natty BumpPo and his fictional offspring. In short, one can find an anti-materialist bias in much of American

1

literature, stemming from Puritan sources—as early as the popular apocalyptic poem "The Day of Doom"—and continuing without a break into the present. This anti-materialism was responding to its opposite, of course. Since the settlement of Virginia in 1603 many have spoken of America in terms of abundance and quick profits. Hyperbolic tracts advertised the New World as a storehouse of wealth or as a virgin continent awaiting exploitation. Recent feminist critics have shown us that these readings of the landscape were patriarchal, but we must also remember that the image of America as raw material awaiting use was not universally acceded to. Just as Irving ironized over Icabod Crane, Henry David Thoreau's first essay was entitled "The Commercial Spirit," and attacked "the blind and unmanly love of wealth" in terms that could easily be applied to the Reagan years of capital accumulation on Wall Street. Yet after calling the businessman a "slave of avarice," Thoreau asserted that even "the most selfish worshipper of Mammon, is toiling and calculating to some other purpose than the mere acquisition of the good things of this world; he is preparing, gradually and unconsciously it may be, to lead a more intellectual and spiritual life." The young Thoreau concluded "that man will not always be the slave of matter...."[3] Today, how many attacks on materialism take his hopeful tone? Indeed, Thoreau himself appears as a potential sweepstakes winner in an ironic poem by Donald Kummings: "Yes, MR. HENRY DAVID THOREAU, you *already* may have won/ the grand prize/ in this year's *Reader's Digest* Sweepstakes."

In "The Young American," Ralph Waldo Emerson wrote:

> Trade.... is a very intellectual force. This displaces physical strength, and installs computation, combination, information, science, in its room.... Trade goes to make the governments insignificant, and to bring every kind of faculty of every individual that can in any manner serve any person, *on sale.* [Trade] ... converts Government into an Intelligence-Office, where every man may find what he wishes to buy, and expose what he has to sell; not only produce and manufactures, but art, skill, and intellectual and moral values. This is the good and this the evil of trade, that it would put everything into market: talent, beauty, virtue, and man himself.[4]

Emerson seems to be making a devastating critique of capitalism, but he goes serenely on to claim that trade fosters liberty, destroys feudalism, keeps the peace, and will help to abolish slavery.

Emerson was analyzing an economic system far different from that of the 1990s. Nineteenth-century authors realized that everything could be put up for sale, but they could not know how completely the marketplace itself would change. It is not merely that many of the goods sold today did not exist in 1840. The marketplace's dimensions have enlarged so much that we seldom engage in face-to-face dealings with those who produce what we buy. As Raymond Williams points out, the word "customer" familiar to Emerson has declined in usage in favor of "consumer;" "customer had always implied some degree of regular and continuing relationship to a supplier, whereas consumer indicates the more abstract figure in a more abstract market."5 In this more abstract market people are less rooted; they belong less to social classes than to what Daniel Boorstin calls "consumption communities."6

Not only are today's consumer and market more abstract, but much of the population works in the service sector, producing things that are intangible, invisible, or arbitrarily valued: including art, service, prestige, education, advice, security, information, protection, psychoanalysis, advertising, and public relations. Even the trade in material things is mediated by electronic impulses centered in banks and exchanges, and we who live in the resulting "culture of consumption" often feel that we exchange only symbols and never touch any tangible object. Advertising, the code of representation that has developed in tandem with this economic system, likewise seems disconnected from the world and often appears to function as an autonomous discourse of images.

Yet tempting as it may be to assume that the experience of late twentieth century life is completely unlike that of the late eighteenth century, Niels Thorsen's introductory paper reminds us that Adam Smith wrote not only *The Wealth of Nations* but also "worked out a theory of consumption, including a highly elaborate theory of the consumer" in *The Theory of Moral Sentiment,* which he published in 1759. Thorsen argues that, "Time and again Smith makes the observation that the demand for consumption is not rooted in utility, but in the need for social attention." Smith's views should be kept in mind when reading the following four essays, which treat communication forms that must be accounted for by any theory of consumption. Roland Marchand probes industrial exhibits at world fairs; David Nye considers photography as a form of discourse; Stig Hjarvand examines the Americanization of European television news, and Barry Shank analyzes rock music in Austin. All four authors explore conflicts between the systems of representation favored by the marketplace and the alternative aesthetics favored by insiders. Sharon Thomas examines the position of another kind of insider, the teacher, with regard to both the debate over "cultural literacy" and contemporary conflicts over teaching methods in American schools. Utilitarian values of the marketplace also come into conflict with other values in Nina Roth's examination of *Commentary Magazine*'s self-contradictory project: defending the traditional family while espousing the *laissez-faire* doctrines that draw women into the marketplace.

The literary consequences of a culture of consumption necessarily include the writer's construction of the text, a topic taken up in three essays. Lis Møller describes Emily Dickinson's free appropriation of a wide variety of sources, presenting her as neither a solitary originator nor as a devotee of canonical works, but rather as a reader who used both popular and literary works for her own art. William Clark assesses how the novelist Frank Norris sought literary forms that could contain his experience of monopoly capitalism, and Alan Shima examines the form of the feminist post-modernist text as part of the morphology of late capitalist society. If the culture of consumption plays a central role in the production of literature, it plays no less a role in social geography. Eric Sandeen writes on the battle between developers and traditionalists over a symbolic site, New York City's Times Square, while Gertrude Øllgaard investigates the tensions and pleasures created by the incorporation of modern technologies into the social construction of the home.

Is anyone outside the apparently ubiquitous culture of consumption? Richard Thomas bears witness to the resistance of many contemporary poets — including himself — to the forms of commodification. And what of African-Americans? By exploring the work of Frederick Douglass and Booker T. Washington, Carl Pedersen confronts the ambivalence of black leaders toward Northern commerical culture in the nineteenth century, and their strategies of resistance to it. Harvard Sitkoff assesses the gains and losses for blacks since the end of the second reconstruction of the 1960s.

Finally, the issues raised by the culture of consumption intertwine with the long-standing debate about America and Europe. Helle Porsdam and Rob Kroes examine how cultural and literary critics have contrasted the two continents, at times using terms drawn from the culture of consumption. Thus we end by taking a long view of our subject, examining texts from Henry James to Umberto Eco, and meditating on the contrasts between America and Europe— a contrast that Sandbjerg itself implied.

David E. Nye and Carl Pedersen

References

1. Washington Irving, "The Legend of Sleepy Hollow," *The Sketchbook of Geoffrey Crayon, Gent.,* in *The Complete Works of Washington Irving,* Richard Dilworth Rust, ed. Boston: Twayne, 1978, p. 280.
2. Jean Baudrillard, "The Ideological Genesis of Needs;" in *For a Critique of the Political Economy of the Sign.* St. Louis, Telos Press, 1974, p . 87.
3. Joseph J. Moldenhaur and Edwin Moser (eds.), Henry David Thoreau, "The Commercial Spirit," in *Early Essays and Miscellanies.* Princeton: Princeton University Press, 1975, pp. 117-118.
4. Ralph Waldo Emerson, "The Young American," *Nature, Addresses, and Lectures.* Boston: Houghton-Mifflin, 1903, pp. 377-378.
5. Raymond Williams, "Consumer" in *Keywords.* New York: Oxford University Press, 1976, p. 69.
6. Daniel Boorstin, *The Americans: The Democratic Experience.* New York: Vintage, 1973, pp. 89-164.

Two Versions of Human Need:
The Traditional and the Modern Understanding of Consumption

Niels Thorsen
Copenhagen University

In recent years the concept of consumption has assumed a prominent place not only among economists, businessmen, and politicians, but also among historians, sociologists, and anthropologists. What is implied in this notion? What kind of world view does it entail? The notion of consumption refers to goods of one kind or another that are used up in order to satisfy human want. It is generally assumed that the Scottish philosopher Adam Smith was the primary author who first sketched the system of modern consumption enclosed in the mode of production. Adam Smith was also one of the significant theorists to teach the first generation of independent Americans how to think in terms of an economy.[1] His most well-known work, *The Wealth of Nations,* was first published in 1776. To gain a better grasp of Adam Smith's contribution it may perhaps be useful to present a contrasting view in which the practices associated with the act of consuming are placed in a traditional context.

An ancient story which played a significant role in the western idea of collective sustenance is related in Exodus, Chapter 16:

> And they took their journey from Elim ...and came unto the wilderness of Sin. ... And the whole congregation ... murmured against Moses and Aaron in the wilderness: ... Would to God we had died by the hand of the LORD in the land of Egypt, when we sat by the fleshpots, and when we did eat bread to the full: for ye have brought us forth into this wilderness, to kill this whole assembly with hunger. Then said the LORD unto Moses, Behold, I will rain bread from heaven for you. ... And when the dew that lay was gone up, behold, upon the face of the wilderness there lay a small round thing, as small as the hoar frost on the ground.... And Moses said unto them, This is the bread which the LORD hath given you to eat. ... Gather of it every man according to his eating, ... according to the number of your persons. ... Let no man leave of it till the morning.

> Notwithstanding they hearkened not unto Moses; but some of them left of it until the morning, and it bred worms, and stank: and Moses was wroth

with them. ... And the children of Israel did eat manna forty years.

The story of wandering in the desert recounts how the congregation of Israel was empowered with their sustenance. It is a story of how the people chose to acknowledge their destiny as inheritors of the land of Canaan. The story of the manna is a counterpart to the story of Esau and Jacob which relates how an individual sold his birthright for a meal of pottage.[2] In both cases material needs are used metaphorically to reconstitute the human condition. At the outset hunger—which signifies necessity and man's dependence upon the powers that provide his sustenance—is distinguished from the order of the covenant with Jehovah, a covenant which involved the believer in an elaborate scheme of rules and proscribed behavior at a distance from the dictates of natural reason. As the story unfolds, material needs are incorporated into the covenant and into a way of thinking and talking about collective livelihood. Thus, the story depicts an understanding of human needs that contrasts with modern ways of thinking such as those associated with the "laws" and the "necessities" that are said to govern the "economic system."

The Biblical story relates how collective identity was foreordained and enacted through material processes that satisfy basic needs. Material needs are, to use Karl Polanyi's term, embedded in the political, i.e. in common forms of life. The satisfaction of these needs is understood to incorporate elements of family, cult, and community.[3] The first feature of the story is that hunger is relieved by what looks like a direct intervention of divine power. But the second feature, which evolves around themes of austerity, temptation, limits, and sharing. is of equal importance. Not only is the congregation admonished to take only for the day, each "for them which are in his tents," but the measurement of the "omer" is instituted. It comes about that although some were able to gather more, and others less, when the result was meted out, "he that gathered much had nothing over, and he that gathered little had no lack; they gathered every man according to his eating."

The manna cannot be accumulated, except on the sixth day of the week in order to cover the seventh day designated to rest. The course of the week is itself understood to militate against hoarding. It is an economy of abundance which is constituted with an injunction against unnatural surplus because it ties need to a rhythm of nature ordained by the highest power. Collective livelihood depends upon the understanding and proper consideration of the limits dictated by the rhythm of material procurement and fulfillment of need. The political meaning of this seems to have been that surplus was dangerous to the integrity of the community, because inequality would inevitably result. Inequality signifies a margin of human self-dependence. Thus the admonition to be careful about nourishment comes together with a conception of limits determined by the end. Each individual is explicitly denied the personal power which is stimulated by the ability to project the future in terms of material security. Collective freedom is revealed as a consequence of immediate dependence upon the rhythm of nature.

The myth of the discovery of manna—which, according to modern biologists seem to refer to the excrement produced by some kind of plant louse—reveals a pre–theoretical conception of an economy with some similarities to the economic practices of stone age societies investigated by what the anthropologist Marshall Sahlins calls the "original affluent society."[4] These kinds of societies were affluent, not because they maintained a high level of production, but because they valued various forms of leisure so highly that they consciously promoted what we would call a low standard of living, that is, a standard of living that reflects an immediate dependence upon particular surroundings.

Although we are perhaps likely to describe the story of the manna as a myth, it is not without theoretical implications that bear the mark of power realism. Jehovah was the embodiment of the greatest kind of power conceivable. In addition, the backdrop to the notion of sharing and abundance is hinted at with the reference to Egypt, the "house of bondage". In Egypt material needs were developed and satisfied through a system of exchange of labor for meat and bread with the Egyptian masters. Adopting a distinction made by Sheldon Wolin it could be said that in contrast to the setting in the desert where needs that are *preformed*, the situation in Egypt suggests material freedom—say, consumer sovereignty or consumer communities—where needs are *performed* rather than preformed.[5]

The story calls attention to an obvious fact. While Jehovah was a vengeful god, and while he was surrounded by tales and rituals that stimulated awe and fear, it is also clear that the believers participated in a complex setting where god and man were in contact, even to the extent that necessities and utilities were negotiated and exchanged. The presence of Jehovah meant that life was lived under conditions of a power which took care of the world. This has changed, obviously. Since we live in the presence of powers that have taken over the attributes of older gods, especially the power over the fate of the world which used to be a divine prerogative, the question is, as Max Weber phrased it: What kind of bearing of man is possible, when man has become "disenchanted and denuded of [his] mystical but inwardly genuine plasticity?"[6] Sheldon Wolin has further sharpened the question by pointing out that modern powers—such as capitalism, administration, and science—each build upon a dynamic which is significantly uncommitted to human needs. Capitalism and administration are committed to a logic of expanding their own powers. Science itself appears to be uncommitted to anything—even science itself.[7]

A certain anxiety surrounds the modern discussion of consumption. A secret and not so secret suspicion is that modern consumption contains destructive capacities that are on the same scale of violence as modern weaponry, although perhaps less sudden and less intense. Thus, defoliation caused by industrial policies rather than by hostile attack have come home to roost in Central and in Northern Europe and elsewhere. The Brazilian jungle represents another example of the ruthlessness of modern enterprise. The fear of the Third World has shifted markedly since President Johnson said that the US must defend itself in Vietnam lest the poor of the third world would claim what the rich world had. The fear is now that if the poor world insists on the level of consumption maintained in the Western world a generation ago, the result would be ecological disaster.

These anxieties may be seen as a consequence of the fact that the post–war generation now knows with objective certainty that the modern way of life and established standards of living impose shocking costs upon the common environment. In itself it may be said that there is little new about such costs. Neither ruthless exploitation of scarce resources or the systematic disfigurement of menial labor are new phenomena in the history of any country. What is new, however, is perhaps less the scale of damage than the fact that knowledge about the social and environmental costs of consumption has become common knowledge. This knowledge is no longer created by conservative Cassandras or by pessimists on the left, but comes to us now with all the quantitative precision and authority that surrounds the natural and the social sciences. And this is not a matter of an esoteric science for the selected few. It is a form of information which is presented to the population almost daily in official statistics, often with outstanding pedagogic trimmings. The political significance of this knowledge has to be assessed in the light of the fact that established leaders in business, administration, and politics for more than a full generation have legitimated their decisions on the basis of infinite economic progress. The powers that determine the fate of the world appear to have grown so much larger than both individual and collective life that modern man has lost the capacity for any kind of communion with those powers.

The idea that the power needed to procure the basic means of life was tied to the settled life of the community—its culture, skills, observance of nature and attention to prescribed rounds of life—persisted virtually unchallenged until the middle of the seventeenth century. It was generally perceived that the skills of cultivation and craft rested upon traditions that were tied to communal rituals. Such beliefs would seem confirmed, not when the proceeds of production were divided between lord and peasant or between master and servant, but when tools were passed on from one generation to another or when fields were cultivated on the basis of cooperation. The Biblical conception of a culture of livelihood was of course transmitted through the Catholic church and was elaborated in doctrines about the different competences assigned to the various orders of society.[8] The Catholic church warned against greed; it prohibited usury, and reverted again and again to the notion of the just price.

The first version of insatiable human wants is usually dated to Thomas Hobbes and his notion of felicity. It has been argued that social norms and behavior in England were very different from the European continent. At least from the thirteenth century a majority of ordinary people "were rampant individualists, highly mobile both geographically and socially, economically 'rational,' market–oriented and acquisitive, ego–centered in kinship and social life."9 Thus, Hobbes' description of man in his restless pursuit of power was probably closer to wide pread practices than was earlier supposed. In any event, Hobbes provided a description that was distinctive, because it sought to picture man as fit for a new science of government which proceeded not from from a notion of structures and inherent limitations upon need but upon the ceaseless generation of needs. The new man, Hobbes stipulated, sought the meaning of life in the "continuall progress of the desire from one object to another," rather than in "the repose of the mind."10 This view of man was futher elaborated by John Locke who rewrote it in his conception of property. Private property was developed to the extent that it was expropriated and withdrawn from the world that mankind owned collectively.11

Adam Smith is of special importance to the theme of consumption because he provides a rich expression of the conception of economics that dominated the Founding Fathers when they created the present Constitution of the United States. As it has been argued recently, Adam Smith completely destroyed the idea that property reverts to the community in extreme circumstances and crises. According to him, the poor were always better off when the inequalities of the market for grain was allowed to run its course.12 Adam Smith is now often used as a codeword for the celebration of private property vis–à– vis the government. In fact, Adam Smith wrote in a field which he labelled political economy.

The title of his work, *The Wealth of Nations,* mirrored the notion of political economy.13 It signified that the book attempted to see private property under the heading of public policies. The idea was, roughly speaking, that private enterprise and industry—which was best encouraged with a minimum of governmental intervention—was the prerequisite for modern forms of state power. Adam Smith, in effect, importantly modified the liberal tradition. Whereas Locke had used his notion of property to argue in favor of political equality and used the notion of private rights to restrain governmental authority, Smith argued that private freedom of enterprise was not to be seen as a check, but as a precondition for the expansion of modern state power understood as political economy and manipulated through its form of rationality. Hence, the wealth of *Nations.*

Adam Smith's notion of the state was distinct from traditional notions of the state which relied on a center of power and authority as typically embodied in the royal court or in Parliament. It is hidden in the logic associated with his famous metaphor of the "invisible hand," which is used to make the claim that despite the inclination of the rich to satisfy only their own desires, in fact they come benefit the poor. The rich are "led by an invisible hand to make nearly the same distribution of the necessaries of life, which would have been made, had the earth been divided into equal portions among all its inhabitants."14 The economy and government were to be viewed as distinct rather than separate phenomena. Smith's distinction between the two powers was intended to preserve the dynamic of both and to endow "private" economic matters with national significance. His attack on outdated forms of governmental regulation was intended to liberate the market mechanism, but as Andrew S. Skinner has shown, it was also a matter of preparing for government intervention where the market mechanism undermined the conditions for further economic expansion.[15]

In England the rationality embodied in political economy was proposed for incorporation into a preestablished mode of government. In contrast, the founding fathers across the Atlantic, particularly Alexander Hamilton, hoped to create a new form of government with the help of political economy. Thus, their question was not what government could do for political economy, but what political economy could do for federal government. While Smith introduced the idea of the system of consumption into a settled country where it had to fight existing cultures of livelihood, the founders created a new nation—predicated on the need for expansion of production. In his famous "Report on Manufacturers" of December 1791, Alexander Hamilton applied the logic of maximation of means of happiness to the federal economy in order to refute the charge that agricultural and manufacturing interests were opposed to each other. He argued that "Mutual wants constitute one of the strongest links of political connection;" and "It is a truth ... that every thing tending to establish substantial and permanent order in the affairs of a country, to increase the total mass of industry and opulence, is ultimately beneficial to every part of it."[16] The reason was that the breakdown of economic self–dependence of the regional economies would stimulate consumption in each of the former colonies.

Adam Smith's famous outline of a new notion of society tied it to the practices of self-interest regulated by competition: "It is not from the benevolence of the butcher, the brewer, or the baker, that we expect our dinner, but from their regard to their own interest. We address ourselves, not to their humanity but to their self-love."[17] But note the "we" that Smith referred to. It is the voice of the consumer, who depends upon the self-interest of the shopkeepers. He or she may want to make a prudent bargain but also may be expected afterwards to go home to use the bread and beer in a social context, say with family or friends. In fact, Smith had worked out a theory of consumption, including a highly elaborate theory of the consumer, already in his work *The Theory of Moral Sentiment* which was published in 1759, sixteen years before *The Wealth of Nations*.

The earlier work was an investigation of the nature of the moral faculty. "Sympathy" or "fellow-feeling" was Adam Smith's term for the human ability to put oneself in a situation as experienced by somebody else. It is the key term of his social ethics. It covers the general ability to appreciate the feelings of other people on the basis of an appraisal of the situation giving rise to their sentiment.[18] In retrospect, the theory is best understood as an anticipation of George Mead's notion of "the self" and "the generalized other."[19] While Smith's doctrine of sympathy is usually discussed as a problem of ethics and moral judgment, his notion would seem to establish Adam Smith as the grandfather of social role theories. The self–directing individual that one is led to deduce from theories that stem from the Protestant work ethic, is simply not to be found in Adam Smith. A wide gulf separates Montesquieu's concept of man "left to his private direction," from Adam Smith's individual who is above all insecure in his craving for social approbation.[21] Sociological criticism about the social primitivism of liberalism is mostly besides the mark.

The notion of "sympathy" implies that human beings judge themselves as well as other people by consulting an outside standard, "the impartial spectator."[22] Outside society the individual "could think no more of his own character, of the propriety or demerit of his own sentiments and conduct, of the beauty or deformity of his own mind, than of the beauty or deformity of his own face.... Bring him into society, and he is immediately provided with the mirror which he wanted before. It is placed in the countenance and behavior of those he lives with, which always mark when they enter into, and when they disapprove of his sentiments; and it is here that he first views the propriety and impropriety of his own passions, the beauty and deformity of his own mind." In order to extract the sympathy they need, they have to form a perception of the expectations of those whose sympathy they seek as well as the expectations of those to whom they want to extend their own sympathy. Thus, the starting point for Smith's theory of consumption was a bleak view of the human ability to engage in meaningful communication with other people, even with close friends. Human emotions were matters of equivalences, of similarities, of concords—but never of real unities. "Our sorrow at a funeral generally amounts to no more than an affected gravity," Smith wrote. To watch friends in affliction was often to note how far "the languid emotions of our hearts" were from their natural outbursts of passion. "We may even inwardly reproach ourselves with our own want of sensibility, and perhaps, on that account, work ourselves up into an artificial sympathy, which, however, when it is raised, is always the slightest and most transitory imaginable; and generally, as soon as we have left the room, vanishes, and is gone forever."[23] Even joy was hard to share: "It gives us the spleen ... to see another too happy or too much elevated, as we call it, with any little piece of good fortune. We are disobliged even with his joy." As Smith noted disparingly, "we are even put out of humour if our companion laughs louder or longer at a joke than we think it deserves; that is, than we feel that we ourselves could laugh at it."[24]

From this communicative inarticulateness comes the celebration of material objects. Adam Smith's next step was to argue that although adversity is more intensely felt by the person principally concerned than prosperity or happiness, it is more difficult to convey one's misfortune in order to solicit the honest sympathy of the observers. Possession of goods then emerges as the most general expression of happiness at a level which appeals to the broadest possible audience:

It is because mankind are disposed to sympathize more entirely with our joy than with our sorrow, that we make a parade of our riches, and conceal our poverty. Nothing is so mortifying as to be obliged to expose our distress to the view of the public, and to feel, that though our situation is open to the eyes of all mankind, no mortal conceives for us the half of what we suffer. Nay, it is chiefly from this regard to the sentiments of mankind, that we pursue riches and avoid poverty.[25]

Much criticism has been directed against Adam Smith for turning economic gain into the sole or at least the dominant end of human behavior. In reality, Smith did almost the opposite. As noted by Albert Hirshman, Smith almost went out of his way to put great emphasis on the non–economic motives behind economic behavior. The struggle for economic advantage and for a high standard of consumption becomes so important because it is fuelled— not by greed or avarice—but by human instincts that drive them towards social life. "The non-economic drives, powerful as they are, are made to feed into economic ones and do nothing but reinforce them."[26] The result is, however, that economic motives can no longer be clearly distinguished from other human passions. Consumption then—either actual or potential— becomes a means to all sorts of ends. So what Smith did was not to narrow the understanding of economic interests, but to enrich it to the degree that it came to encompass the essential aspects of the social totality.

Time and again Smith makes the observation that the demand for consumption is not rooted in utility, but in the need for social attention. Isolated man has almost no need for things. Man in society lives with an intensified need for everything. The reason is that "we constantly pay more regard to the sentiment of the spectator, than to those of the situation principally concerned, and consider rather how his situation will appear to other people, than how it will appear to himself."[27] Smith leaves no doubt that there is a great element of self-deception in this. It leads ordinary men to stuff their pockets "with little conveniencies...some of which may sometimes be of some little use, but all of which might at all times be very well spared, and of which the whole utility is certainly not worth the fatigue of bearing the burden."[28] The situation is even more bleak for the rich: The rich man, when forced to observe his own situation with attention, will note that his riches are "enormous and operose machines contrived to produce a few trifling conveniencies to the body, consisting of springs the most nice and delicate, which must be kept in order with the anxious attention, and which in spite of all our care are ready every moment to burst into pieces, and to crush in their ruins their unfortunate possessor. They are immense fabrics, which it requires the labour of a life to raise, which threaten every moment to overwhelm the person that dwells in them."[29]

In retrospect, it is interesting that Adam Smith, who watched and celebrated the building of an industrial empire, should focus his view of human nature on characteristics that have a strong resemblance to the views of Karen Horney, Eric Fromm, and modern social psychologists, who emphasize the deep–seated needs for social recognition rather than for material aggrandizement. What is "that great purpose of human life which we call bettering our condition?" Adam Smith asked. "To be observed, to be attended to, to be taken notice of with sympathy, complacency, and approbation, are all the advantages which we can propose to derive from it."[30]

In *The Wealth of Nations* Adam Smith formulated the stern definition of consumption as what is left over and used when savings are deducted from total income.[31] His earlier work, however, provided a full depiction of the psychological needs fulfilled by goods. He was clearly aware that he lived in a society in which material necessities were reshaped by social conditions, while at the same time, goods of questionable utility began to fill up the world. In fact, the disjunction between basic necessities that appeared to him to be available in abundance and the scarcity that seemed to rule the market for superfluous goods is a recurring theme which indicates his distance from utilitarianism:

> How many people ruin themselves by laying out money on trinkets of frivolous utility? What pleases these lovers of toys is not so much the utility, as the aptness of the machines which are fitted to promote it. All their pockets are stuffed with little conveniencies. They contrive new pockets, unknown in the clothes of other people, in order to carry a greater number. They walk about loaded with a multitude of baubles, ... some of which may sometimes be of some little use, but all of which might at all times be very well spared, and of which the whole utility is certainly not worth the fatigue of bearing the burden.[32]

Superfluous goods served as a striking paradigm of a logic which unfolds as private foolishness is turned into public benefit. The irrationality of individual wants buttressed the rationality of the system as a whole. As Smith goes on, "we rarely view it in this abstract and philosophical light. We naturally confound it in our imagination with the order, the regular and harmonious movement of the system, the machine or the economy by means of which it is produced. ...And it is well that nature imposes upon us in this manner. It is this deception which rouses and keeps in continual motion the industry of mankind."[33]

In his famous claim in *The Wealth of Nations* Smith asserted that the means of happiness were maximized without the individual's own intention: "Every individual necessarily labours to render the annual revenue of the society as great as he can. He generally, indeed, neither intends to promote the public interest....he intends only his own gain, and he is...led by an invisible hand to promote an end which was no part of his intention."[34] In

The Theory of Moral Sentiment Smith had first developed his notion of the invisible hand to refer–not to the maximation of goods, but to the consumption of goods. The produce of the soil maintains at all times nearly that number of inhabitants which it is capable of maintaining. The rich only select from the heap what is most precious and agreeable. They consume little more than the poor, and in spite of their natural selfishness and rapacity, though they mean only their own convenience, though the sole end which they propose from the labours of all the thousands whom they employ, be it the gratificate of their own vain and insatiable desires, they divide with the poor the produce of all their improvements. They are led by an invisible hand to make nearly the same distribution of the necessaries of life, which would have been made, had the earth been divided into equal portions among all its inhabitants, and thus without knowing it, advance the interest of the society, and afford means to the multiplication of the species."[35]

The mechanisms of social approbation of material achievement is the key, first to the dependence of the poor, who benefit from the inability of the more fortunate to consume everything within their possession. Since the rich only have a limited capacity for consumption, they are inclined to hire the poor to procure the trappings of happiness: "The capacity of his stomach bears no proportion to the immensity of his desires, and will receive no more than that of the meanest peasant. The rest he is obliged to distribute among those, who prepare, in the nicest manner, that little which he himself makes use of ... among those who provide and keep in order all the different baubles and trinkets, which are employed in the oeconomy of greatness; all of whom thus derive from his luxury and caprice, that share of the necessaries of life, which they would in vain have expected from his humanity or his justice."[36]

Secondly, the social order as a whole is seen as a monument to the desires for social approbation as society comes to be governed by things rather than by men:

> Nature has wisely judged that the distinction of ranks, the peace and order of society, would rest more securely upon the plain and palpable differences of birth and fortune, than upon the invisible and uncertain differences of wisdom and virtue. The undistinguishing eye of the great mob of mankind can well enough perceive the former: it is with difficulty that the nice discernment of the wise and the virtuous can sometimes distinguish the latter.[37]

As political theorist Nicholas Xenos has pointed out, the theory of social emulation identifies an important part of human psychology in a commercial society where goods have become the all–important social standard. When luxury goods are desired for the apparent happiness they bring to their possessor, the individual who succeeds in acquiring these goods inevitably contributes to competitive race for consumption. The acquisition of desired goods entails one of two discoveries that may be made simultaneously:

14

Either the luxury goods have now become available to so many that they are no longer perceived as luxuries, in which case the race for whatever now counts as a luxury begins, and/or the possession of those goods, if they are still luxuries, doesn't bring much happiness....It turns out that having other people think that he is happy, just as he perceived the happiness of the wealthy before, brings satisfaction and a kind of happiness.... So if his desire for luxuries gets the rat race going, his desire for the envy of others keeps it going. It's true that Smith thought this to be a debased way to live a life from the point of view of true happiness, but it is a way to get the economic machine in motion and keep it in motion.[38]

The result is progress in a society where goods come to stand for social approbation which advertises itself as a virtual social identity. There is but a short way from Smith's anxious strugglers for approbation to the modern idea of self–respect. As social scientist Lee Rainwater argues:"What is distinctive about industrial society is the proliferation of material objects and services that are offered for sale and through which individuals in society live out their identities, perform roles, forge their sense of personal meaningfulness."[39]

Adam Smith's account of the dynamic of social emulation projects a house of bondage beyond Egyptian proportions. It depends on a logic of power, hardly less demanding than that required by Thomas Hobbes' great *Leviathan*. But unlike the Leviathan, it is in no way founded on a moment of consent. It is based on the stipulation of a social psychology which has been allowed to invade all possible realms, private as well as public. Most cultural restaints appear to have vanished before this new fiction which was introduced under the name of a "system" as a synonym for the "invisible hand" operating within the political economy.[40]

A system stands for an organization of control "made possible by a tightly integrated set of functions whose performance assures the survival and adaptation of the whole." It includes "a conception of rationality embodied in its structure."[41] Unlike the myth of the manna, a system embodied a theory which left power relationships, domination and dependence, largely inexplicable. When inequality is absorbed into the logic of the economic system, the result is a peculiar placidity of disbelief and mystification: "The rich only select from the heap what is most precious and agreeable," as Adam Smith put it.[42]

The new understanding of consumption was one which replaced the approach to needs as the nurture of collective livelihood with inquiry into the power hidden in psychological cause-and-effect relationships that could be be produced endlessly. Power is therefore dissociated from needs restrained by cultural and religious observance. The economy of need which had been implicit in the livelihood sustained by myth and ritual was replaced by an economic system which took pride in scientific "laws" that sustained their claim to autonomy. Needs were liberated to become restless and endless. And if they tend to settle down, the modern world has produced powerful institutions—elaborate sciences, whole professions, world fairs, etc.—to renew their dynamic. In due time the *system* of consumption even aspired to be dignified as a *culture* of consumption.[43]

References

1. Paul K. Conkin, *Prophets of Prosperity: America's First Political Economists*. Bloomington: Indiana University Press, 1980.
2. Sheldon S. Wolin, "Contract and Birthright," *Political Theory*, Vol. 14, No. 2, 1986, pp. 179-193.
3. *Ibid.,* p. 180.
4. Marshall Sahlins, *Stone Age Economics*. London: Tavistoc Publications, 1974, pp. 1-40. Nicholas Xenos, *Scarcity and Modernity*. London: Routledge, 1989, investigates the classical Greek culture of self-sufficiency.
5. Wolin, *op.cit.,* p. 180.
6. "Science as a Vocation," *From Max Weber,* ed. by H.H. Gerth and C. Wright Mills. New York: Free Press, 1948, p.148.
7. Sheldon Wolin, "Postmodern Politics and the Absence of Myth," *Social Research,* Vol. 52, No. 2, 1989, pp. 217-239.
8. Istvan Hont and Michael Ignatieff, "Needs and Justice in the *Wealth of Nations*: An Introductory Essay" in *Wealth and Virtue: The Shaping of Political Economy in the Scottish Enlightenment*, ed. by I. Hont and M. Ignatieff. Cambridge: Cambridge University Press, 1983, pp. 1-44.
9. Alan Macfarlane, *The Origins of English Individualism: The Family, Property and Social Transition*. Oxford: Basil Blackwell, 1978, p. 163.
10. Hobbes, *Leviathan*, pp. 160, 161, quoted after Wolin, "Postmodern Politics," p. 238.
11 John Locke, *Two Treatises of Government,* ed. by Peter Laslett. Cambridge: Cambridge University Press, 1960, pp. 326-344.
12. Istvan Hont and Michael Ignatieff, *op.cit.*
13. Adam Smith, *An Inquiry into the Nature and Causes of The Wealth of Nations,* ed. by Edwin Cannan. Chicago: University of Chicago Press, 1976.
14. Adam Smith, *The Theory of Moral Sentiment*, ed. by D. D. Raphael and A. L. Macfie. Oxford Press, Clarendon Press, 1976, pp.184-5.
15. Andrew S. Skinner, *Adam Smith and the Role of the State*. Glascow: University of Glascow Press, 1972.
16. *Alexander Hamilton's Papers on Public Credit, Commerce and Finance,* Ed. by Samuel McKee, Jr. New York: Liberal Arts Press, 1934, pp.

230-32.
17. Smith, *Wealth of Nations,* p. 18.
18. Smith, *Theory of Moral Sentiment*, p. 10.
19. George Mead, *Mind, Self, and Society*, ed. by Charles W. Morris. Chicago: University of Chicago Press, 1962, pp. 152-163.
20. Glenn R. Morrow, *The Ethical and Economic Theories of Adam Smith.* [1923] New York: Augustus M. Kelley, 1969, pp. 28-44.
21. Baron de Montesquieu, *The Spirit of the Laws.* Translated by Thomas Nugent. New York: Hafner Press, 1949, p. 3.
22. Smith, *Theory of Moral Sentiment.*, p. 110.
23. *Ibid.,* p. 47.
24. *Ibid.,* p. 16.
25. *Ibid.,* p. 50.
26. Albert Hirshman, *The Passions and the Interests: Political Arguments for Capitalism before Its Triumph.* Princeton: Princeton University Press, 1977, pp. 108-109.
27. Smith, *Theory of Moral Sentiment*, p. 182.
28. *Ibid.,* p. 180.
29. *Ibid.,* p. 183.
30. *Ibid.,* p. 50.
31. Smith, *Wealth of Nations,* I, p. 359.
32. Smith, *Theory of Moral Sentiment.*, p. 180.
33. *Ibid.,* p. 183.
34. Smith, *Wealth of Nations.*, I, p. 477.
35. Smith, *Theory of Moral Sentiment,* pp. 184-5.
36. *Ibid.,* p. 184.
37. *Ibid.,* p. 229.
38. Xenos, "Neoconservatism Kristolized," *Salmagundi*, Vol. 74-75, Summer 1987, p. 144. "Liberalism and the Postulate of Scarcity," *Political Theory*, Vol. 15, No. 2, pp. 226-233.
39. Lee Rainwater, *What Money Buys: Inequality and the Social Meanings of Income.* New York: Basic Books, 1974, p. 21.
40. Smith, *Theory of Moral Sentiment*, p. 185.
41. Wolin, "The New Constitution," *New York Review of Books,* June 1, 1978, p. 20.
42. *Theory of Moral Sentiment,* p. 184.
43. *The Culture of Consumption: Critical Essays in American History, 1880-1980,* ed. by Richard Wightman Fox and T. J. Jackson Lears. New York: Pantheon, 1983.

Corporate Imagery and Popular Education:
World's Fairs and Expositions in the United States, 1893-1940

Roland Marchand
University of California, Davis

"No man ever leaves the Machinery Building a bit disappointed. If he surveys all that is to be seen carefully and intelligently he has obtained an amount of information concerning mechanic arts that he had never dreamed of."
— *History of the World's Fair* (Chicago, 1893).[1]

"The exhibitors who best understood that people came not to be educated and not to be sold but to be thrilled and entertained and amazed drew the biggest crowds."
— Ford Motor Company, "World's Fair: A Study of Circulation and Reactions. ....." (1939).[2]

Over the years since the first great world's fair, London's "Crystal Palace" Industrial Exposition of 1851, these exhibitions have served a multitude of purposes. People have come seeking knowledge of new technologies, vicarious experiences of distant peoples and places, visions of the future, lessons in everyday living, thrills and entertainment, or simply the pleasures of joining in the flow of eager and expectant crowds. Businesses have set up displays at such expositions to sell their goods, show off their new products and technical capacities, cultivate public admiration and goodwill, and strike heroic or beneficent poses. All of these elements appeared to some degree in the American expositions of the late nineteenth century and continued to play a role in the fairs of the mid-twentieth century and afterward. But the balance among these elements shifted decisively by the 1930s — in ways that signalled larger trends within the society.

Although historians have devoted most of their attention to the architecture, anthropological displays, amusement zones, and official themes of such expositions, the industrial exhibits of the business corporations are also worthy of close scrutiny. During the half-century from the Columbian Exposition at Chicago in 1893 to the New York World's Fair of 1939-1940, American corporations not only intensified their participation but also decisively transformed the content and style of their displays. These changing exhibits, in turn, marked a significant maturation in the deliberate fashioning of corporate images. They also reflected a steady blurring of conventional assumptions within the business community about the distinctions between education and entertainment, between business and show business.

We can best analyze the nature of this change by asking four simple questions. When the corporation came to the fair, during each phase of this era,

1) *What* did it bring?
2) *Where* did it display what it brought?
3) *How* did it display what it brought, and
4) *What expectations about the audience* did its method and style of display suggest ?

A quick, elementary answer to the first of these questions, although it ignores the diversity of corporate displays at each individual fair, still highlights the fundamental transformations between the 1890s and the mid-twentieth century. First, during the late nineteenth century, the corporation brought its *products* to the fair; then, beginning roughly with the Panama-Pacific Exposition of 1915 in San Francisco, it tried to bring its *factory*. Ultimately, with increasing self-consciousness throughout the 1930s, it sought to bring its *corporate image*. And this basic pattern of change, in turn, influenced *where* the display took place and *how* and *for whom* it was designed.

To postulate such a tidy progression — from product to factory to image — is, of course, to obscure the typical disorderliness and lack of steady, sequential progression in historical change. Even at the end of the 1930s, few corporations neglected to put some of their products on exhibit in their fair displays. Conversely, one might well argue that the massive locomotives of the Pennsylvania Railroad or the elaborate towers of bottles of Heinz pickles at the nineteenth-century expositions were intended to convey corporate images more than to display simple products. Still, a decisive change of emphasis did take place as American corporations came increasingly to see the great fairs and expositions primarily as aspects of public relations programs rather than as arenas in which to carry on technical exchanges or sell products.

The shift in "what" corporations brought to the fair brought immediate changes in "where" and "how" they displayed it. When the predominate purposes were the mutual display of technical advances and the direct promotion of sales of products, most companies were quite content to stage their displays within large halls along with the exhibits of other manufacturers of similar products. Such halls insured a large flow of traffic and enabled interested visitors to educate themselves by examining various technical advances in the same field within close proximity to each other. They also relieved companies of the costs of erecting their own buildings and of carrying out individual activities to promote attendance at isolated display sites.

But as concern with the promotion of a distinct corporate image became dominant, companies became less willing to accept the low visibility and modest corporate stature inherent in inclusion amongst a plethora of exhibits in a standard exposition building. As John Cawelti has noted, while only 9 out of the 137 buildings at the 1893 Chicago Exposition were built by individual business corporations (and nearly all of these nine represented amusement zone concessions or the idiosyncratic impulses of small companies), by the time of the 1933-34 Century of Progress Exposition in Chicago, some twenty corporations — including such giants as General Motors, Ford, Chrysler, Firestone, Goodyear, Sears, Roebuck, and A&P — had come to insist on erecting their own structures.[3] An early (1928) proposal for the Century of Progress Exposition, which called for the firms in each industry to cooperate in "composite" exhibits rather than stage individual "competitive displays," was utterly crushed by the stampede of corporations to exercise total control over their exhibit environments. By making striking architectural statements, they now demonstrated their willingness to incur large costs to impress the public with their unique images.[4]

As corporations increasingly focused on conveying general conceptions of themselves to a broad public, they not only situated their exposition displays in their own distinctive buildings; they also altered the style and content of their exhibits. A focus on the transmitting of technical information gradually gave way to an emphasis on entertainment values, simplicity of message, and command over audience attention. A Ford Motor Company report on the impact of corporate displays at Chicago in 1934 praised exhibits that made their points simply and dramatically rather than providing a "technical discussion" that would only "mystify the layman." The next year, designer Walter Dorwin Teague advised his client, the Du Pont Company, that it should be happy if each visitor to its exhibits went away "gratified by the entertainment and with a mental picture of the broad range of Du Pont activities and their importance to himself."[5] Paradoxically, Ford and Du Pont would be the two major corporations that would hold out the longest — but not without notable compromises — for an older vision of the great fairs as places of popular education in new technologies and industrial processes.

We can best view the process of transformation in corporate industrial exhibits by looking first at the practices that dominated displays during the late nineteenth century and persisted up through the Panama-Pacific exposition of 1915. Two modes of presentation dominated the displays of this area, almost all of which were located in huge halls of associated industries. One mode amassed impressive quantities of products in the most eye-catching or awe-inspiring way. Thus spectators confronted pyramids of pickle bottles, towers of incandescent lamps, massive stacks of steel ingots and rows upon rows of lathes or motors.[6] The other major strategy of presentation sought to induce empathy with the corporation by instructing visitors in the company's complex methods of manufacture or its impressive technologies of service. Thus in 1893 AT&T instructed fairgoers in its technological expertise through sectional drawings of various instruments and the display of "an elaborate switchboard of the latest design." In a studiously didactic style, its official fair brochures goaded visitors to "Let us see how this is done."[7] Although most manufacturers were slower than the utilities to recognize a political need to cultivate public understanding and respect, by the early twentieth-century some of the industrial giants had also begun to view industrial expositions mainly as public relations forums.

Production-oriented executives had always liked to show off their factories. As they recognized the need to cultivate broad public favor, they typically concluded that people would readily sympathize with them if only they could be shown the complicated, coordinated steps of manufacture and the intense effort and sophisticated expertise involved. Once the public observed the miraculous processes by which "useless" raw materials were transformed into functional products, then they would appreciate the immense service provided by the large corporation. Through a plethora of scale models, working demonstrations, diagrams and dioramas, companies sought, at least figuratively, to bring their factories to the fairs.

By the time of the Panama-Pacific Exposition in 1915, the General Electric Company was displaying the manufacturing of light bulbs through a "miniature lamp factory" and the giant United States Steel Corporation was operating scale models of a blast furnace, a Bessemer converter and an open hearth furnace "equipped with ladles, ladle cars, etc." to demonstrate "the process of the actual manufacture of steel from the raw materials to the most highly finished products." The persisting tradition of the fair as a place of technical education for the masses influenced even the use of new media to dramatize such sagas of production. U.S.Steel supplemented its scale models in 1915 with a six-and-a-half hour series of silent films that pointed out every detail of production "in a clear, concise, yet comprehensive manner, and in logical sequence." Lecturers provided simultaneous explanations "so that the audience may clearly understand the processes being shown upon the screen." Supremely conscious of its educational role, the corporation observed that a "careful study" of its exhibit would "commend itself to all observant and investigative minds."[8]

The unchallenged champion among corporate displays at San Francisco in 1915, however, was the Ford Motor Company exhibit. Henry Ford, the epitome of the production-oriented entrepreneur, gave literal form to the manufacturer's instinct to bring the factory to the fair. As the centerpiece of his exhibit, he constructed an operating Ford assembly line which produced between 18 and 25 Model-T's a day. Frank Vivian, the Ford exhibit manager for that fair, later recalled the strenuous efforts that had been required to keep the surging crowds at a safe distance from the machines and workers. On opening day, the mob of visitors had simply crushed the railings in its eagerness to get close to the conveyor belt. The overwhelming success of this exhibit seemed to prove that demonstrations of manufacturing processes were exactly what the public wanted to see.[9]

How quickly this emphasis on education-laden exhibits of factory processes might have been supplanted had a constant parade of national and regional expositions continued after 1915 we can only surmise. But the long hiatus between the Panama-Pacific Exposition in 1915 and the next exposition of significant size in 1933 (the Philadelphia Sesquicentennial of 1926 attracted little popular or corporate attention) may have actually delayed the evolution of new presentational strategies. Not only had modernist styles in art, fashion and architecture begun to attract corporate attention in the meantime, especially in the wake of the Paris Exposition Internationale des Arts Décoratifs et Industriels Modernes in 1925 and the concurrent rise of the new profession of industrial design in the United States, but the flourishing advertising agencies had begun to pay more heed to audience behavior. Department Stores had fully embraced the values and techniques of showmanship and emerging experts on window dressing were beginning to recognize the attention-grabbing value of extreme modernism in style and of displays with moving parts.[10]

When 1933 arrived, with Chicago's long-planned centennial exposition now assigned the responsibility of reviving the nation from its depression listlessness and pessimism, designers would convince corporate leaders to apply the new insights into audience-stimulation that advertising agents and public relations experts had formulated over the previous decade. Their new techniques would challenge the now-traditional corporate assumptions about expositions as places to educate the citizenry in manufacturing operations while promoting products. But the new display concepts would not immediately vanquish the lingering educational aura of the typical corporate display. Only over the course of several major expositions between 1933 and 1939 would the full implications of modernist styles and public relations objectives be fully realized within the substance of corporate exhibits.

A number of companies still sought to bring their factories to the fair in Chicago in 1933 and 1934. The strikingly modernistic architecture of the Century of Progress, with its celebration of a machine aesthetic, seemed to provide a fitting and dramatic scene for such displays. But exhibitors had also become more conscious of the need for popularization and showmanship. The fair planners cautioned that, while the fair's theme had to embody "those higher concepts of education, science and culture," exhibitors should remember that "people visit an exposition with a carnival spirit, hoping to be amused and diverted." The Kelvinator Corporation responded by telling its story through a marionette show while Sinclair Oil erected a "dinosaur zoo." To an "uncritical public," one advertising man remarked scornfully, the zoo successfully served as "visual and physical proof" of the superiority of Sinclair

Oil.[11] John Cawelti, observing to what an extent the 1933-34 Chicago fair had moved away from an earlier mode in which all amusements had been sternly segregated from "the monumental vistas of industrial progress," has characterized the 1933 Century of Progress as "a carefully mixed blend of entertainment and education, showmanship and science."[12] I would dissent only in suggesting that the mix was not always so carefully blended and that some deep fissures of intention and supposition underlay the incongruous elements of many displays.

The new showmanship blossomed in a variety of forms. At least a half-dozen corporate displays in 1933 included mechanical manikins or talking robots. Standard Oil suggested the "live power" of its gasoline through a "Cage of Fury" animal act while Swift & Company supplemented its dioramas of meat-preparation with "humorous moving figures." Both General Motors and Firestone constructed operating assembly lines, but visitors at General Motors could also listen while "Chief Pontiac" (a robot) joked with the crowd and Firestone guests were treated to a "pantomime pageant of the history of tires" in which, for each chronological period, "a female performer dressed in the costume of the time appears and prances around a bit as a hidden announcer recites the significance of Firestone tires in that particular era." One advertising man observed that an uncritical public made successes of some exhibits in which there was "no inherent relation between the entertainment and the firm or product."[13]

Seeking to associate themselves with the cutting edge of technological advance and to assure audiences that corporate science would cure the depression, many companies now sought less to bring their *factories* than their *research laboratories* to the fair. Most did so through some form of theater. Westinghouse's "House of Wonders" presented dramas of invention and household electrification on a revolving stage while Union Carbide and Carbon demonstrated the wonders of science at its "Liquid Air Theater." Kelvinator demonstrated its technology through "magic tricks" conducted by a company magician who was occasionally interrupted by "a feminine voice from the refrigerator" to "get over a bit of the sales story." Although General Electric spoke of making "educational features...easily available to the mass of people," it unflinchingly adopted the language of showmanship to describe what went on in its "House of Magic." There, "Maestro" W. A. Gluesing, a former professional magician, served as a "scientist-magician," operating various devices with "a wave of his wand." The *GE Monogram* significantly characterized the effects of this exhibit not as the education of visitors in technical processes, but as "a thrilling presentation of electrical wonders."[14]

The Ford Motor Company's film, "Rhapsody in Steel," seemed to go even further than the "House of Magic" in embracing the concept of the industrial exhibit as a show rather than a classroom. A Ford brochure characterized this film, created "especially for Century of Progress visitors," as "an amusing fantasy." Its protagonist was a "Ford imp," a "whimsical character" who cast a "magic spell over a staid collection of parts, making them behave in a most surprising and frivolous manner."[15]

For all of the emphasis of their displays on entertainment and showmanship at the Century of Progress, however, many corporate leaders clung tenaciously to the conviction that the main thrust of their exhibits was educational. General Electric insisted that its huge dioramas and miniature reproductions and cut-aways of turbines and power stations responded to the desires of "people who want to see what makes the wheels go round." General Electric also assumed that visitors were learning about science through its "House of Magic" show and might well have taken umbrage at the observer who charged that the House of Magic "plays with the stroboscope and makes it entertaining" in contrast to the MIT exhibit which "really illustrates its principle." Especially earnest in insisting upon the educational role of its exhibits was the Ford Motor Company. Ford's fair manager, Fred Black, zealously assembled reports of visitors who had praised the educational effects of the Ford displays and passed their words along to Edsel and Henry Ford. Comments such as those which characterized the Ford building as "the most complete and instructive exhibit ever produced" or proposed that "every boy and girl in the country should see this if nothing else in the fair" gained the fondest reception among Ford executives.[16]

Even when it ballyhooed the "amusing fantasy" of its "Rhapsody in Steel" film, the Ford Company still seized upon opportunities to reemphasize the educational thrust of its exhibits. The film was set "against the serious background of the drafting room" it noted, and it provided "a good conception of the magnitude of the Ford industry and the many operations in the building of a Ford car." Just as the Ford exhibit had employed such techniques as photographic murals and demonstrations of selected manufacturing processes as a way of continuing to "bring the factory to the fair," so even this "frivolous" film reproduced something of the factory aura. Its musical score, Ford boasted, had been "actually composed in the Rouge plant." Ford publicity materials stressed the intent of its 1934 display to explain the evolution of the automobile from the raw materials of the earth; its designer, Walter Dorwin Teague, affirmed that Ford had specified that this evolution "must be portrayed in a way to make it both educational and dramatic." Ford publicity particularly stressed such elements of its exhibit as the "educational display" in which two trained Ford mechanics disassembled and reassembled a V-8 motor in 23 minutes, thus making "understandable to the layman the operation of the modern auto engine."[17]

For all of the fervor of such corporate tributes to the central educational purposes of industrial displays, those observers of the Chicago fair who counted most said little to promote a faithfulness to the duty of educating the layman. Those who counted the most, of course, were the designers, the advertising experts, and the emerging cadre of corporate public relations men who would shape the patterns of future displays. From the Century of Progress Exposition in 1933-34 through the Texas Centennial Exposition in

Dallas in 1936, these experts would scrutinize the effects of corporate displays on fair audiences as never before. With unanimity they concluded that animation and visitor-participation were the elements crucial to a successful display.

Almost as invariably, they called for radical simplification. One advertising man observed at Chicago that "an exhibit had to be clearly interpreted for the public, since the public resents the necessity of making its own interpretation." A Du Pont lecturer remarked in 1936 that "(t)hey like to see something moving - something that can be understood at a glance." Visitors seemed to recognize that Du Pont's chemical demonstrations were "useful to them in some way," but they were "not especially interested in knowing how." Such observations led Walter Dorwin Teague, the fair designer for both Ford and Du Pont, to recommend that Du Pont "carry the process of simplification still further." For its 1939 display, he recommended the "complete elimination of all details not familiar to the public, with the whole complex process [of production] reduced to a few dramatic steps."[18]

The drive for simplification had also gained an impetus from the modernistic style of the Century of Progress. *Advertising Arts* praised the new styles and devices that led exhibitors to "concentrate on the quick dramatization of pertinent facts." Teague, as he pared down the extent of Ford's fair displays of manufacturing processes by observing and selecting just those processes which most appealed to plant visitors, sought to impress upon Edsel Ford that unity was crucial to good design. Through simplification and dramatization, a few key elements could be brought into a visual harmony. The resulting aesthetic effect would trigger immediate understanding. The kind of understanding that Teague and the public relations experts had in mind was neither technical nor educational in the older sense. It involved primarily a popular "understanding" of the social and economic services performed by the great corporations and, in the particular case of Du Pont in the wake of the "merchants of war" charges of the 1934 Senate hearings, the "tearing aside of general ignorance and misunderstanding."[19]

The rising predominance of such a goal for corporate exhibits was also apparent in the campaigns of such corporate exhibitors as General Motors to convince the public that private industry would cure the depression through science. GM President Alfred Sloan, convinced by 1934 that the celebration of technological expertise represented the best way both to build GM's own reputation and to restore confidence in the economic system, highlighted the new GM research exhibit when the Chicago fair reopened for its second year in 1934. He staged an impressive dinner, to which he invited hundreds of scientists, businessmen and civic leaders and solicited from each a statement about the future marvels to be anticipated from the merging of science with industry. It was "tremendously encouraging," Sloan exulted, to hear from men who could speak with authority that science (and not the New Deal) was "ready to show the way to greater industrial progress." The General Motors research exhibit now accentuated an educational mission that looked beyond the earlier goal of initiating laymen and technically-minded citizens into an understanding of manufacturing processes. Its central purpose was to educate all visitors to associate General Motors with scientific progress and to teach them to rely on technological innovation, not New Deal "regimentation," as the proper response to the depression. [20]

Whatever the public may have learned at the 1933-34 Century of Progress Exposition, the most intense educational experience at that fair — and at the large regional fairs at Dallas, San Diego and Cleveland over the next three years — was the schooling of a new group of experts in the techniques and psychology of corporate industrial displays. The rising level of financial commitments to fair displays brought increased pressure for accountability. Nearly every major corporate exhibit now amassed statistics on the number of visitors, their composition by age and sex, and the duration of their attention to the display. AT&T constructed detailed profiles of those who won free long-distance calls from its exhibit, noting not only their age, sex, and home-town but also the content of their conversations. Ford commissioned a surveying agency to record "overhead conversations" at its exhibits between 1934 and 1936 and Du Pont insisted upon detailed biweekly reports from its exhibit lecturers. As a speaker at a private forum of the J. Walter Thompson advertising agency observed, the visitors to the Century of Progress Exposition had been "on display" as much as the exhibits. To emphasize this point, he gave the title "Twenty-Two Million Gold Fish" to his report on this "great human-nature laboratory." Never before had the responses of audiences come under such intense — and occasionally systematic — scrutiny. [21]

By the time of the great 1939 fairs in New York and San Francisco, the full impact of this scrutiny of exposition audiences would become apparent. The lingering ambition of a minority of corporate executives to see themselves in the role of educators of the masses in modern technology would confront even greater pressures to simply provide entertainment and call it education. Observations of fair crowds increasingly impressed public relations executives and designers with the short attention spans of visitors and the need to elicit quick impressions. Survey after survey concluded that only animated displays could command attention. Visitors seemed so easily distracted that it was hard to envision them as serious. The technical advisor to the Board of Directors for the 1939 New York's Fair observed that "(t)he morbidly curious appear to be present in large numbers at all exposition crowds." Visitors were impelled less by the desire to see or understand something than by the rush to avoid missing some sight or spectacle. "Exposition visitors," he concluded, "prefer attractions in tabloid doses." [22]

While such derisive views stemmed partly from surveys of exposition audiences, they also owed much to the increasing emphasis on corporate exhibits as displays of a corporate image for public relations purposes. With such goals, companies came to see the audiences for their exhibits as little different from the heterogeneous mass audience for magazine, newspaper and radio advertising. Gender images played a significant part in this shift. Early

26

in the century, corporate exhibitors had easily assumed that fairgoers would segregate themselves sexually and that most industrial exhibits could anticipate an audience composed primarily of men. Here they could "talk shop" about industrial processes to visitors on a "man-to-man" basis. It was no mere linguistic convention that prompted the monumental 1893 *History of the World's Fair* to pontificate, "No *man* ever leaves the Machinery Building a bit disappointed (emphasis mine)." 23

But with even such corporations as United States Steel, Westinghouse, General Electric and Du Pont now heavily engaged by the late 1930s in selling consumer goods directly to female shoppers and with their public relations campaigns aimed at the broad public, the corporations came to attribute to the fair audiences those same characteristics — ignorance, emotionality and frivolousness — that advertisers had long associated with a feminine audience of consumers. And, as observers at expositions increasingly characterized men as behaving in as distracted, uncomprehending and inattentive a manner as women, the drive toward greater simplification and showmanship in industrial exhibits proceeded apace.24

In 1939, with broad, impressionistic, public relations objectives now foremost in their minds, exhibitors gave full reign to the impulses of showmanship as they brought their corporate images to the fairs. In New York, Chrysler Motors adopted what it called "the new concept of what an industrial exhibit should do" and refused to focus on "the complicated processes of production." It rejected demonstrations of assembly lines in favor of an exhibit entitled "60 Minutes of Magic" and billed as a "Five Star Show." Visitors made their way past a "frozen forest" (a demonstration of the powers of air conditioning), to gaze curiously at "engineering wonders," listen to a "talking car," and experience a simulated rocket ride to London. In 1940, the *Chrysler Motors Magazine* boasted that the company had rejected "the old formula of product and manufacturing demonstrations and displays" in favor of "a central carnival theme." 25

Meanwhile, General Electric astonished visitors with ever more spectacular tricks in its updated "House of Magic." *Business Week* characterized the General Electric show as "pure science served to the public as unalloyed entertainment." Du Pont's designer, Walter Teague, proposed that the company acquire public understanding through a "key statement" at the entrance, perhaps a symbolic figure, given simulated motion by flashing electric lights, "the object being to create an impression of...invincible action." Ultimately, he created a dramatic corporate signature to call attention to the Du Pont building — a shaft in which a series of magnified and abstracted models of the apparatus for chemical reduction formed a 100-foot "Tower of Research" which emitted rising bubbles to incorporate the crucial ingredient of action to command attention.26

Inside, Du Pont concluded its presentation with a marionette show and boasted that its exhibit would not include any of the "mysterious, too-deep-for-me science of the textbooks." Du Pont public relations man Emerson Evans made several visits to the company's 1939 display in New York to "form an impression of its effectiveness from the standpoint of showmanship." At one point he noted: "The magic element in this process will make a more striking appeal than the present emphasis on research and will link it closer to the spectator's experiences, while at the same time make the spectator acutely conscious of Du Pont research." Few observations could have exemplified more pointedly the shift from the technical education of the public to impression management.[27]

In quite different ways, the two largest manufacturers of automobiles reflected the shift in exhibit styles that had become fully apparent by 1939. General Motors evaded the frivolity of pure entertainment by conveying a sense of grand and public-spirited vision in its "Futurama," the "hit show" of the New York fair. In the promotion of its corporate image, General Motors no longer sought to bring the factory to the fair. Instead, it brought its vision of the future. Pioneering in what was subsequently to become a popular exhibition technique, General Motors induced visitor participation through an automated "armchair" ride into a General Motors' world of the future. At the outset of his work in designing the Futurama, designer Norman Bel Geddes had insisted to the company that this display would "emphasize *entertainment*" (rather than science or education). Through the visitors' experiential tour in Futurama — over a futuristic super-highway system and a city of tomorrow — Bel Geddes and General Motors managed to blend science, technology and showmanship more decorously than most other exhibitors. Still, if the Futurama provided "education" in any sense, it was now an education for visitors in the benevolence and foresightedness of this great corporation and in the capacity of free enterprise to lead the people in envisioning a better future.[28]

In contrast to General Motors' smooth passage into the new ("come experience our world") mode of industrial display, the Ford Motor Company awkwardly reflected the unresolved tensions that still marked the transition into a new style of corporate image-making. For Henry Ford, and to a considerable extent for his son, Edsel, the old image of the great manufacturer — as simply the "hard-working, no-nonsense, axle-grease mechanic with an inventive flair" writ large — was too deeply ingrained to easily surrender. Such an image implied an educational obligation to other laymen with a hankering to understand how things worked, an obligation that Ford sought to capitalize as a public relations asset in ads for its 1939 exhibit entitled "Young Henry Ford Came to the Fair." These ads ascribed epic significance to that moment at the 1893 fair "when a thirty-year old mechanic named Ford forgot everything else as he studied a small gasoline engine mounted on a fire hosecart." Out of that experience, the company contended, had come its "conviction that expositions are *education*." Henry Ford still expected that his exhibits would "help eager young people to gain inspiration for inventions."[29]

But the actual Ford exhibit, for all its inclusion of such traditional Ford demonstrations as the disassembly and reassembly of the Ford V-8 motor, had moved toward an awkward compromise with the penchant for assimilating education into entertainment. Ford still stressed the methods of production of the automobile from the raw materials of the earth, as it had in 1934. But at New York in 1939, it did so through an immense revolving "cyclorama" entitled the "Ford Cycle of Production." This exhibit "educated" visitors in the transformation of raw materials into automobiles by enabling them to watch typical production activities as carried out by 87 groups of animated, carved figures of men and animals, their appeal enhanced by "humorous details...added through plastic noses, eyes, horns and tails." Visitors could then view a cartoon film in which the animated figures from the Ford Cycle of Production were "brought to life as actors and actresses." Ford's publicity director bemusedly characterized the film as "a puzzling combination of 'Snow White' and an educational, industrial reel."[30]

If this aspect of the Ford exhibit conveyed a confused message, it only amplified the ambiguity introduced by the visitors' first experience upon entering the Ford building. Here, an immense "animated" mural, composed of a maze of protruding shafts, connecting rods, and "whirling gears and pistons," sought "dynamically" to reproduce "certain phases of the Ford plant at Dearborn." This activated mural was intended to present viewers with an abstract vision of "the increased accuracy and precision of modern mass production." The mural's creator frankly insisted that its central purpose was "not to instruct but impress." Even so, a Ford press release insisted that the mural played "the dual role of gratifying the eye and of satisfying the mind by dramatizing for the world the complex story of the making of automobiles." In assessing the "benefits it had gained from its 1939 exhibit in New York," the Ford Company noted that it had "increased our prestige by assisting the Fair...in performing a great educational function." But it also defined the major "educational" results of its own exhibit as "educating the public in the vast labor necessary to build an automobile" and in "the importance of the automobile in the economic structure of America." Such public relations achievements were quite different from the education at an exposition that "young Henry Ford" presumably had gained in 1893. [31]

While General Motors had more decisively made the leap into a mode of presentation in which the incorporation of "education" within entertainment was accomplished with an untroubled, almost casual sense of assurance, the awkward incongruities and forced explanations of the Ford exhibit serve to remind us of the significance of the transition. What had once been an assumed and reassuring cultural boundary between education and entertainment, between the serious and the frivolous, was now being destroyed — complacently by some business leaders but with agonized reservations by others — in response to the dictates of modern public relations.

References

1. Benjamin C. Truman, ed. *History of the World's Fair*. 1976 Arno Press reprint of Chicago, 1983 edition, p. 322.
2. Ford Motor Company, "World's Fair: A Study of Circulation and Reactions....." (1939) p. 2, Acc. 146, Box 16, Ford Motor Company Papers, Edison Institute, Dearborn, Michigan.
3. John W. Cawelti, "Amcrica on Display: The World's Fairs of 1876, 1893, 1933," in Frederic Cople Jaher, ed., *The Age of Industrialism in America: Essays in Social Structure and Cultural Values*. New York, 1968, pp. 347-48.
4. "Chicago World's Fair Centennial Celebration," (typescript of plan, July, 1928), p. 6 and unsigned to George K. Burgess, Aug. 21, 1928, Box V, folder 8, Julius Rosenwald Papers, Regenstein Library, University of Chicago; Lenox Lohr to Rufus Davis (telegram), Apr. 30, 1931, folder 354, Lenox Lohr Papers, University of Illinois, Chicago.
5. Ford Motor Company, "1934 Report on the Fair," p. 10, Acc. 554, Box 4, Ford Papers; Walter Dorwin Teague, explanatory caption in Oversize Scrapbook, Acc. 77.242, photographic collection, E.I. Du Pont de Nemours Company Papers, Hagley Museum and Library.
6. J. W. Buel, *The Magic City*. St. Louis, 1894, *passim;* John Allwood, *The Great Exhibitions*. London, 1977, p. 87; Photograph #1354 (1908), H. J. Heinz Company, Photographic Collection, Pittsburgh; Frank Morton Todd, *The Story of the Exhibition,* 5 vols. New York, 1921, IV, pp. facing 122, 166 and 206.
7. "Telephone Switchboard in Operation in the Exhibit of the American Bell Telephone Company in the Electricity Building, World's Fair, Chicago," brochure (1893), and "Exhibit of the American Bell Telephone Company, Electricity Building, Columbian Exposition, Chicago, 1983," pamphlet, pp. 12, 18, 25, Box 1061, AT&T Corporate Archives, Warren, N. J.
8. *The Edison Sales Builder,* 2 (June, 1915), p. 56; Todd, *The Story of the Exposition,* IV, p. 297; "Description of Exhibits of the United States Steel Company and Subsidiary Companies, Panama Pacific Exposition, (1915), pamphlet, pp. 5, 17, 19, 54, USX Archives, Pittsburgh.
9. "The Reminiscences of Frank Vivian," pp. 7-10, 14-15, 31, typescript of interview, 1952, Oral History Section, Ford Archives; *Ford Times,* 8 (July, 1915), p. 455; David L. Lewis, *The Public Image of Henry Ford*. Detroit, 1976, p. 118.
10. Jeffrey L. Meikle, *Twentieth Century Limited: Industrial Design in America, 1925-1929*.Philadelphia, 1979, pp. 21-24, 39-67; Susan Porter Benson, *Counter Cultures: Saleswomen, Managers, and Customers in American Department Stores, 1890-1914*.Urbana, 1986, pp. 102-104; Paul H. Nystrom, *Economics of Fashion*. New York, 1928, pp. 91-92; Edison Lamp Works of the General Electric Company,

Edison Blue Book, 1923.Harrison, N. J., 1923, p. 102.

11. Ford, "1934 Report on the Fair," p. 27; Walker Rohe, "Twenty Million Gold Fish," Minutes of the Creative Staff Meeting, Jan. 3, 1934, J. Walter Thompson Company Archives, New York (now at Duke University and hereafter cited as JWT). The fair planners are quoted in Cawelti, *op.cit.,* p. 354.

12. Cawelti, *op.cit.,* pp. 353-54.

13. Ford, "1934 Report on the Fair," pp. 4, 15, 20, 22, 26-27, 31, 36; Minutes of Creative Staff Meeting, Jan. 3, 1934, p. 4, JWT Archives.

14. *American Machinist,* June 20, 1934, p. 430, clipping, Acc. 285, Box 1540, Ford Archives; Ford, "1934 Report on the Fair, " p. 27; *GE Monogram,* 10 (Jan. 1933), p. 11; (Apr. 1933), p. 12; (June, 1933), p. 17; General Electric Publicity Department, "General Electric in a Century of Progress," mimeo [1933], pp. 1-2, L 5335, Hammond Files, General Electric Library, Schenectady.

15. Ford Motor Company, "Ford at the Fair," (booklet, 1934), folder 16-269, Century of Progress Papers, University of Illinois, Chicago.

16. "General Electric in a Century of Progress," (mimeo, Publicity Department, [c. 1933], p. 3, L 5335, Hammond Files, General Electric Library; *GE Monogram*, 10 (May, 1933), p. 15; Fred L. Black to Frank Campsall, June 30, 1934, July 4, 1934; Black to Edsel Ford, June 29, 1934, Acc. 285, Box 1540; Black to Edsel Ford, Oct. 9, 1935, Acc. 6, Box 332, Ford Papers.

17. "Ford at the Fair," *loc. cit.*; Walter Dorwin Teague, "Designing Ford's Exhibit at A Century of Progress," *Product Engineering,* August, 1934, p. 282, clipping, Acc. 450, Box 2, "Engine Assembly Story," (press release, n.d.), Acc. 450, Box 3, Ford Papers. Another testimony to the Ford passion for educational seriousness appeared in a "ready for mailing" souvenir in 1934 entitled "Man must go to the earth for all materials." Within a small box, twelve individual compartments displayed tiny labelled samples of 12 natural ingredients, from iron ore to soy beans, that went into the making of Ford cars. One of these souvenirs has been retained in folder 16-269 of the Century of Progress collection at the University of Illinois, Chicago.

18. Minutes of Creative Staff Meeting, Jan. 3, 1934, p. 12, JWT Archives; Harvey Watts, "Report," August 1, 1936, Series II, Part 2, Box 51, Du Pont Archives; "Oversize Scrapbook," Acc. 77.242, photographic collection, Du Pont Archives; Walter Dorwin Teague to William A. Hart, June 22, 1936, reel 16:21A, Walter Dorwin Teague Papers, Syracuse University.

19. *Advertising Arts*, 4 (July, 1933), p. 17; Walter Teague to Edsel Ford, June 14, 1934, Acc. 6, box 167, Ford Papers; Martin Dodge to E. I. Du Pont Company, July 23, 1937, series II, pt. 2, Box 34, Du Pont Papers; "Du Pont Presentation," (memo, Nov., 1936), reel 16:21A, Teague Papers; *Advertising and Selling* 31 (Oct. 1938), p. 32.

20. *Scientific Monthly*, 39 (July, 1934), p. 17; *General Motors World,* 13 (June, 1934), p. 4 , (July, 1934), p. 6; "Press Release," May 26, 1934, General Motors, New York, 1934 folder, Charles F. Kettering Papers, GMI Alumni Foundation Collection of Industrial History, Flint, Michigan.
21. A. W. Page, "Memorandum," Nov. 14, 1933, "The Bell System at A Century of Progress," pp. 16-17, and S. L. Andre to A. W. Page, Mar. 15, 1934, Box 1061, AT&T Archives; Fred Black to Edsel Ford, June 9, 1934, Acc. 285, Box 1540 and "Comments Overheard at Ford Exhibit, Texas Centennial," Attendance Record Binder, Acc. 450, Box 2, Ford Papers; Rohe Walker, "Twenty-Two Million Gold Fish," Minutes of the Creative Staff Meeting, Jan. 3, 1934, pp. 1-2, JWT Archives; Ford, "1934 Report on the Fair," *passim*; R. H. Coleman to W. A. Hart, n.d., Acc. 500, Box 56 and "Case History and Final Report, Texas Exhibit," Series II, pt. 2, Box 51, Du Pont Papers.
22. Ford, "1934 Report on the Fair", pp. 23, 33, 38; P. H. Erbes, Jr., "Some Advertising Slants at the Century of Progress, *Printers' Ink*, June 15, 1933, pp. 47-48; Cawelti, *op.cit.,* p. 352; "Report by George M. McCaffrey," Minutes of the Board of Directors, Annual Meeting, Feb. 2, 1938, New York World's Fair, 1939-40 Papers, New York Public Library.
23. Truman, ed., *op.cit.,* p. 322. Commenting on the 1915 Panama-Pacific Exposition, Ford's fair manager, Frank Vivian observed: "They always said at that fair, 'If you're looking for a woman on the fair grounds, go up to the Food Building, but if you want a man, you've got to go down to Ford's,'" "The Reminiscences of Frank Vivian," p. 27.
24. For an extended discussion of the conception of consumers as female and an analysis of the characteristics thus imputed to them, see Roland Marchand, *Advertising the American Dream: Making Way for Modernity, 1920-1940.*Berkeley, 1985, pp. 53-72.
25. "What to See Today at the Chrysler 5-Star Show: 60 Minutes of Magic," flyer, (May, 1939), Vol 330, T. J. Ross Scrapbooks, Ivy L. Lee Papers, Princeton University; *Chrysler Motors Magazine,* 6 (June 1940), p. 6.
26. *Business Week*, Nov 4, 1939, p. 27; "Outline for Extension of 'Wonder World of Chemistry,'" (1939), Acc. 77.242, Du Pont photographic collection; Walter D. Teague, "Suggestions for Rebuilding 'The March of Chemistry,'" Series II, part 2, Box 51, Du Pont Archives; Helen Harrison, *Dawn of a New Day: The New York World's Fair, 1939/40.* New York, 1980, p. 99; *Life,* Aug. 7, 1939, p. 4.
27. "Script for 15-minute interview over radio Station WWRL," May 16, 1940, Acc. 1410, Box 44 and Emerson Evans to Matthew N. Chappell, July, 1939, Series II, part 2, Box 34, Du Pont Archives.
28. Norman Bel Geddes, untitled memo beginning "The proposed exhibit...", c. Apr. 7, 1938, pp. 3, 14, file 381 (Correspondence); "Description of the Conveyor Ride Model," file 381 (GM Building); and GM Press

Release, Apr. 15, 1939, file 384, Norman Bel Geddes Papers, University of Texas, Austin. Good descriptions of the Futurama and its implications appear in Meikle, *op.cit.,* pp. 200-09 and Alice Marquis, *Hope and Ashes: The Birth of Modern Times*.New York, 1986, pp. 202-04, 208-10.

29. *Saturday Evening Post,* May 6, 1939, pp. 68-69; "Young Henry Ford Went to the Fair," brochure (1939), Acc. 554, Box 21, Ford Papers; Fred L. Black, "Interview, March 10, 1951," p. 198, in Oral History Collection, Ford Papers; *San Francisco Chronicle,* Feb. 26, 1939, p. A4.

30. *Advertising and Selling,* 32 (Feb. 1939), pp. 22-23; "The Ford Exposition, New York World's Fair," (brochure, n.d.), Box 1005, New York World's Fair Papers, NYPL; N. W. Ayer & Son, "Ford Cycle of Production, 1940, Revised," (enclosure to H. L. McClinton to Fred Black, June 18, 1940) Acc. 554, Box 21, Ford Papers.

31. "Press Release," May 6, 1939, and May 13, 1939, Acc. 544, Box 14 and Henry Billings, "Mural Decoration for the Entrance Hall of the Ford Motor Building," typescript, n.d. Acc. 544, Box 1; Plummer Whipple to Fred Black, n.d. [1939], Acc. 56, Box 3; Ford Motor Company, "Benefits Received from Our Participation in the New York World's Fair, 1939," (typescript, n.d.) Acc. 554, Box 2, Ford Papers; *Saturday Evening Post*, May 6, 1939, pp. 68-69.

The Emergence of Photographic Discourse:
Images and Consumption

David E. Nye
Copenhagen University

In Don DeLillo's *White Noise* two university professors take a short trip.

> Murray asked me about a tourist attraction known as the most photo-
> graphed barn in America. . . . . We counted five signs before we reached
> the site. There were forty cars and a tour bus in the makeshift lot. We
> walked along a cowpath to the slightly elevated spot set aside for viewing
> and photographing. All the people had cameras; some had tripods,
> telephoto lenses, filter kits. A man in a booth sold postcards and slides—
> pictures of the barn taken from the elevated spot. We stood near a grove
> of trees and watched the photographers. Murray maintained a prolonged
> silence, occasionally scrawling some notes in a little book.
> "No one sees the barn," he said finally.

Murray concludes, "Being here is a kind of spiritual surrender. We see only
what the others see.. . . We've agreed to be part of a collective perception.
This literally colors our vision. A religious experience in a way, like all
tourism." Through a complex cultural mechanism, the barn has been selected
as an icon of rural life. Its owners have designated it as "the most photographed" barn in the United States, and through roadside signs they ensure
that this assertion becomes fact. The physical textures of the barn, its
intended day-to-day uses, and even its appearance from other vantage points
have all become secondary matters, subservient to its existence as a collective
representation, as an idealization of American "barn-ness." Significantly, the
passage in *White Noise* scarcely describes the barn itself, but deals with the
organization of collective attention, specifying neither its color nor its architectural style. In short, it is the activity of going to see the barn and returning
with its image that is important to the tourist, who, as Murray suggests, is
engaged in a modern form of pilgrimage.[1]

DeLillo's comment is particularly apropos one hundred and fifty years
after photography's invention in 1839. Few cultural practices are as central to

the culture of consumption as photography, which has long been useful to advertising and public relations and essential to the mass-appeal of newspapers and magazines. It is the shorthand that seems to be everywhere at work, transforming the physical world into appearances and visual clichés. Photography is a central cultural practice, whose products the public accepts as being accurate and true. Of the billions of photographs made each year, a few become universally recognizable representations of a particular person or event. Some become "official" records. Many are used for advertising or persuasion. An enormous number become prized private possessions, which anthropologists have found to be among the most cherished objects in the American home. Society is saturated in imagery, and photography is said to be intimately related to religion, consumption, cultural values, memory, desire, repressive desublimation, the collective unconscious, propaganda, and the work of art's loss of aura.

The first standard histories of the field treated photography as a hierarchy of images in the art history tradition, making it into a minor field related to painting. These histories themselves were the outcome of a successful hundred year struggle by photographers to have their work taken seriously as art. For most others, Susan Sontag's *On Photography* and Walter Benjamin's "The Work of Art in the Age of Mechanical Reproduction" are perhaps the most common reference points. Sontag approaches photography in a neoplatonic spirit of condemnation and reproduces not a single image. Many combine her unfootnoted attack with Benjamin's ruminations on how mechanical reproduction robbed the fine arts of their sacred aura and conclude that photography is a spurious, degenerate art of false consciousness.[2] Less commonly, photography has been understood as a fundamental mode of perception and communication in modern society, requiring courses in visual literacy. From this point of view, restricting photography to one department is no more sensible than restricting literature courses to students who aspire to be novelists. A few have treated photography as a form ideological expression, and therefore as a part of intellectual and social history. They stress not on the sequence of inventions or the work of "great" photographers, but rather on the development of what Alan Sekula has called "photographic discourse."[3] Roland Barthes began to move in this direction in his later work on advertisements and personal snapshots, but unfortunately he generalized from them to all photography, a procedure analogous to studying a few prose forms, such as personal letters or public relations handouts and, based on this material, generalizing to define writing *per se*. [4]

What generalizations are possible about the photographic medium? Even if someone with a camera would like to "present things as they are" this is technically impossible; the photographer necessarily constitutes the subject, regardless of what the "straight" practitioner may claim.[5] Photographs appear to be objective, yet they are interpretations of the world, not mechanical reproductions of it. They eliminate four of our five senses, and reduce the one remaining, sight, to a two dimensional plane. As a result, relative size, proportions, and the distances between objects become problematic. The flattening and distortion of the perceptual field is further complicated by the angle chosen and by the framing of images in a rectangular form borrowed from painting. This initial and unavoidable interpretation of reality is only supplemented by other, also unavoidable. choices of lenses, films, cameras, and darkroom techniques. Nevertheless, the public has long believed that "a picture is worth a thousand words," a superstition reinforced by the use of photographs as evidence by insurance companies, the police, and courts of law. Nor have intellectuals been immune to the public's naive faith in the literalness of the image. In the 1970s, perhaps because of a loss of faith in referentiality in literature as a result of the deconstruction movement, some otherwise sensible people proclaimed photographs to be literal representations. Roland Barthes wrote that, "In the photograph—at least at the level of the literal message—the relationship of signifieds to signifiers is not one of 'transformation' but one of 'recording,' and the *absence of a code* clearly reinforces the myth of photographic 'naturalness': the scene is there, captured mechanically, not humanly (the mechanical is here a guarantee of objectivity)." In such pronouncements, Barthes, who had little experience as a photographer and who seems to have read virtually nothing on the subject, spread a good deal of confusion, not least because he yoked his belief in the photograph's literal record to Sausurrean dichotomies. (In one of his last works Barthes abandoned the mechanics of his earlier structuralism, and meditated on the intensely personal meanings he ascribed to images of his childhood and his mother. Yet however intriguing, this document cannot substitute for a general theory of photography.) By the early 1980s most within the field realized that photography was not, as Barthes once claimed, "a message without a code," nor was it susceptible to an analysis based on structural linguistics.6 In photography, unlike language, there is no double articulation, no equivalent to the alphabet, no dictionary of visual elements, no system equivalent to the phonemes used in the study of language. As Victor Burgin put it, "there is no language of photography, no single signifying system (as opposed to technical apparatus) upon which all photographs depend." 7

Yet if there is no single signifying system, photography must nevertheless be understood as a form of communication, or discourse, consisting of the system of image classes deployed in a society at a given time.8 Within each culture these image classes compose a changing, self-contradictory system of seeing the world. We are only beginning to recover the history of these photographic image systems, which might be called socially constructed visual realities, but it seems clear that the basic form of American photographic discourse was already defined by the 1900 at the latest, and to grasp what that discourse entails, it is useful to sketch its development.

II

Before photography portraiture was restricted to the wealthiest classes, who alone had enough money to buy a painter's time and skill. Even the pre-photographic vogue of miniatures should not be seen as a popular movement, for despite their small size they were too costly for most people. Rather, the growing demand for representations of the self was filled by two inventions, the silhouette and the physiotrace, which mechanically traced a likeness of the face.9 After Daguerre's and Talbot's inventions in 1839, however, virtually anyone could possess a self-image, in this way establishing another social reality. Images of the self could be publicized, exchanged, sent in the mail, and handed down in the family, permitting the ordinary individual to enter into a new realm beyond immediate space and time. A discourse of social appearance once limited to the very few who could command the services of a portrait painter now became a common cultural possession. In the United States alone, by 1853 2,000 daguerreotypists were making more than three million images each year.10 For the first half century, portraits were still made almost exclusively by professionals, often former painters, who carried into photography the rectangular frame and the conventions of the canvas. Their formal studio portraits dignified the ordinary person in the poses and settings formally the province of the rich alone. The sitters had only to stand in front of a studio backdrop dressed in borrowed clothing, and they appeared to be rich gentlemen and ladies. In this way, the nineteenth century public began to use photography to embellish the truth, to hide defects, to equivo-cate. Yet all the same came the familiar realization that someone did or did not look good in photographs, a popular recognition that the medium was neither a mirror of nature nor unproblematic.

One might expect to find that picture-making formulas became more fluid once the Kodak camera began to deprofessionalize photography in the 1890s. Suddenly an amateur could make images without owning a darkroom, and yet pushing a button did not destroy the old portrait genres. Amateur photography only spread more widely a limited number of ways of seeing the family and the self. An anthropologist who studied American snapshots found that they fall into a few relatively small number of poses and subject matters; amateur photographers but repeat the images they have seen before. Snapshot photography suggests how a visual codification that might be compared with but not subordinated to the linguistic code is at work, creating a system of standard views that are imposed on the body.11 In other words, it is misleading to speak of images as being external, or imposed on the eye. Rather, repeated visual representations standardize a collective perception, which is internalized. It becomes difficult, logically perhaps it even becomes impossible, to see oneself in a portrait, any more than DeLillo's characters can see "the most photographed barn in America."

Novelists have often noted the substitution of the photograph for the person and the allure of the image. Edna Pointellier in Kate Chopin's *The Awakening* fantasizes over the image of a popular actor. Likewise, in Theodore Dreiser's *The Titan*, Frank Cowperwood is not drawn to Berenice so much by her presence as by her photograph, which he purchases secretly and hangs in his private "Chicago rooms, where sometimes, of an afternoon when he was hurrying to change his clothes he stopped to look at it. With each succeeding examination his admiration and curiosity grew. Here was perhaps, he thought, the true society woman, the high born lady, the realization of that ideal. . . ." Cowperwood thus reifies Berenice, transforming her into a bloodless ideal. Perhaps the most pathetic example of the substitution of the photograph for the person can be found in the recent vogue of home pornography. As John Updike noted in *Rabbit is Rich*, the polaroid SX-70 Land Camera allows every couple to have "personal" pornography.[12] Couples can make images privately that were once confined to the seamy underworld of Victorian image-making and later the stock-in-trade of "dirty" magazines. Now they are self-produced with no telltale negatives, no embarrassing third parties in the photo-lab, presumably for their eyes only. But Updike's Harry goes upstairs to use the bathroom, and, inquisitive about his friends' sex life, he looks in the drawer of the bed-side table to see what kind of contraceptives they use. He finds eight polaroid images of Cindy and Webb.

> The top photo, flashlit in this same room, on this same satiny bedspread, shows Cindy naked, laying legs spread. . . .At arm's length he holds the glazed picture closer to the bedside light; his eyes water with the effort to see everything, every crease, every hair. Cindy's face, out of focus beyond her breasts, which droop more to either side than Harry would have hoped, smiles with nervous indulgence at the camera. Her chin is doubled, looking so sharply down. Her feet look enormous. [12]

Harry notes the camera's distortions of scale, but he makes mental corrections and is sexually aroused nonetheless. The camera has made it possible for him to violate his neighbors' privacy, to see what is forbidden, to observe their awkward self-observation. He knows that when he leaves the bedroom the room's "mirror will erase his image instantly." Unlike the camera, it leaves no trace of his presence, of his secretive encounter. Sociologists have found that, as one might suspect from Updike's account, these apparently exotic private images fall into a rather small number of poses, signifying not a new freedom achieved through technology but rather the further penetration of visual clichés into the sense of self, commodifying the body.

Before photography, most visual experience was confined to what one had personally seen. Paintings and engravings were not widely dispersed, and the only way to see something was to travel. After photographs appeared, they quickly became both a substitute for travel and a preparation for it. Henry James noted in 1888 that, "When Americans went abroad in 1820 there was something romantic, almost heroic in it, as compared with the perpetual ferryings of the present hour, the hour at which photography and other conveniences have annihilated surprise."[13] As soon as it was technically feasible, photographers journeyed around the world, to "take" the most famous cities, natural wonders, mysteries of the Far East, and the exotic destinations of explorers. The American middle class was particularly avid for "stereograph" views of their own West, which taught them to understand it in terms of the painterly tradition of the Hudson River School.[14] As James suggests, the tourist's experience soon became that of seeing in person what had already been seen in photographs, and of having preconceptions confirmed or disappointed. The world had been codified in advance, and the tourist learned to interpret sites according to how well they lived up to their photographs.

Yet photography did more than annihilate surprise. Natural scientists used it to gather more precise information than had been possible before. Astronomers photographed the heavens, using time exposures that revealed stars too dim to be seen with the naked eye. Their images also showed the arrangement of heavenly bodies at a given moment more precisely than drawings. Likewise, the botanist and biologist found photography an indispensable form of exact record-keeping, especially when microscopic photography became possible. Engineers and physicists learned to use high-speed cameras to study operating machinery or other objects in rapid motion. Archaeologists found that aerial photography revealed the faint traces of earlier settlements. In science, then, rather than "annihilate surprise," photography extended human vision into new areas.

Thus photographic discourse is not simply a system of visual clichés that filters much of the world to us; it also contains entirely unexpected vistas and fundamentally new information. While this point is obvious in astronomy or micro-biology, it is valid for everyday objects as well. Many ordinary things can be made much more interesting, or "seen anew" when framed in a photograph. This realization, formally expressed in the pre-World War I Russian theory of "ostranenie," underlay a whole movement in the 1920s and 1930s dedicated to using photography to "make strange" the world, as in the images of Moholy-Nagy and Man Ray. By the 1930s, however, this impulse had largely "dissolved into the general modernist need for constant stylistic innovation, seen as an end it itself."[15] Even aside from such a formal dedication to the image's misprisoning of the reality it represents, photographers have long known how to transform their subjects through manipulating angle, focus, lenses, or other technical aspects of the camera. Indeed, each generation of American photographers seems distinguished by a new set of practices that produce a revisioning of the world. By means of a special soft focus lens turn-of-the-century pictorialists produced images that looked like impressionist paintings. A generation later, through close-ups and unusual angles, Edward Weston made a urinal or a green pepper sculptural. A list of further examples would include the Farm Security Administration (FSA) photographers, Robert Frank, Diane Arbus, Lee Friedlander, and the usual litany of the art history tradition.

Thus within photographic discourse there seem to be two contrary movements, the one codifying the world and reducing it to visual clichés, the other expanding the reach of the eye and the range of vision. Depending upon which of these two a theorist emphasizes, photography as a whole may seem to be a prison house of images or a liberating expansion of information and human awareness.[16] Both of these viewpoints, however, are rooted in a romantic view of the self, in which a pure and undifferentiated childhood vision is corrupted by conventions. In this view, the great photographer, like the poet, breaks through the conventions, liberating us to see the world afresh. Yet photography need not be viewed in these terms. Like literature, photographic studies can be passed through the alembic of structuralism, post-structuralism, and deconstruction. Just as Michel Foucault declared the death of the author, one must also declare the death of the photographer. Rather than examine photographs as emanations of genius, we can study them as systems of images.

To return to the example of tourist photography, granting that the postcard, snapshot, and travel book overdetermine the tourist's response to the foreign or the exotic, at the same time their visual conventions become the necessary precondition for counter-images, or revisionings of these sites. Even in their routinized form tourist images increase the visual information available to those who never visit the sites, despite the fact that it comes in the form of a two-dimensional conventionalized transcription. Rather than condemn photography as a corruption of vision, then, it is more accurate to understand it as a continually changing complex of image classes, some of which invert or oppose others, and all of which are social constructions of reality, not mirrors of it.

One can develop this point further by examining how nineteenth century photography transformed the popular understanding of war. Before the American Civil War the public had a rather grandiose and heroic ideal of battle. After seeing images of dead bodies strewn over the battlefields, however, war seemed far more terrible. Yet given photography's slow technology at that time, it revealed only the aftermath of battle, not the battle itself, and as Alan Trachtenberg has argued, images of the Civil War turn out to be quite problematic: "The simplest documentary questions of who did what, when, where, and why may be impossible to answer. And much more consequential matters of meaning and interpretation, of narrative and ideological tropes, of invisible presences and visible absences, have rarely even been asked."[17] Only by a rigorous investigation, he argues, can one hope to free these images from "authorized functions and meanings" and begin to see them. William Frassanito made one such determined investigation of the photographs taken after the Battle of Gettysburg. He found that because it took photographers several days to reach the battleground and because each wet-plate negative required about half an hour to be prepared immediately before exposure, the cameramen had trouble keeping ahead of the grave diggers. To cope with their rapidly disappearing subject, photographers brought along their own props, such as rifles, they moved some bodies into more picturesque positions, and they took the same fallen men from different angles. They apparently felt no compunctions as they recomposed the scene to fit their vision, and the shocking war-images they created were ready-made clichés, another codified class of images.

Such practices were already common before photographic discourse expanded into many other areas after 1870, as a series of technical changes created entirely new possibilities. The half-tone newspaper photograph, first employed after 1880 and perfected in the following decade, came into widespread use by c. 1895.[18] A little earlier the dry plate appeared, which permitted cameramen to carry far less equipment and travel more easily, no longer needing a small chemical laboratory nearby at all times to prepare wet plates immediately prior to exposure. These innovations together facilitated the deployment of four additional photographic forms: photo-journalism, advertising, documentary work (e.g. Lewis Hine and Jacob Riis), and commercial photography. These four, together with the already established traditions of scientific image making, portraiture, and landscape, coalesced into a tacit photographic discourse in the 1890s. The major genres had been established, and the world had been carved up into a set of stylized representations, each with its appropriate audience. The rapidly growing ranks of professional photographers, linked together by associations and journals, institutionalized this representational system. The United States Government further facilitated the circulation of images when it legalized the picture post-card in 1898, initiating what some scholars have called a mania or a craze. One decade later almost one billion post cards were being sent annually, while millions more were purchased as mementoes.[19]

Indeed, photographers soon outnumbered professional writers, as their work penetrated into every American community by the turn-of-the-century. Anthopologist Bill Jay's work demonstrates that by 1900 even tiny hamlets in rural Pennsylvania were saturated with stylized commercial images, including standardized post-card views, stereo slides of famous places, formal portraits, and images of local homes, stores, and small businesses.[20] "View" photographers made the local images, as they traveled the countryside in wagons, inducing families to pose before their homes. They returned a few weeks later with the eight-by-ten inch contact prints that sold for as little as $1.50 each. Ruby's work shows that the new photographic discourse addressed virtually all citizens, not merely the urban middle class.

As this sketch indicates, the history of photography need not be the story of gradually evolving technical means mastered by a few artists, but rather the story of social practices that developed in the half century after 1839 to the point where images blanketed and defined the world. Certainly by 1900 a set of discursive practices had become conventionalized, each serving quite different social functions, and each institutionalized in publications. It is no accident that Alfred Stieglitz and the Photo-Secessionists defined the artistic tradition at precisely the end of the 1890s, for at this historical juncture the whole discursive apparatus of photography found definition. At a time when some images were being reproduced by the million in popular magazines, Stieglitz refused to make more than a few prints from a negative, employing meticulous darkroom techniques and special papers. The resulting images were presented to the public as unique art objects; like paintings they could not be reprinted in magazines satisfactorily. Instead, in *Camera Work* Stieglitz championed the expensive technique of photogravure, while stressing that even it could not capture every nuance of an "original" platinum paper print. His movement was only possible, in a sense, because the new commercial and documentary forms had emerged as its foils.

The development of this discursive apparatus after 1900 can only be hinted at here. Obviously the forums available increased, as both journalistic and advertising photography had greater scope once popular magazines shifted away from engravings to photographs. Documentary photography, building on the work of Hine and Riis, became the stock-in-trade of reformers and was also briefly common in sociology. After c. 1920 it suffered a decline, and then briefly became a dominant form again during the 1930s, before being largely absorbed into the conventions of corporate imagery by the 1940s.[21] By the later 1930s the enormous circulations of mass magazines indicated that photography had become a determinant way of seeing. *Life* and *Look,* with their human interest and news photography, most obviously display the period's dominant image systems, but perhaps the most intriguing mass publications of these years were *Vogue* and *Fortune,* both proponents of modernism and the international style. They captured the upper-class audience, marking its appropriation of *avant guard* artistic forms, as can also be seen in the architecture of world fairs before World War II.

While the development of documentary photography is reasonably well-known, it is perhaps more important to recognize that the large corporations by the 1920s had made photography a crucial form of public relations. Every major company had a full-time staff devoted to mass-producing images of its products, workers, and social environments, and they deployed these images in a wide variety of contexts, including public relations, scientific publications, advertisements in national magazines and newspapers, and in-house journals whose circulations could be as large as 100,000. During the inter-war years these corporate images, distributed by the billions each year, shaped and defined the social construction of reality, providing what might be called a visual rhetoric of everyday life.[22] The images that corporations disseminated constituted photography's "ordinary language" that was sporadically "answered" by documentary and artistic photographers, when they were not working on corporate payrolls themselves, as almost all were at times.

Photographic discourse since World War II has been marked by several developments whose complex interconnections can only be hinted at here. Television news largely replaced the mass-circulation magazine, and *Life, Look,* and many other weeklies went bankrupt, returning in a few cases as monthlies that no longer command the same national attention. As Barbara Rosenblum has shown in her ethnographic study *Photographers at Work,* now that these glamorous forums have disappeared, most professional photographers do routinized work in advertising or journalism. Employers and clients largely determine the subject matter of widely disseminated images, as well as the time available to create them and the audience who will receive them. To deal with these constraints photographers rely upon standard techniques and formulas of composition as much as possible. Only those who aspire to be artists seem to be free to make photographs as they wish, and yet as Rosenblum found in her participant observation, they also confront gatekeepers, in the form of the curators of museums and galleries, who determine whose work is to be supported.[23] Even as artistic production has been valorized, creating a boom in the photographic print market, however, the most prolific image makers certainly are the amateurs, who each year have access to ever more automated cameras and faster films, and who, as noted, endlessly repeat themselves in front of the most photographed barns in America.

III

This sketch of photographic discourse and its development only outlines the historical background. At present, we know far too little about the history of this discourse to make many definitive statements. Furthermore, the reconstruction of this history is complicated because photography is a discourse which usually hides the interpretive function it performs. Complicating the problem further, while every photograph is legible to an intended audience when it is made, its meaning erodes or slips away over time. Eventually its meaning can be controlled by the caption affixed to it, particularly if it passes on to a new audience and a new interpretive situation. This process is most obvious in old photographs that elude explanation, such as one that Ruby found of five women sitting in a field with their spinning wheels. The image is less than a century old, and yet has already lost much of its first meaning. We do not know who these women were, why they had the image made, or why they wanted it taken out in a field. One can *guess* that they represent three generations of one family, carrying on a traditional craft. But in fact such work had been mechanized before the Civil War, and virtually no one made yarn or thread by hand in 1900. It is tempting to think that these women were among the last spinners and they wanted a memorial to their passing, but this is sheer speculation. Or they may have been devotees of the arts-and-crafts movement. My point is the image's resistance to our interpretation. By comparison, few *written* documents from the popular culture of 1900 are so hard to read.

This particular image invites speculation, but every photograph is exposed to a similar, if less obvious, erosion of its first meaning. This slippage occurs because the meaning of an image is established by a network of codes, which are a heterogeneous complex of technical features (such as focus), artistic conventions (e.g. framing, poses, parallels with famous images), kinesic codes (e.g. gestures), language inside the image (e.g. shop signs), social codes (e.g. dress), and, not least, the other images known to the viewer, either similar photographs or representations of the same people.[24] Over time each image loses contact with some of the codes that gave it meaning for the photographer and first viewers. As these layers of signification are stripped away, a photograph is unmoored from its context and can gradually be emptied of its content, making it more and more possible to impose entirely new meanings upon it. Photography is thus the quintessential form of consumption, as it translates a tangible physical object into a system of representation. It appears to remain faithful to its referent, and yet permits the erasure of one meaning and the substitution of countless others. As Wittgenstein succinctly put it, "A picture can depict any reality whose form it has."[25] Photographic content is inexorably recontextulized with the passage of time, and an image will be further redefined by placement in a new location and by the changing stance of the viewer. For example, Farm Security Administration images originally made as government public relations work to publicize New Deal programs have been presented in museum shows as art. Likewise the popular "Family of Man" exhibit of the 1950s welded together a wide variety of images from different contexts, transforming their meanings in the process. As Eric Sandeen has noted, Edward Steichen, who organized the "Family of Man," reused images from previous contexts to create his own narrative. To do so he did not hesitate to manipulate them by cropping, enlarging, or remounting them. The result was a powerfully integrated show which was eventually seen by nine million people during a six year world tour. The power of the exhibit stemmed not only from the excellence of many of its 503 images, but also from their skillful arrangement in a larger pattern. Some of the photographers protested, however, that the aesthetic distinction of their work had been sacrificed to achieve a unified effect. As Sandeen concludes, "the photographs were not in fact the same, neither in terms of technique, nor aesthetic values, nor symbolic impact."

As this example suggests, an immediate problem for all who study photographs is how they have been seen over time, a problem that can be formulated as one of "viewer response."[26] Another important area for future research is the process of recontextualization, which can be studied by tracing an image through its various encodings. One study of this kind has been done by Henning Hansen, who examined the multiple uses and meanings of Eugene Smith's "Garden of Eden" photograph in the forty years it has been used since first appearing at the end of World War II.[27] Such research recognizes that it is not the photographer but the photograph itself which has a "career" as it passes through successive contexts.

The synchronic parallel to such chronological analysis of individual images must be study of the organization of photographic archives. Alan Trachtenberg has examined how the Library of Congress classified its FSA collection into clusters of images that invite the user to insert them into pre-formed narratives. The file was conceived as a "machine for the re-combination of images into stories, a device for identifying the best approximate denotative description of an image in order to release an unlimited fund of connotational relations."[28] Likewise, my investigation of the more than one million images in the General Electric Photographic Archives revealed not a mere chronological file, but clusters of images, organized according to anticipated uses in particular kinds of forums. It could be described in the same terms that Trachtenberg uses to describe the FSA. In each case, the file presents itself as a "'story' in its own right" that fuses many "tropes into an implicit narrative of human society as such." The archivists at large institutions have thus done more than create a meta-structure that circumscribes the meanings a researcher is likely to give an image. They have also used photographic files as a way to map an institution's activities onto the larger society, constructing a multifaceted representation of its relation to the world.

To take account of the continually recontextualized image and of the archive as a representation of the world is to locate photography as a discursive apparatus in intellectual history. The emergence of this apparatus at the end of the nineteenth century marks a fundamental shift in society, as the historical subject was divided into an array of images, a subdivision that was a vital part of the larger transformation of American society, as it moved from a culture of production to one of consumption. The change was not merely that often-noted shift from the complexities of the wet plate process mastered only by a few to the simplicities of the Kodak camera, rather it was the shift from a limited production and distribution of photographs to the multiplication of the subject in images, casting its historical position, its solidity. and its certainty, into flux. Given the pluralities of photographic representation, reality began to seem so elusive that it could no longer be described by the magisterial third person narrators of William Dean Howells or Balzac, and it is hardly accidental that in the same years that photography became a dominant form of representation novelists became fascinated with the use of stream of consciousness and multiple narrators in fiction.

The photographic discourse that emerged at the turn-of-the-century was inherently modernist. As used in advertising, public relations, documentary, and news reporting, it expressed not a single vision, but the intersection and rupture of many codes. Yet if the discourse as a whole was fractured, internally contradictory, and discontinuous, individual images functioned as forms of belief in momentary solidities, replacing monolithic interpretations of the world, or traditional ideology. During the period of photography's

45

greatest social power, from 1900 until 1950, photographs became a primary form of representing the world. They seemed to express fixed meanings; when in fact they could only temporarily validate interpretations of the world. They permitted the development of a new kind of hegemonic system which seemed to be no more than the expression of facts, and which therefore no longer required absolutes. Even at the moment of its first use each image was already part of a discourse built up as a series of oppositions established by traditions of representation. Over time each photograph's meaning could only change and disintegrate. The instability of photographic vision thus signifies far more than a mere variety of techniques adopted in the search for novelty; it represents the transformation of the historical subject into a multiplicity of contradictions, each of which appears to be accurate and true. Despite the photograph's apparent stability, it can only fracture over time, unwinding into a series of interpretations, sliding into an indeterminate state as its meanings are continually reinvented.

References

1. Don DeLillo, *White Noise*. London: Picador, 1986, p. 12.
2. See Beaumont Newhall, *The History of Photography from 1838 to the Present Day*. New York: Simon & Schuster, 1949. Helmut Gernsheim, *The History of Photography, 1685—1914*. New York: McGraw Hill, 1969. Susan Sontag *On Photography*. New York: Delta Books, 1977. Walter Benjamin, "The Work of Art in the Age of Mechanical Reproduction" in *Illuminations*. New York: Harcourt Brace & World, 1968.
3. The term "photographic discourse" was perhaps first used by Alan Sekula, in his influential article, "On the Invention of Photographic Meaning," *Artforum*, 13:5, (1975).
4. Pierre Bourdieu's *Un Art Moyen*. Paris: Les Editions de Minuit, 1965. an essay on the social uses of photography in France, takes a broader view of image making and consumption, yet his work has had less impact in America than Barthes, whose works were not only translated but issued in paperback, such as *Image, Music, Text*. New York: Hill and Wang, 1977.
5. For an extended discussion of this point see Roman Gubern, *Mensajes Iconicos en la Cultura de Masas*, Barcelona: Editorial Lumen, 1974, pp. 29—31, *passim*.
6. Barthes, *op. cit.*, pp. 44, 17.
7. For a more extended critique of Barthes, see David E. Nye, *Image Worlds: Corporate Identities at General Electric*. Cambridge: The MIT Press, 1985, pp. 47—54. Victor Burgin, "Looking at Photographs," in his edited volume, *Thinking Photography*. London: Macmillan, 1982. For another view, see W. T. J. Mitchell's important *Iconology. Image,*

Text, Ideology. University of Chicago Press, 1986.

8. For an analysis of "Photography as Communication," see *Journal of American Culture* 9:3, (Fall, 1986), pp. 29—37.
9. Gisèle Freund, *Photography & Society.* London: Gordon Fraser, 1980, Chapter Two, "Precursors of the Photographic Portrait, pp. 9—19.
10. *Ibid.,* p. 33.
11. Richard Chalfen, "Redundant Imagery: Some Observations on the Use of Snapshots in American Culture," *Journal of American Culture* 4:1 (1981), 106—13. Also see Chalfen's "The Sociovidistic Wisdom of Abby and Ann: Toward an Etiquette of Home Mode Photography," *Journal of American Culture,* 7:1 & 2, (Spring/Summer, 1984), pp. 22—31.
12. Kate Chopin, *The Awakening.* New York: Avon Books, 1972. [Reprint of 1899] Theodore Dreiser, *The Titan.* Cleveland: World Publishing Company, 1946. p. 348. John Updike, *Rabbit is Rich.* Harmondsworth: Penguin Books, 1982, pp. 282—284. Also see Charles Edgeley and Kenneth Kiser, "Polaroid Sex: Deviant Possibilities in a Technical Age," *Journal of American Culture,* 5:1, (Spring, 1982), pp. 59—64.
13. Henry James, *Aspern Papers* in *The Novels and Tales of Henry James,* Vol. 12. New York: Scribner's 1961, p. 49.
14. Barbara Novak, *Nature and Culture.* New York: Oxford University Press, 1980, pp. 176—196.
15. See Simon Whatney, "Making Strange: The Shattered Mirror," in Victor Burgin, ed., *Thinking Photography.* London: Macmillan, 1982, p. 170.
16. For the "prison house" view, see Susan Sontag, *On Photography.* New York: Delta Books, 1977; for a thoughtful argument of the opposite view see William Crawford, *The Keepers of Light.* New York: Morgan and Morgan, 1979.
17. Alan Trachtenberg, "Albums of War: On Reading Civil War Photographs," *Representations* 9, Winter, 1985, pp. 2—3.
18. William Frassanito, *Gettysburg.* New York: Scribners, 1976. Raymond Smith Schuneman, , "The Photograph in Print: An Examination of New York Daily Newspapers, 1890—1937" Doctoral Dissertation, University of Minnesota, 1966, pp. 97—100.
19. Steven Dotterer and Galen Cranz, "The Picture Postcard: Its Development and Role in American Urbanization," *Journal of American Culture,* 5:1, (Spring, 1982), p. 44 and *passim* .
20. Jay Ruby, "The United States View Company of Richfield, Pennsylvania," *Studies in Visual Communication* 9:4, pp. 45—64.
21. See Nye, *op.cit.,* pp. 155—160.
22. *Ibid.,* pp. 9—58.
23. Rosenblum, Barbara, *Photographers at Work.* New York: Holmes and Meier, 1978.
24. See Burgin, *op. cit.,* pp. 143—144.
25. Cited in Mary Douglas, ed., *Rules and Meaning,* London: Penguin

Books, 1973, p. 53.

26. Eric J. Sandeen, "The Family of Man at the Museum of Modern Art: The Power of the Image in 1950s America." *Prospects*, Vol 11, (1986), p. 388. A useful short guide is Richard Rudisill, "On Reading Photographs," *Journal of American Culture*, 5:3, (Fall, 1982).

27. Henning Hansen, *Myth and Vision: On the Walk to Paradise*. Lund: Lund University Press, 1987.

28. Alan Trachtenberg, "Of This Time, of That Place: Reading the FSA File" unpublished paper, courtesy of the author, p. 2. The essay is incorporated in his *Reading American Photographs*. New York: Hill and Wang, 1989.

Americanization of European Television:
An Aesthetic Approach

Stig Hjarvand
Copenhagen University

In October 1989 The European Common Market ministers adopted the EEC-directive on European television. Earlier that same year — in May, 1989 — the Council of Europe's "European Convention on Transfrontier Television" was ready for signature by member nations. These two decisions represent the latest attempt on a political level to regulate the new television situation in Europe. These attempts towards regulation — or rather re-regulation — come after a 10-year period of continuing *deregulation* of broadcasting activities in Europe. The process of deregulation has radically changed the television situation in two ways. First, the opening for more commercial activities (private ownership, advertising etc.) in the television field has resulted in many new television stations challenging the old national public television monopolies. Second, the introduction of "new" distributions technologies (cable and satellite) has changed the traditionally national basis of broadcasting and thus created a much more diversified and complex situation, with a growing number of both local, national, and transnational television stations.

The growing competition from privately-based and/or advertising-financed television has put great pressure on the old national channels. At the same time as they are losing viewers they are financially strained by increasing expenditures and by political reluctance to raise the license fees. More importantly, because the old stations no longer are the only national broadcasters, they are forced to reconsider their institutional role and program policy. From being old national monopolies based on the public service concept with obligations to broadcast news programs and many educational, cultural and entertainment programs, they are now one of many channels in a milieu where television is increasingly understood as an entertainment medium. However, the European public service stations will probably not be marginalised as in United States. Most public service stations have already chosen to use their still considerable resources to compete with the new commercial stations, not least in order to legitimate their license fees. More likely the television situation in Europe will end up as a hybrid of business and public interests, and the tension between these interests will not only characterize the relations between TV-networks but also the internal policy of individual institutions, including the public service stations.

In the light of this, the previously mentioned directive and convention can be seen as attempts to regulate and counter the "worst" consequences of deregulation. They reflect the fact that although deregulation in many countries has been a deliberate policy to create a new dynamic in the television sector, there is a growing understanding of the problems of leaving televisual communication to market forces alone. And in this debate U.S. television takes its place as the most extreme experience.

The "responsible" call for a third way of broadcasting, which would not be modeled after either the old European public monopoly or American television, is clearly expressed by the European Television Task Force, a study group headed by Giscard d'Estaing:

> ...between a return to the authoritarianism of the public service monopolies and the anarchy which would result from unbridled competition, there is a third way. This option would enable organizations with a different legal status and financed in different ways to co-exist, bringing real diversity into the content and spirit of programs, accepting responsibilities over and above the search for immediate profit, and accepting certain minimum operating standards within a European framework.1

In accord with this viewpoint, the European Council's TV-convention stipulates different restrictions on advertising and sponsorship and pays special attention to young viewers. Furthermore, both this convention and the EEC-directive stipulate that at least half of all programs must be of European origin, allowing the European TV stations to import no more than 50% of their programs from non-European countries.

Not surprisingly this last restriction is primarily directed against the import of American programs, especially "fiction" programs, here defined as films, series, and dramatic programs. The need for this restriction, however, reveals a contradiction in the deregulation-policy: although meant to revitalize the European broadcasting industry (and the industry at large by increasing advertising possibilities) and in that way stimulate the production of European programs, the competition has created a massive demand for TV-programs which the European TV-stations themselves have not been able to meet. As a result, the import of American programs, especially "fiction," has in many cases increased. Deregulation of the broadcasting sector has in this way contributed further to the most direct expression of Americanization.

In order to make the European television industry more competitive, deregulation as such has proved insufficient. Not only for cultural considerations but also for strictly commercial reasons a regulated commercialization is needed. As a result both the European Council's TV-Convention and the

EEC-Directive are taking steps to enable the European television industry to compete with its U.S. counterpart. By making clearer and more uniform rules for the transnational exchange of television programs in Western Europe a larger home market for the European program industries can be created, thus reducing the American advantage of a big home market.

This short sketch of some major trends in the deregulation process and the attempts to re-regulate the new television situation shows some of the simplicity and confusion which characterizes the usual political discussion about the consequences of the deregulation process in general, and the discussion of Americanization in particular. Two aspects of Americanization can be distinguished. The first aspect, the adoption of a commercial model of broadcasting, is primarily understood as a way to attract more money to the television sector and to create more dynamism through competition. It is not understood as a transformation of the social aim and character of televisual communication. Given this view, the political task is simply to impose some regulations on the market.

Table 1. National Distribution of Supply and Consumption in Danish Television [1*] during Ten Selected Weeks in the Period 1984-1987.

Percent of total programming supply & consumption, from:

	Nordic	Europe	USA	Total	Denmark
Import Supply					
Factual	2	8	1	11	89
Sports	4	45	8	57	43
Drama	1	42	32	81	19
Music, light entertainment	2	8	4	14	86
Other	0	0	0	0	100
All hours	3	21	9	34	66
Consumption					
Factual	3	18	2	23	77
Sports	4	36	6	46	54
Drama	4	34	48	86	14
Music, light entertainment	3	3	2	8	92
Other	0	0	0	0	100
All hours	3	19	15	38	62

Source: Preben Sepstrup: "The Transnationalization of Television," Working Paper No.13, Department of Marketing, Aarhus School of Business, 1988.

[1*] The old network of radio and television is called Denmarks Radio.

The second aspect of Americanization, the unequal trade balance in the program field, likewise requires simple countermeasures: the political task is to limit the import of American programs. Americanization in this rather simple sense is not so pronounced, however, as is often assumed. In a small European country like Denmark, in which TV-stations traditionally use many foreign programs due to financial restrictions, the actual share of American produced programs nevertheless is not very high, and this is true of both the share of supply and the share of actual consumption. Table 1 shows that American programs are only relatively dominant in the case of the genre of drama/fiction programs. In genres like news and documentary or sports, and entertainment Danish and Western European productions predominate. If these figures do not correspond with the Danish daily experience of television, it is probably due to fact that American fiction programs are very popular and therefore are placed in prime time. In the light of these statistics Americanization cannot be perceived as the huge import and consumption of American programs. The term must be considered to be part of a protectionist argument in the trade competition between the United States and Western Europe, rather than as a description of the actual situation.

However, it is still hard to ignore the fact that some kind of Americanization follows from the deregulation process. To get a more complete understanding of the consequences of deregulation, it is useful to look at deregulation, commercialization, and Americanization as different aspects of the same process, a continuing transformation of the *social form* of televisual communication from a public and legal form to a *commodity form,* in which communication increasingly serves the realization of capital. It is not a complete or unambiguous shift from one form to another. It is rather an interaction between two different social forms that shapes the final social form and use of television. Nor is the communication entirely subordinated to this commodity form. But due to this shift in social form, the communicative relation itself is changed. In the commodity form the communicative *intention* is divided into two rather opposite considerations. On the one hand the intention to communicate becomes empty. The interest is solely to arouse the viewers' interest as such. There is no intention of telling the viewers anything, only the intention of telling, as such. On the other hand, to achieve this first goal the needs and wishes of the viewers must be anticipated so that the actual communication can be as attractive and pleasurable as possible. In the public form neither the wish to get attention nor the satisfaction of the viewer is the primary communicative intention. The communicative intention is to a large extent committed to non-individual, social interests.

Compared to other mass media, television has occupied a special position outside the capitalist market in Western Europe for more than 40 years, a situation that, depending on one's point of view, can be considered either unique or old-fashioned and outmoded. The current change in the social form of televisual communication has not only financial and institutional consequences, but also consequences on the level of program content and aesthetics. If the level of program content and aesthetics is taken into consideration, Americanization is not only about the volume of imported programs or the introduction of a commercial organization of broadcasting (although the last is a very important aspect), but also about the usage, adaptation and transformation of the aesthetics developed within American television. An aesthetic analysis is traditionally outside the scope of politics and economics. Nevertheless, it is on this level that the actual changes in the communicative practice can be analyzed and the phenomenon of Americanization can be more thoroughly comprehended.

Within this broad framework I will try to outline an analysis of the changes in the evening news, which traditionally has served as the principal program for maintaining the public service-institution's self-conception as a performer of public communication. More specifically, the analysis will deal with the changes in the old Danish public service-institution television news program "TV-Avisen." These changes were made in the late 1980s as a reaction to increasing competition from commercial stations at the local, national and international level. Before looking at these changes, it is necessary to characterize the initial position and aesthetics of traditional public service news.

The model for the European public service-stations was to a great extent the English BBC, but public service is not a specific organizational model. Both license and advertising financed stations can have more or less public service-like obligations. Public service stands for a special conception of the social role of radio and television: on the one hand it must be independent of private and commercial interests, and on the other hand it must be independent of the public authorities. Instead, as the holder of a national monopoly, it is committed to society as a whole, that is to a postulated common, national interest among the audience. This ideal of public service, with some national variations, was the result of specific historical circumstances in the 1920s. Conservatives and Social Democrats were afraid of leaving the new powerful medium of radio in the control of market forces, but direct state control of broadcasting was (by some at least) also considered dangerous. The Social Democrats were especially in favor of the independent public model, according to which radio and later television could serve a broad educational role. They wanted radio and television to stand above social contradictions as a national unifier.

As a result of this social construction of broadcasting public service-based communication had a very abstract character, especially in news programs. The enunciative stances had a very unclear shape. The voices and faces addressing the audience did not express clearly identifiable personal, political, or private interests. The voices and faces on the screen were not persons but embodiments of the institution. It was rather the idea of a common will which found its expression through television and gave public service television its unmistakably paternalistic mode of address. The anticipated receivers were equally abstract in character. They were not specific social groups or persons but the public in general, everybody as citizens interested in the common national (bourgeois) culture and political life.

In the BBC's radio and later television news programs, which became a model for many other European news programs, this abstract character was very profound. To depersonalize the news service not even the names of the newsreaders were mentioned. Rather characteristically, the first time the BBC departed from this practice was for considerations of national security: The fear of a German invasion at the beginning of the Second World War made it urgent that the voice of the BBC was clearly recognized, and tying a name to the acoustic image of the newsreader would help to establish this. As an internal document read: "The aim is not to publicize the announcers, but to ensure that listeners get acquainted with their voices, so that there may be no confusion in times of emergency."[2] After the war the BBC returned to anonymous announcers. In the first years of television after the war, the BBC did not try to visualize the news. Instead the radio news program was repeated over a photo of Big Ben on BBC television.

When the BBC began "real" television news with images, the news studio was made as neutral as possible. In the words of the former editor of BBC Television News, Michael Peacock: "The style of our studio presentation is simple. There is no attempt to simulate a newsroom atmosphere, or to present stills, photographs, maps, charts, and the like on back projection screens in the American manner. We decided on a straightforward down-to-earth approach....The simpler the style, the longer it will remain acceptable to the viewer."[3] This last assumption about the audience's taste is certainly doubtful, but his description reveals the deliberate attempt to diminish the viewer's attention to the communicative relation itself. By reducing the news studio's interior to the absolute minimum, a chair to sit on and a table to put the manuscript on, a room with no social indications and no trace of the journalistic work process was produced, and this style emphasized the authoritative and socially neutral mode of address. The reluctance to use visual material along with the reading of news items also shows an old-fashioned dislike of pictures and an attempt to produce authority by stressing the written/spoken word.

Although not entirely identical to broadcasting on the Continent, the aesthetic characteristics of BBC news was rather similar to that of other European television news programs, including Danish television. When Danmarks Radio began to prepare itself for the new multi-channel situation in the 1980s, the initiative for renewal of the news program "TV-Avisen" was called "Project New Face 87." It was not an initiative to change journalistic criteria or editorial priorities, but it was exactly what it said, a face-lift, a change in the enunciative structure and modality. The aim was twofold: first, to give the program a more uniform appearance along with other programs so the viewers' identification of what station they were watching became much easier; second, to modernize the program's mode of address by stressing the separate qualities of the communicative relation itself. The role of the newsreader was changed and emphasized by the introduction of two newsreaders or hosts, who were both present at the same desk. This creates a more dynamic presentation, as the newsreading alternates between them and the previously very formal tone and language are replaced by a more informal and everyday language, occasionally making room for some "happy talk" between them, a practice taken over from American local news programs. Furthermore, the hosts are of the opposite sex, which increases the identification possibilities and occasionally gives the talk between the hosts a touch of flirtation. The dynamic presentation is also stressed through the use of animated logos, charts, and graphics. On Sundays the news is read by a TV-star from a prime time entertainment program. The weather forecast is given a more thorough and separate treatment by a special announcer, whose comments on the weather often assume a chatty and humorous form. The news is now read from a tele-prompter, a rolling manuscript behind the camera allowing the host to simulate eye-contact with the viewer at the same time as he/she is actually reading from the manuscript. As a result, the host becomes a "newsteller" or narrator rather than a newsreader. He or she no longer seems to be reading news items produced by the news institution, but is presented as the narrator or originator of the news. It is the person, not the institution, who addresses the viewers.

These innovations change the communication's relation to the social spheres. Where the old public service mode of address established a public communication in a public space characterized by anonymity and non-individual regulation, the new mode of address establishes a communication characterized by intimacy and proximity between newsreader and viewer. The old mode of address stresses the relation from the announcers *back* to the institution: that is, the newsreader gains authority from the institution. The new mode of address emphasizes the communicative relation *forwards*: from the announcer to the viewer, with whom he/she seems to be on familiar terms. This new mode of address breaks down the public form of communication and places it in a private space, the sphere of intimacy, with the home as the principal location. As a result the newsreaders in their address to the viewers alternate between the public sphere and the sphere of intimacy. And similarly, the viewers can alternate between taking a more serious attitude towards the news and enjoying the company of famous TV-personalities.

This aesthetic shift towards a *semi-private form* of communication reflects a commodification of televisual communication in two ways: First, such communication increasingly addresses the viewers in their capacity as private individuals and consumers rather than as citizens. Second, the new mode of address itself has qualities which make the program more pleasurable and as a consequence its commodity character is further stressed. These changes in news programs are not necessarily negative. There is no reason to be sad about the disappearance of the old abstract and paternalistic mode of address. On the contrary, the personal mode of address can strengthen the interest in news and perhaps also contribute to an understanding of news not as something socially neutral or objective but as the result of choices made by individuals.

However, the new mode of address also creates a contradiction between form and content. The content of news — political, social and financial affairs — is ruled by quite different determinants than those regulating the personal communicative relations of intimacy and proximity, which the new mode of address simulates. The new mode of address positions the viewer as a private individual and consumer, and as a consequence of this his or her reception of the news will probably also tend to change. Increasingly, the news will be interpreted by viewers in categories taken from the sphere of intimacy, and the news will be turned into an object of consumption. One possible solution to this contradiction could be an increased commodification, in which both the journalistic criteria and the structure of the news narrative are changed correspondingly, making both the news selected and the way of presenting it more pleasurable, and making room for interpretations closer to the individual experiences in the sphere of intimacy. This adjustment of news content to the mode of address has taken place in the news programs of local, commercial TV-stations. In the case of public service stations such as Danmarks Radio, however, this has not happened. The content of public service news is to a large extent committed to the premises of the political public domain. It is a hybrid form, in which a personalization of mass communication has taken place on the aesthetic level, but the public character is stressed on the level of content.

As mentioned earlier, these changes in televisual communication are the result of a transition from a public, juridical form to a commodity form. However, the connection between commodity form and aesthetics is neither direct nor unbroken. The public service station's programming in most cases is not directly subordinated to a commercial logic, and the communication (the programs) does not completely assume the commodity form. This is especially true of public service stations that are solely financed by a license fee. In such cases there is no direct pressure on the individual programs to be "saleable." The existence of privately owned, commercial competitors does, nevertheless, create an indirect pressure on the programming of public service stations to achieve high viewing figures; not for a single program, but for the programs as a whole. If viewing figures drop permanently, political support for the license fee will also gradually decline.

Still, the change in aesthetics cannot be solely explained as an adjustment to the new financial situation. It is also a reaction to the past and an attempt to modernize public service programming. The old abstract mode of address has prevented public service television from using some of the aesthetic possibilities of television, especially the possibility of simulating a direct, personal address to the viewer in his/her most intimate space, the home. In the attempt to modernize, public service television is also looking for a new aesthetic identity, which is in accord with the audience's contemporary social and psychological experience. The problem is, however, that modern aesthetic ideals are developed within a commercial, mainly American, television culture. As a consequence, modernization most often also means Americanization.

When West European television stations use elements of an American television aesthetics, the immediate reason is its popularity and thus suitability for achieving higher ratings. On a more fundamental level this use reflects the fact that American television aesthetics is more attuned to modern experience than its European counterpart. Trying to anticipate the audience's wishes, commercial American television has developed an aesthetics which is much more sensitive to some very urgently felt social and psychological needs of the audience. This is not to say that commercial aesthetics really satisfies these needs, but only to point out that a commercial aesthetics very effectively expresses the contradictions, hopes, and anxieties of a modern television audience.

An outline of one argument behind this assumption can perhaps make the connection between aesthetics and the psychological experience of the audience more plausible. Several sociologists, Jürgen Habermas and Richard Sennett in particular but also others, have argued that the relation between the social spheres has changed concurrently with the modernization of society.4 Both Habermas and Sennett argue that the balance between the public and private spheres has been disrupted. The sphere of public life is eroding; one no longer participates in public life, but increasingly attends it as an observer or part of an audience. Instead, the private sphere and especially the sphere of intimacy, becomes a refuge from the disagreeable outside world of public politics as well as private business. In the sphere of intimacy the preoccupation with the self dominates. The self is stripped of social determinations and considered as a value in itself, an inner authentic truth about the individual.

According to Sennett there is not only a different balance between the public and private spheres, but the public sphere is subordinated to the private sphere. The world of intimacy, connoting warmth, feeling and authenticity, becomes the yardstick by which public life is measured. Public life is increasingly experienced and evaluated through categories of inner feelings, thus creating an intimate "filter" in the perception of public life. But as public affairs and social life in general do not adjust well to the categories of feelings and self, public space becomes dead. Instead of being a social activity in its own right, public life becomes part of the individual's search for identity. Through the disclosure of personal feelings in public appearances, the individual can authenticate himself.

Following this line of argument, the use of new aesthetic forms in television can be considered in a broader social context. The simulation of a direct, personal address marked by intimacy and proximity constructs a communicative relation which is in close agreement with the audience's general attitude towards the public sphere. Television news is no longer capable of producing authority by referring to institutional legitimacy. Instead, authority must be produced by stressing the personal authenticity of the address. Correspondingly, the relevance of public affairs to the individual is no longer self-evident. The relevance of public affairs must be produced through the construction of an engaged personal address to the audience. By giving public affairs an emotional value they become interesting and real. As a result, the communicative relation becomes increasingly important and tends to dominate at the expense of the actual content of the communication.

In short, apparently small and insignificant aesthetic changes have a "large" meaning and considerable social implications. The newsreader's use of a tele-prompter is not only a technical innovation, because through it the relation between addressee and recipient is changed. The use of a more informal language is not only an accommodation to a new generation of viewers: it also reflects a general change in the social form of televisual communication. The development is irreversible. It is neither possible nor desirable to return to the old paternalistic mode of address. The new competition in the field of television has definitively loosened the authority held by public service monopolies. After the deregulation of television, the authority of institutions is no longer indisputable, as has been the case for a longer time in other social areas. Authority is now something to be produced and evaluated through daily practice.

On the European television scene not all communication assumes a direct commodity form. This creates the possibility of (but by no means the certainty of) a new television aesthetics, that produces a non-authoritarian relation between television producers and audience in which a mutual engagement in social problems is stimulated. This, however, requires a profound consciousness of the social implications of aesthetic choices, not least the usage, adaptation and transformation of aesthetics developed within a commercial, mainly American, television culture.

References

1. European Cultural Foundation, "Europe 2000: What Kind of Television?" *The Report of the European Television Task Force,* Media Monograph No. 11 . Manchester, 1988, p. 11.
2. Cited in Philip Schlesinger, "Putting 'reality' together: BBC News." London: Methuen, 1987, p. 29.
3. Michael Peacock, "News in Television," Geneva: *EBU Review*, part B, no., 77, January, 1963.
4. Jürgen Habermas: *The Structural Transformation of the Pubic Sphere.* Cambridge: MIT Press, 1989; Richard Sennett, *The Fall of Public Man.* London: Faber and Faber, 1977.

"In Your Eyes:"
Identification, Consumption, and Production in Austin Rock'n'Roll

Barry Shank
University of Pennsylvania

Winter in Austin, Texas means grey skies and forty degree temperatures. Radio disc jockeys remind their listeners to wear hats, and people rummage through their closets looking for space heaters. Liberty Lunch is one of the larger nightclubs in Austin, with an audience capacity near one thousand. Touring shows of nationally famous acts along with the more popular local bands perform here. Often, people will stand outside to listen, since the club's only solid wall is the brick outer surface of the building next door. This brick is covered with a multicolored mural depicting an early seventies vision of a back- to-nature utopia. The stage and the rear three-quarters of the club are covered by a wooden plank roof. When it rains, as it often does in the winter in Austin, dancers and listeners huddle under the roofed portion of the club. When the skies are clear, the temperatures drop a little lower and fans of Austin music snuggle around the blasting gas heaters that shoot from the back corners of the room. Lights warm the stage, but still the ubiquitous leather jacket, draped over anorexic shoulders, achieves something like utility.

Wearing his leather jacket and a Texas Rangers cap, John Croslin of The Reivers slashes at the strings of his beaten Telecaster. Cindy Toth dances in black behind her bass; Garrett Williams still manages to sweat and smile while pounding the drums; and Kim Longacre sways with her eyes half-closed, nodding in time, strumming chords on her guitar and opening her voice, singing, "I see myself in your eyes, and it looks so right."[1] The fans huddled near the back move towards the heat now coming from the front of the club—some dancing, some drinking, some pouting, yet each consuming images and stories, melodies and rhythms that blaze from the stage. This consumption that is also a production—of identities, of communities, of subject positions and pleasure and musical texts—is one of the central defining practices of the rock'n'roll scene in Austin, Texas.

Through consuming musical texts, live performances, and the representations of a discursively constructed social reality, individual participants in the

Austin scene identify with aspects of what is offered, producing within themselves (although by no means consciously controlling) new subjectivities.[2] Through her experiences within and among the practices of the Austin scene, a single individual might be situated in a variety of mirroring relations. By (mis)identifying with some component or attribute of the scene, appropriating and incorporating that aspect, thereby changing positions and finding herself in a new set of relations, this individual can be transformed from a casual fan attracted by a sense of possibility, to an established musician celebrated in the discourses and practices of Austin rock'n'roll.[3] Produced by the scene while contributing to its production, consuming aspects of the scene and, in turn, being consumed herself, Kim Longacre of the Reivers personifies the "reciprocally constitutive effects" of the Austin music scene and a continually self-producing subject. Specific discursive constructions channel desire through this concomitant production of both subjectivities and a social reality organized around a particular cultural practice.[4]

Viewed from this analytic perspective, the rock'n'roll scene itself becomes the site where the consumption and production of popular music texts reciprocally and mutually recreate the conditions of their own possibility. This scene—exemplified by nightclub performances of local bands, commodified through record releases and ticket sales, inscribed in local and national press coverage—is experienced at many different levels by a diverse array of participants—musicians and fans, workers in the culture industries and casual occasional listeners. Austin is the capital of the state of Texas and home of the major campus of the state university. The population of Austin now exceeds four hundred thousand. The number of students attending the University of Texas at Austin surpasses fifty thousand. There are one thousand six hundred fifty-two musicians actively playing country, jazz, blues, pop, folk, and rock'n'roll in the city of Austin. Close to fifty independent labels and eleven recording studios call Austin home. Ninety-three records or tapes produced by Austin acts were released in the first six months of 1989.[5] Since 1976, Austin has been nationally recognized as a viable and important music scene, capable of supporting a variety of both touring acts and local musicians.[6]

From that time to the present, a series of popular musical styles have flown through Austin, each representing specific and differing desires and ideologies, yet each displaying underlying regularities—regularities connected to traditions of Texan music as well as to the structures of the national music industry. Kim participates in the "New Sincerity" scene that grew out of a nightclub called the Beach. The music associated with performances at this club is characterized by a post-punk assertion of aggressive noise grafted onto a self-conscious (at times, almost ironic) appropriation of traditional Texan musical styles. In "(I'm Sorry) I Can't Rock You All Night Long," Austin's Wild Seeds combine standard "cock-rock" musical conventions with a deadpan vocal style delivering a lyrical message that parodies the sexual posturing typical of cock-rock.[7] Texan macho and guitar-hero hard rock are simultaneously evoked and dismissed in this typical example of the New Sincerity brand of rock'n'roll.

While the New Sincerity label described the dominant musical trend in Austin in 1985, it also encompassed bands that extended and disrupted the generic conventions of this style. The songs of Glass Eye, Scratch Acid, the Hickoids, and the Butthole Surfers, among other bands, feature modernist violations of traditional pop song form along with hardcore-punk high-speed attacks that signify relatively "difficult" musics. The Surfers recorded a version of the Guess Who's early seventies hit, "American Woman," that, buried in industrial rhythms and electronically manipulated voices, is nearly unrecognizable. A strategic anti-commercial stance contributes to the status of these bands. The recorded musical commodities produced by bands like the Butthole Surfers are not only difficult to understand, they are even difficult to purchase. Limited pressings and erratic distribution demand a certain consuming skill from the fans. The prestige associated with these difficult bands, admittedly on the fringe of the New Sincerity scene, affects the structured hierarchies of taste developed and displayed by fans of Austin music.[8] Greater cultural capital accrues to those with the knowledge of how to consume or understand the more difficult to acquire or appreciate textual commodities. Austin insider fans demonstrate their status, their distinction within the scene as well as their distinction from the mass of popular music consumers, by consuming the textual productions (songs, performances, records) of local bands—the more difficult, or "anti-commercial" the band, the more prestige accruing to these fans.[9]

Since the opinions of prestigious fans carries comparatively more cultural authority within the discursive construction of the scene, even the more pop-oriented bands take on some of this anti-commercial discourse. Despite the overt commercial orientation and structures of popular music—its undeniable commodity form—Austin musicians insist that they a) play their music only for the music's sake, and b) only want to make a living from playing music; they have no desire to become stars.[10]

The most prestigious knowledge within the scene is that available to insiders only: information about the personal histories of the musicians, perhaps some sense of specific lyrical references in the songs, or information about the career decisions made by performers as they negotiate the national, commercially oriented streams of the music industry. In turn, possession of this knowledge partially defines the status of insider. Using some of this valued information, representing some of the structured knowledge of the Austin insider fan, I hope to create an image of the reciprocal constitution of subjectivities and cultural fields. Following Kim Longacre's narration of her experiences in and through the Austin rock'n'roll scene, we can watch her tastes, her sense of her own identity, and her position within the field change, and thereby we can gain a sense of the fluidity within structures that the over-determination of popular culture allows.

Kim Longacre moved to Austin with her family in 1978, the summer before her senior year in high school. She received classical voice training as a child; her parents (an Arts administrator and a singer) wanted her to sing opera professionally. Her early tastes in pop music consumption centered on massively popular bands like Fleetwood Mac and Journey. But the move to Austin gave her "an opportunity to start all over again. Just start from scratch." She met a young man in high school who played records for her by the Ramones, Ian Dury, and Elvis Costello, but most importantly, he introduced her to the club scene in Austin. According to Kim, "I just went haywire (...) I remember going to Raul's and being really intimidated. It was the whole scene, the clothes, the attitude. People were very strange and a lot older than me and seemingly sophisticated. (...) They seemed to have soul. Hardship, they knew hardship. (...) It was like a real eye-opening experience for me—that people could actually do something they believed in."[11]

Here we see Kim responding to the cultural authority of prestigious fans, but it is important to note exactly what attracts her—"the clothes, the attitude"—various signifiers of difference. These sophisticated fans are strange and intimidating because they display mastery of a cultural field, thereby constituting representations of discursively defined subject positions that Kim finds attractive. And this attraction, already marked by difference, takes on some of the standard codings of difference within American rock'n'roll. These people, who knew hardship, had "soul" by virtue of that hardship, and since they had soul, they could "actually do something they believed in." The linkage between soul, hardship and action motivated by belief is a typical American discursive construction of authenticity. Enunciated by an educated middle class WASP, this authenticity is located in the experience of a (generally) racially defined Other that is instantly eroticized. Within the discourses of American rock'n'roll, authenticity is linked to soul and soul refers to expressions of the experience of African-Americans in general and (sometimes) lower-class whites—any experience but that of the hegemonic group.[12]   For Kim specifically in 1978, the coded desire for authentic experience fired the drive to consume rock'n'roll since the possibility of this experience was signified by the instantly authentic group of oddly dressed rock'n'roll fans hanging out in Raul's. Immediately attracted to this Other, Kim incorporated aspects of the fashion and the attitude, "dressing real outrageously and being real vocal about my opinions." (KL:89) Driven along this chain of signifiers (opinions and clothing) appropriated through consumption, Kim was beginning to construct within herself the romantic bohemian artist, mediated through Texan rock'n'roll.

But simply wearing the clothing did not bring authentic experience. Soon, Kim says, "I saw myself and I didn't like it. It wasn't very genuine. It wasn't genuine at all." (KL:89) While costuming is important, the cultural field of Texan rock'n'roll remains overcoded by discourses of authenticity. At each point in the signifying chain, aspects of authenticity constitute the partial objects of desire. Once appropriated by Kim, the fashions and the attitudes lost their capacity to signify authentic experience, instead appearing as false constructions, spurious structures, empty signs. Since these signs no longer belonged to an imagined Other, they lost their value, their marked position, in the discourses constructing Kim's experience. More than a change in fashion is needed in order to achieve this enhanced experience of authenticity. Nevertheless, by a partially successful introjection of the signs of authenticity, Kim moves along a metonymic chain through the visual attraction of fashion into the practices of rock'n'roll music production. In 1980 Kim began bashing out rock'n'roll songs on a guitar (the classic Sears Silvertone) with a friend of hers. "We never had a gig but we had a great time. We drank a lot of wine. That's where I learned about alcohol and drugs, was with her. Things like, this is rock'n'roll, you know. This is angst." It was at this point that her interest turned from fashion to being "focussed more on the music."(KL:89) The performance of rock'n'roll, through an historically constructed romantic association with a condition of inner torment (the blues, angst— again a representation of marginalized painful authenticity), becomes the way for Kim to gain what Bataille calls "inner experience"—a pre-discursive no-place of authentic feeling. Drugs and alcohol appear in Kim's narration as the standard bohemian attempts to smash western discursive constructions of consciousness. With intoxication comes freedom and freedom is necessary for the "banal felicity" of "authentic inner experience."[13]

Once Kim joined her first performing rock'n'roll band (the Dynah-Nihilists), "drinking (became) a celebration of that (the potential for freedom that performing rock'n'roll could bring). And it also helped me to feel like a child, to get in touch with being uninhibited. (...) I always had a problem with that, being classically trained. (...) What a joy to watch that (childlike uninhibited performance) and what a joy to be that. And that was what I wanted. I wanted to feel that. Even in this uptight, anal-retentive, intellectual band, it was like so weird and so fun. It was like being a kid again." (KL:89). Within the cultural field of rock'n'roll, Kim's self-described problem is her training, the force of western traditions of expression, but her solution derives from an alternative that is equally discursively constructed. The desire for authentic experience, free of inhibitions—the that that she wanted to feel—is linked to a specific subject position believed by Kim to be keyed by rock'n'roll and wine. Wine destroys the constrictions of classical western training which then must be replaced by a different set of constructions—the necessarily bounded, because historically enacted, discourses of rock'n'roll. While this is not freedom, it is an alternative, a discursively shaped experience that carries a coding of freedom through the shock of change.

As Kim moves from band to band, listening to various records, hanging out in the clubs of the Austin scene, she consumes the commercially oriented, industrially produced commodities of popular music. She develops the articulated taste of an insider fan of Austin music, structured by the very type of private knowledge I am representing in this paper. Her list of favorite bands moves from the Clash and the Ramones, to Flying Lizards and Yaz, to Austin bands like the Butthole Surfers, the Dharma Bums, and the Wild Seeds. Her tastes in musical consumption meld with the styles of her musical production as her own bands move from punk thrash to post-punk techno-pop to Austin-oriented combinations of experiment and tradition. In the spring of 1983, John Croslin asks her to work with him on a new project that would become first Zeitgeist and then the Reivers. In Zeitgeist, Kim's self-production as romantic bohemian artist achieves fruition. She describes the early days of the band using the classic conventions of musicians paying their dues. "We were having the best times of our lives in the worst possible conditions. We had a terrible practice room and it was just so romantic. It was your wildest dreams come true." Kim goes on, "There was no pretense. It was just—we're gonna get together; we're gonna play; we're gonna have a good time; we're gonna be nice, decent people."(KL:89)

Within a year Zeitgeist had become very popular in the Austin scene, and in 1985 they released an album, *Translate Slowly*, on DB records. They are the headlining act during one episode of MTV's new music program, "The Cutting Edge," and are voted the best band in Austin by the readers of the Austin Chronicle. Two of Kim's then favorite bands—the nationally known acts, Love Tractor and REM—were touring through Austin at this time. Kim refers to them as, "Normal people. They were college kids. They wore normal clothes. They weren't trying to be outrageous. They were good musicians. They had something to say. (...) It was very interesting that they could be so mundane and melodic. And they were nice (...) I mean, they could have been in your class."(KL:89)[14]

Filled with the elaboration of equivalences, not differences, these comments indicate Kim's successful self-construction as romantic bohemian artist within the discourses of rock'n'roll. The cultural field of the Austin rock'n'roll scene is no longer intimidating but instead appears natural and evident. This enables her to describe REM as normal, Zeitgeist as a band with no pretense and the Beach scene as "a real socialist thing. It was real organic and not like anybody sat down and wrote the rules out. (...) what was magical about it was that it could be mundane. And that you could look normal. You didn't have to wear make-up."(KL:89) Kim's position as singer/guitarist for Zeitgeist contributes a perspective of normality, focussed on an everyday reality heightened to an intensely romanticized yet seemingly organic and free experience. Kim's experience is free of make-up, free of artifice—all natural. She *is* the bohemian romantic artist, the preferred marginalized commentator (partially) constructed by the bourgeois hegemony.

But marginalized conscience often sells. Their popularity on the college circuit grows and within two years, Zeitgeist signs a contract with the major label, Capitol Records. For legal reasons they are forced to change their name to the Reivers. As employees of a major label record company, the Reivers are contractually obligated to produce commercially viable recordings, suitable for the machines of mass reproduction and systems of distribution that are set up to exploit economies of scale. Industrially positioned as commercial entertainers, the Reivers struggle with contradictions between the anti-commercial discourses of romantic bohemianism central to the Austin scene and the strategies of professional performance. When she tries to articulate these contradictions, Kim slips back into a language of displaced authenticity. "What I'm interested in (...) is that I want to tap into that which I think a lot of black people have. And it's not to be a black singer— you know, gospel and stuff like that. What I want is the way it feels. And it probably wouldn't change my music. I don't want to change that. I want, I want to feel that spontaneity. I want to feel that kind of assuredness and confidence. I wanna be unconsciously competent (...) so it all just comes right through and it's effortless. Just this voice comes out. (...) That's how I want it to be. But it's hard. It's like trying to be sincere. (...) What we've had to learn is to be more sensitive to what we're getting back from the audience. (...) It's just a matter of being more sensitive to what the feedback is."(KL:89) Echoing some of her earlier statements, Kim wishes for a specific inner experience that she imagines to be the property of a discursively shaped different group of people. Kim describes a desire to effortlessly, spontaneously, unconsciously use her voice as a channel through which the feelings of her audience speak back to them, a talent based on sensitivity, that she believes "a lot of black people have."

Here Kim legitimizes her new role as entertainer, mitigating the contradictions between this position and the position of the romantic artist. The association between the performing styles of black musicians (spontaneity, confidence) and Kim's previously unthinkable desire for successful professional communication derives in part from what Andrew Ross describes as "the different historical relation which black musicians have had to the rules of commercial entertainment." Without many alternative means of earning a living, African-American efforts to profit from pleasing or entertaining an audience did not carry the same stigma as would similar strategies developed within the (European) artistic traditions encumbered by the switch from patronage to a dependence upon the support of the bourgeois market.[15] For Kim, techniques of professional entertainment can still retain their effectiveness as expressions of authenticity when coded through this legitimating historical difference.

Secondly, her role as entertainer, as performer, has become a facilitator of consumption, of audience identification. As lead singer she occupies an overcoded position that can function somewhat in the way that a charismatic leader can form a group or as a psychoanalyst can become the locus of transference. Inviting projection, Kim becomes a vessel through which pass expressions of authentic experience, but no longer her experiences, not her feelings, but rather the feelings and the experiences of a mirrored other—her audience. By becoming an object of identification, the professional lead singer returns the desires of the audience in such a way that these desires can be recognized.[16] By remaining sensitive to the specific desires "spoken" by each audience, by encouraging this sort of structural identification and by responding spontaneously, Kim hopes to manage the contradictions between being a bohemian artist concerned with the expressions of authenticity and being a commercial success who entertains unknown masses.

A number of textual strategies encourage and utilize this identification at the level of the single song. Many of the very techniques traditionally scorned in popular music effectively foster this process. According to Theodor Adorno, "The fundamental characteristic of popular music is standardization. This follows not only from the industrial production of music but also from the industrial production of the subjects to whom it is addressed."[17]

"In Your Eyes" is an industrially produced hit song, written and sung by Kim Longacre. It completely fills the empty form of the standardized pop-rock single, taking the shape of Adorno's interchangeable commodity but exploding the restrictions he puts on its significance. The structures that encourage multiple identifications are produced within the standardized significations of popular music.

The lyrics of the song are as follows:

There's something in my hand,
There's something in my stereo,
But I can't stop it, stop it from happening.

Ooh-ooh, it's just a little fear.
And I see myself in your eyes,
And it looks so right and it looks
so right.

It could be the lights,
You could call it poetry,
But I can't hear you, spin above my
record player.[18]

Notice how in the first verse, the central object remains unnamed. In the classic hit song fashion, the central signifier remains as polysemic as possible to encourage maximum identification. Yet we have some information about it. It is material—it can be held in one's hand; it is capable of technological mediation—it can be in the stereo; and it is determined—it cannot be stopped. After the first descriptions of this object come Kim's trademark empty vocalizations—the ooh's. These soaring tones rise and fall, leading metonymically (through these purely vocal, not lyrical, signifiers) into the first named emotion, fear, followed by the specification of a scopic relation, of subjective identification, "I see myself in your eyes," a tired pop cliche magically revived into meaning. This structure of significance is repeated in the second verse: it could be lights, it could be poetry. Again the object of desire remains unnamed, although the structures and practices through which it can be approached are specified—both discursive and technological, they are the consumption of popular music. Musically, the song also follows very standard hit song conventions. The harmonic structure alternates between the sub-dominant and the tonic, resolving through the relative minor into the dominant—the chords are C G C G C Em D. The bridge eliminates the Em and the chorus doubles the alternating pattern of the bridge, creating an effect of greater intensity.

Melodically, the song contains two sections of pitch variation, each covering the same interval—a sixth. The verse ranges from G below middle C to the E above it; the bridge moves from the dominant D to the B-natural above that. The chorus unites the two melodic phrases, beginning with the highest note in the song, the B-natural, and resolving with the low G. The rhythmic pulse is steady throughout. These are all very traditional, almost stereotypical hit song conventions. So why does this song work? Richard Middleton argues that popular music operates through the interplay of the two basic psychoanalytic drives—Eros and Thanatos—celebrating the victory of the pleasure principle over the death instinct.[19] This process functions in "In Your Eyes" through the stunning majesty of Kim's lead vocals over the variations and repetitions within the standardized structures of the song. The emptiness of the lyric, the simplicity of the harmonic, melodic and rhythmic relations, and the imbricated repetitions all provide a framework through which Kim's voice weaves a pattern of mystery, a beckoning towards possible identification, an erotic offering tinged with fear, the offering of her voice, her body, and, even more, the possibility of being, the pleasure of authentic experience.[20] Yet this individual achievement is entirely generic. In the classic female singer role, Kim becomes the simultaneous partial object of and channel for the desires of her audience.

When Kim Longacre sings "In Your Eyes" at nightclubs like Liberty Lunch, these three objects (the scene, Kim, the song) reciprocally constitute each other through the ongoing processes of production and consumption, projection and introjection. As the fans move toward the front of the drafty club, they identify with and participate in the continual construction of the overlapping cultural fields that enable the experiences they each desire. Although the motivations of desire remain unconscious and the structures of identification are constituted before the arrival of the subject, identification is an active process. Producing in the very act of consuming, seeing themselves in the eyes of others and mirroring back the constitutive effects of a misrecognized identity, the subjects of Austin music dance away the discontent of winter within the incomplete structures of the social reality they know as the Austin rock'n'roll scene.

References

1. Kim Longacre and John Croslin, "In Your Eyes" copyright 1987, Midsnicker Music, administered by Bug Music Inc., BMI.
2. In *The Language of Psycho-Analysis*, Laplanche and Pontalis state that the identification is "the operation itself whereby the human subject is constituted." J. Laplanche and J.-B. Pontalis, *The Language of Psycho-Analysis*. New York: Norton, 1973, p. 206. According to Freud, "Identification endeavours to mold a person's ego after the fashion of the one that has been taken as a model." *Group Psychology and the Analysis of the Ego*, trans. James Strachey. New York: Norton, 1959 (1921), p. 38.
3. By using terms like "mirroring" and "misidentification," I mean to invoke Lacan's concept of the mirror stage as the constitutive moment in subject production. The mirror stage has been expanded by film analysts to provide a theory of continual subject production, through identification or misidentification (retermed "suture") with characters or gazes constructed in or by a film. If this expansion is valid, it is not difficult to take the next step and conceive of cultural relations, however mediated, as a field for mirroring and misidentifying. See Jacques Lacan, "The Mirror Stage in the Function of the I," in Alan Sheridan, trans. *Ecrits: A Selection*. New York: Norton, 1977, pp. 1-7. See also Christian Metz, *The Imaginary Signifier*, trans. Celia Burton et al. Bloomington: Indiana University Press, 1981 and Stephen Heath, *Questions of Cinema*. London: Macmillan, 1981.
4. Teresa DeLauretis discusses experience as "an ongoing process by which subjectivity is constructed semiotically and historically." Her description of social reality and subjectivity as "reciprocally constitutive effects" can be found in *Alice Doesn't: Semiotics, Cinema, Feminism*. Bloomington: Indiana University Press, 1984, pp. 178-186. Freud maintains a distinction between the states of being-in-love and of identification based on the difference in placement of the introjected aspects of the object (whether simply in the ego or as a replacement for the ego ideal). Lacanian psychoanalysis does not seem to recognize the distinction. In Lacanian terms, desire becomes a more abstract notion that, through its actions, blurs the distinction between these two states.
5. The number of active musicians comes from the "Musicians's Register," *Austin Chronicle,* November 13, 1987; the list of records released and the number of independent labels and studios comes from Luke Torn, "1989 (So Far): An Austin Discography," *Austin Chronicle,* June 23, 1989.
6. See, for example, Larry L. King, "Redneck," *Texas Monthly,* August,

1974 and "The Passions of the Common Man," *Texas Monthly,* August, 1976; William Martin, "Growing Old at Willie Nelson's Picnic," *Texas Monthly,* October, 1974; Jack Hurst, "The Pickin's Pickin' Up in Austin," *Chicago Tribune* March 31, 1976; Jan Reid, *The Improbable Rise of Redneck Rock.* Austin: Heidelberg Publishers, 1974.

7. Simon Frith and Angela McRobbie discuss the category of cock-rock in "Rock and Sexuality," *Screen Education* 29 (1979), pp. 3-19.

8. For an interesting discussion of the value of prestige in avant-garde music as well as an acknowledgement of the differing articulations of prestige found in popular musics, see Susan McClary, "Terminal Prestige: The Case of Avant-Garde Music Composition," *Cultural Critique* 12 (Spring, 1989), pp. 57-81.

9. Bourdieu's notions of distinction and cultural capital apply even within the relatively provincial field of the Austin rock'n'roll scene. See *Distinction: A Social Critique of the Judgement of Taste* trans. Richard Nice. Cambridge: Harvard University Press, 1984, especially chapter 4, "The Dynamics of Fields," pp. 226-256. The distinction associated with the Butthole Surfers has broached national borders; see the graffiti gracing the wall surrounding the Rosenberg Gardens in Copenhagen.

10. Simon Frith has argued that the historical moment signified within popular music by the prominence of ideas like anti-commercialism, authenticity, sincerity and community has disappeared. While this might be true in terms of a national or international "rock culture," many regional scenes, along with certain musical trends in pop (college rock and, perhaps, certain strands of hip-hop), are still organized around these terms. Frith's argument is found in *Sound Effects.* New York: Pantheon Books, 1981.

11. From an interview with Kim Longacre, conducted on June 2, 1989. (...) indicates an editorial elision. (with text) indicates an editorial addition for clarity. All further references to this interview will be cited in the text: (KL:89).

12. An early and important discussion of this link can be found in Charlie Keil, *Urban Blues.* Chicago: University of Chicago Press, 1966. A more recent discussion of the discursive connections between African-American cultural expression and "authenticity" can be found in Andrew Ross, "Hip and the Long Front of Color," *No Respect: Intellectuals and Popular Culture.* New York and London: Routledge, 1989, pp. 65-101.

13. Bataille's obsessions with inner experience, ecstasy, communication and poetry (in effect, the sublime) are documented in *Inner Experience* trans. Anne Boldt. Albany: State University of New York Press, 1988, p. 112 and *passim.* It shouldn't be necessary to document the historically reinforced link between musical expressions of ecstasy and the intoxications of liquor or drug use.

14. It is tempting to take advantage of the possible slippage in meaning in that last phrase. I know that Kim was consciously referring to college

classrooms, but certainly even that distinction is available only to a particular class of persons.

15. Ross, *op.cit.,* p. 72. In the realm of the Imaginary, binary relations dominate. One of the most powerful binary oppositions within American rock'n'roll is, of course, the opposition of race: black/white, which then takes on aspects of another traditional opposition: nature/culture. It is not surprising that Kim would locate this "effortless" talent in the "natural" make-up of black Americans. However, if Wynton Marsalis has his way, western notions of autonomous self-referential art will come to dominate African-American musical practice as well.

16. Freud discusses the ways in which sublimated love for a singer can unite a gathering of fans into an identifying group on p. 52 of *Group Psychology.* The metaphor of the analyst (entirely my own gloss--not Kim's) is rooted in the readings of Lacanian psychoanalysis given by a number of American feminists. In particular, I have found Shosona Felman, *Jacques Lacan and the Adventure of Insight: Psychoanalysis in Contemporary Culture*, Cambridge: Harvard University Press, 1987, and Jane Gallop, *Reading Lacan*, Ithaca: Cornell University Press, 1985, to be quite helpful.

17. Theodor Adorno and George Simpson, "On Popular Music," *Studies in Philosophy and Social Sciences* 9 (1941), pp. 17-48.

18. John Croslin and Kim Longacre, "In Your Eyes," copyright 1987 by Midsnicker Music, administered by Bug Music Inc., BMI.

19. Richard Middleton, "Play It Again Sam: the Productivity of Repetition in Popular Music," *Popular Music* 3 (1983), pp. 235-270.

20. For a discussion of the erotic effects produced in the grain of the voice, see Roland Barthes, "The Grain of the Voice," in *The Responsibility of Forms* trans. Richard Howard. New York: Hill and Wang, 1985, pp. 267-277. Unfortunately, I am not able to include a recording of this song and, so far as I know, the music of the Reivers has not been released in Europe. However, this song is intended as an example, not a unique instance, and I am certain that any number of other recordings could stand in for "In Your Eyes," once intertextualized.

Education in a Consumer Society

Sharon Thomas
Michigan State University

There is an idea circulating in certain educational circles in the United States —usually among teachers of history, literature, and (sometimes) foreign languages — that some insidious disease called "process" is destroying the teaching of humanities in American high schools and that, as a result, students do not enroll in humanities programs in colleges and universities. The proponents of this theory, among them Lynne Cheney, chairman of the National Endowment for the Humanities, believe that "the culprit is 'process'—the belief that we can teach our children how to think without troubling them to learn anything worth thinking about."[1]

In a 1987 report entitled, *American Memory: A Report on the Humanities in the Nation's Public Schools*, published by the National Endowment for the Humanities, Cheney suggests that transmitting culture ought to be the goal of teaching and that without this transmission of culture, we will not be able to affirm our humanity or learn the lessons of the past that will help us plan our future. Along the way, Cheney admits that the learning of dates and names "are not all that students should know, but such facts [she claims] are a beginning, an initial connection to the sweep of human experience."[2] According to Cheney, progressive educators have transformed education into curriculum guides and scope and sequence charts that direct teachers to focus on substeps, skills, drawing conclusions, and predicting outcomes. Cheney also attacks Scholastic Aptitude Tests (SAT's) for not testing knowledge of content taught in high schools as well as textbooks that are "meaningless and dull" and consist of "disconnected facts."[3]

Obviously, teachers' manuals, SAT tests, and dull textbooks all serve to discourage both the teaching and learning of humanities. The proponents of process, however, did not bring about these evils. The process movement is a reaction against those teachers, kindergarten to college, who teach penmanship, spelling, grammar, and the five-paragraph-formula essay in the misdirected belief that they are teaching writing. These are people who focus on the correctness of the end product rather than on the process of producing the product. Of course, a polished finished product is the final goal, but another lesson in the use of the semi-colon doesn't help students whose thoughts put down on paper are too confused to be saved by a semi-colon, or any other punctuation mark. Nor does covering the final product with red ink corrections help many students to avoid the same mistakes in the next assignment. More likely, the emphasis on an error-free final product too early in the process directs so much attention to the proper form that connected discourse becomes impossible. In a similar manner, too much emphasis on correct, error-free oral reading in the round-robin reading groups of early reading instruction can also destroy the students' comprehension of the text, not to mention enjoyment of reading.

Process proponents are reacting to an emphasis on correctness that impedes both the understanding and production of meaning. They are not against content. In fact, hundreds of professors, teachers, writers, and researchers across the United States who are advocates of the whole language approach (a broader view of instruction that is built on the teacher's knowledge of the processes of both reading and writing) have been fighting for some years now to bring content back into the curriculum. Like Cheney, they are also opposed to both teaching and testing that emphasize substeps, skills, and bits of unrelated information. These are the elementary teachers who put the *See Spot Run* readers on the shelf and bring into the classroom classic children's literature even if they have to pay for it themselves; the junior high teachers who turn in to the principal their scope and sequence chart lesson plans but, secretly, in their classrooms, introduce their students, through novels, plays, poetry, and historical biography, to the richness of life; the high school history teachers who throw out the dull and boring texts and, with their students, explore a history rich in real people, fascinating events, and compelling ideas. Whole language teachers do indeed wish to teach their students to think and they've gone to great trouble to provide their students with not just "something" to think about, but the very best the humanities has to offer to think and read and write about. Process is not the culprit. Yet, textbooks and tests do remain a problem. I would argue, however, that the real reason textbooks and tests are problems is due to big business enterprise.

As Cheney points out in *American Memory*, textbook publishers try to sell as many books as possible. Thus, driven as they are by the profit motive, publishers target the biggest markets they can, and California and Texas—the two biggest states with state-wide adoption policies—are the biggest markets. In these states, various interest groups attempt to influence textbook adoption and, especially in Texas, some groups wield considerable power. In one segment of a televison series entitled, *Learning in America,* that was aired on American television in March and April of 1989, some of the meetings of the Texas textbook adoption committee were shown. One particularly aggressive, fundamentalist, religious woman dramatically unfurled a sixteen-foot long continuous roll of complaints she had against a single textbook. Nor do various political groups fail to let their concerns be known. Another woman, a textbook writer who was interviewed for the program, complained she had

72

attempted to help American children understand the geography of a certain part of the Soviet Union by comparing it to the far western regions of the United States. This description was deleted from the text because it offended a conservative political group.4 Unfortunately, the Texas contract is so valuable to publishers that, too often, what Texas wants the rest of the nation gets. Enlightened teachers, many of them whole language advocates, have attempted to change the way text books are adopted in their states by convincing state departments of education to change their definiton of reading from the subskills model Cheney describes to a reading as constructing meaning model. As a result, new types of textbooks are now in more demand.

As Cheney, herself, points out, California's new curriculum now calls for history textooks "that put the facts of the past into compelling narrative and stimulating intellectual form."5 And teachers have gained more control. Recently, Arizona decided to let the teachers, themselves, decide which texts they will use (an event greatly celebrated at a meeting of whole language teachers in April in New Orleans). At the same time, publishers are getting nervous. Multiple adoptions and teacher choice adoptions will require a greater variety of books, higher production and marketing costs, and decline in profits. Scores of participants in this year's meeting of the International Reading Association received letters from publishers asking them to meet to discuss the concerns of publishers.6

Tests are also big business. The Educational Testing Service (ETS) which develops, administers, and scores the Scholastic Aptitude Test (SAT) which determines, along with financial resources and parental "clout," which students get into which universities and colleges, has a virtual monopoly on this type of testing. Aside from charges that such tests are racially biased, reflect white, protestant, middle class values, are elitist, and don't measure what they claim to measure, such tests also drive instruction. The subskills, substeps, predicting outcomes, and drawing conclusions that Cheney abhors in teachers' manuals simply reflect what students will be tested on. Unfortunately, these kinds of tests are easy to administer, efficient, and cost effective—for the publishers of tests. Fortunately, some changes are occurring as new definitions of reading call for new tests as well as textbooks. Several states have recently redesigned their state achievement tests in order to include longer texts that give students the opportunity to construct meaning as they read. Even ETS is currently testing a new form of the SAT that will also use longer passages, vocabulary in context rather than in isolation, and, possibly, a writing section.

On the other hand, ETS has historically developed, administered, and evaluated a staggering array of tests that are used to control admission to both two- and four-year colleges, to graduate study, to special professional schools such as architecture and podiatry, and to independent secondary schools. In addition, ETS supplies tests to determine admission at all levels of schooling, including preschool, as well as professional examinations to determine certification for such diverse fields as insurance, obstetrics, gynecology, and speech pathology and audiology and to determine who can be appointed by the federal government to foreign service jobs. In other words, ETS has control of the gateway to most professions in the corporate world.7 Of course, ETS tests reflect big business values because ETS is, itself, a product of the corporate world. ETS was started by corporate wealth (a grant from the Carnegie Corporation) and continues to be supported by corporate wealth— often with grants from the Carnegie Foundation—only one of many foundations that seek to exert control over educational policy.8 The point is that we can squabble all we want over process vs content and never arrive at the real reasons for the problems that beset American schools—the poor teaching of the humanities being only one of many problems. I agree that the humanities are not well taught in some elementary and secondary schools and, therefore, not pursued by students in colleges and universities, but I want to argue that the cause is not process. Rather, I want to argue that the humanities are so poorly taught because corporate America has other plans for American education. Moreover, corporate America and its predecessors have always had their own agenda for the schools.

Today, as the United States races against Japan for world markets, the pressure from business to restructure the schools can be seen everywhere. In America, today, one can hardly pick up a newspaper, magazine, professional teaching journal, or even a business publication without reading about the mess the schoools are in. Articles with titles such as "Retooling the Schools," "The Education Crisis: What Business Can Do," "Saving the Schools: How Business Can Help," and "Business Offers a Hand to Education" are commonplace.9 And not much mention is made of the humanities. Frequently some rhetoric about the need for better informed citizens to participate in a democracy is woven in somewhere in these articles, but the possiblity of an educational system that could produce truly independent, literate, critical thinkers is studiously avoided. Thus, American schools continue to be the battleground where wars are waged over economic policy as they have been for more than 150 years. The latest battle is merely a new twist on an old theme: education for participation in a democracy versus education for economic preeminence. As David Nasaw has pointed out in his book, *Schooled to Order*, from small town industrialists in the nineteenth century to corporate magnates in the 1980's, the business community has always had its hand in the educational pot. In the 1830's, supported by the business community, Horace Mann spearheaded the common school movement designed to get the dangerous classes of people, accused of threatening not only America's democratic institutions but also her economic well-being, off the streets and into the schools where they could be socialized into obedient, submissive workers as well as citizens who would defer to the judgements of their betters in both economic and political matters. Horace Mann's studies, which showed educated workers were better workers and that a prosperous economy was the result of better educated workers, instituted a theme that has reverberated through the halls of education (and business) ever since. And, the transformation of the high school at the turn of the century heralded the beginning of yet another well-known educational theme—imposition of the business model on the educational system.10

If business had prospered through consolidation and centralization into the massive, efficient, industrial giants of the day, the early twentieth century high school reformers argued, then schooling would also benefit if locally controlled school boards were replaced with centralized, city-wide boards that would bring the same efficiency to education. The fact that the school board candidates supported by the business community's generous funding and superior media clout frequently won over the former school board members with scant funding and limited local neighborhood support was only an additional bonus. Once control of the schools was firmly established in the hands of the business community, a rapid transformation of the high schools occurred.11

American industrialists, having exhausted home markets, increasingly felt the need to compete in the foreign export market. Thus, they began to push for the transformation of the American high school into something more closely approximating the German system of vocational and technical schools which educated the workers for German industry.12 Transforming the American high school into an entity that would produce better workers had another advantage, too. As Nasaw has pointed out, control of the labor force by the unions was pushing up the cost of labor. If the training and certification of skilled labor could be moved into the schools, then the unions would lose control, business could pay lower wages and, as a result, compete successfully in the world export market.13

The high school reformers were immensely successful. In less than 25 years, the American high school underwent a radical transformation. In 1892, the Committee of Ten, established by the National Education Association, had reaffirmed classical studies as the proper curriculum for all high school students. Only twenty-one years later, in 1913, a new NEA commission, known as the Committee on the Reorganization of Secondary Education, adopted seven cardinal principles for secondary schools: health, command of fundamental processes, worthy home membership, vocation, civic education, worthy use of leisure, and ethical character.14 The classics were not mentioned. Cheney has suggested that we ought to learn the lessons of the past in order to plan for the future. Here, then, are some lessons about education we ought to study. For nearly 150 years, now, American schools have danced to the tune of the economic pied piper and the tunes issuing forth these days are not much different from those heard in the past: restructure the schools so that corporate America can compete in the world market; impose the latest business organizational model on schools (what's good for America's business must be good for America's schools); and produce more literate workers (the economy depends on well educated workers).

One of the strongest advocates of restructuring the schools is David T.

Kearns, chairman and chief executive officer of Xerox Corporation. In his book, *Winning the Brain Race*, written with Denis P. Doyle, Kearns argues for a free market entrepreneurial school model. Working from the premise that tomorrow's workers have to be better educated than ever before because profits depend on well-educated workers, an all too familiar refrain, Kearns proposes a "choice" model in which students and their parents can choose any school they want and educational funding—federal, state, or local—will follow that student to the chosen school.[15] Thus, the schools become corporate-like entities, students and their parents become customers, education is the product, and schools must compete with each other to provide the best customer service.

This latest suggestion is merely an extension of earlier business-supported transformations of American schools. Once the schools had been consolidated, made more efficient through centralized, city-wide school boards, and restructured as producers of future workers rather than institutions of classical learning, the imposition of the free-market, entrepreneurial model was probably inevitable. The recent transformation of telephone books (after the break up of I.T.&T.) into a "business" and "other" format in which schools are to found in the "business" section, should come as no surprise to those who have read *Winning the Brain Race*. In Kearns' scenario for the future, the concept of schooling for participation in a democracy has been so totally replaced by education for economic preeminence that the schools, themselves, must now compete for economic preeminence.

Other advocates of restructuring the schools would impose different models on education or, at least, they would get rid of the current mass production model in which students, like products on an assembly line, move passively from one class to another receiving a dose of history at one stop, an exercise of grammar at the next, a bit of chemistry at the third, and so on. Even the American Federation of Teachers has criticized this model. In their ad in the premier issue of *Teacher*, a new educational journal, they point out that if businesses were organized like schools, they would soon be out of business. "Imagine it....Employees wouldn't have their own desks. They would change offices, bosses and work every 45 minutes at the sound of a bell. And if employees tried to get help with their work from their colleagues, they'd be called on the carpet."[16]

In place of the assembly line model, some have suggested that schools follow in the footsteps of business and reorganize along the lines of Japanese work groups — a model that is hastily being implemented in many American businesses whether or not they are Japanese owned and managed. In the meantime, businesses across America adopt schools, send their employees into the classrooms, set up satellite schools at the factory, open their own private schools (available tuition free to those who qualify), and give students summer jobs in order to start their business training early.[17] The business community is so intent on making sure that they will have the workers they need in the future that they have taken to directly interfering with the "business" of education and, for the most part, fail to hear what educators, like Joan Canella, director of the Bank Street School for Children, have to say. According to Canella, "The best thing business can do for schools is to make it possible to combine work and family, allowing working parents to get involved with the schools." 18

Herein lies the problem. The profile of the working parent is about to change. As of 1985, white males dominated the American work force, comprising 47% of those working. From 1985 to the year 2000, however, these statistics will change drastically. Of those entering the work force during these years, women will constitute a whopping 42% while the percentage of white males entering the labor force during these years will drop to a mere 15%. Percentages for non-whites and immigrants, both male and female, will also rise, though not so dramatically.19 Non-white and immigrant workers are traditionally less well educated than white males, and women who work outside the home have special needs—like day care which consistently fails to receive funding from Congress.

Small wonder that the business community is suddenly interested in education, particulary the literacy level of those who, traditionally, do not do well in our nation's schools. Thus, business leaders call for higher literacy and, in some cases, attempt to define what that literacy should be like even when they lack the expertise to do so. In their special report on the schools, *Business Week* breaks down literacy into six levels, defines each one, and projects what the mismatch will be between what is needed and what will be available. According to these estimates, the biggest problem will occur at level 4, defined as, "Can read journals and manuals, and write business letters and reports." At level four, the projections indicate that the need will be nearly eight times greater than the actual skill level of new workers.20

On the surface, a demand for an increase in literacy among America's future workers and a commitment from the business community to help schools help students achieve those higher levels sounds promising and is often heralded as a new, and long overdue, partnership between business and education, devoted to the increased well-being of Americans. In fact, the partnership has resulted in some gains—at least at lower levels of achievement. Gains in higher level thinking skills, however, have not been achieved and Richard Coe, of Simon Fraser University in Canada, points out the reason. According to Coe, white collar work has been deprofessionalized. At one time, Coe argues, white collar work meant a professional/managerial status, but increasing technology has made white collar work more simple and less professional. These days, even though white collar work does not resemble the blue collar, manual labor of the past, it is, nevertheless, white collar assembly line work. Further, such workers do not have the autonomy accorded to white collar workers of the past. The increase in the size of corporations means that the decision makers are further and further removed from the point of production and these decision makers can only make decisions if they have a corps of middle management workers who can accurately read the instructions they receive and, in return, write the reports the upper level managers need in order to make their decisions.21 According to Coe,

> What they need, in short, is many workers who can read for information, follow instructions, and (perhaps) write short reports (probably on forms) clearly and accurately; some workers with specialized reading, writing, and thinking abilities to write longer reports and handle "decentralized" implementation decisions, which require the ability to make low-level inferences and deductions correctly; and a few really educated professionals with genuinely critical reading, writing, and thinking abilities to serve in (and educate) the centralized managerial elite.22

Further, Coe suggests that students educated to fill these positions, mostly students from "non-traditional" groups, will receive a college education designed to make them literate enough to cope with these jobs but not so literate as to make them overqualified. Certainly, they will not receive much education in the humanities and the result will be alienation and anti-intellectualism as these graduates come to realize that their educations neither led to satisfying jobs nor even gave them the critiical ability to understand their lives and social universe.23

The real question, of course, is what *kind* of literacy do Americans need to have? And, further, *how* will this literacy be achieved? E. D. Hirsch, author of *Cultural Literacy: What Every American Needs to Know*, claims to have the answers to these questions. Starting with the familiar claim that "only highly literate societies can prosper economically,"24 Hirsch sets out to define what makes a society literate and concludes that literacy depends on shared background knowledge. That is, literate speakers and writers can communicate to one another effectively only because they share common background knowledge. Further, this knowledge held in common is culturally specific. While Americans might be able to "decode" (that is, correctly pronounce) the words to the Australian song, "Waltzing Matilda," without the cultural knowledge of a "Swagman," a "billabong," a "coolibah," or a "billy," they cannot truly understand the song.25 Given the national character of the knowledge literate citizens need to understand one another, Hirsch suggests that Americans should define what that national knowledge is and teach it in the schools. Hirsch's book concludes with an appendix that lists what he believes Americans need to know to be culturally literate and he suggests that this content be dispensed, in a systematic manner, by teachers across America.26

Hirsch, quite correctly, supports his definition of literacy with schema theory research. And he understands that readers and writers not only have to have shared schema/background knowledge/cultural literacy in order to understand one another, but that this shared schema/background knowledge/ cultural literacy also plays a significant role in how readers understand a text. Hirsch's views on these areas are quite acceptable even though his definition of what constitutes sufficient background knowledge is rather narrow. However, when he turns his attention to how literacy is achieved (or, more specifically, how reading is taught in American schools), he latches on to a theoretical model of reading that is incongruent with the schema theory research he cites.

It is true that a skills model of reading has dominated much of reading instruction in America; however, the important lessons to be learned from schema theory research have not gone unnoticed by those who teach reading. New definitions of reading as the construction of meaning are rapidly replacing the old skills model that Hirsch so vehemently attacks. And reading as construction of meaning is built on the very schema research that Hirsch finds so illuminating. Yet, Hirsch largely ignores the advocates of whole language who offer a theory of reading build on an understanding of literacy that is congruent with schema theory research. Worse, Hirsch, having dismissed the skills model as inadequate, goes on to suggest that the kinds of facts that he includes in his list be dispensed to students who would then be tested, at appropriate intervals in their schooling, on their general knowledge of the items on the list. Dispensing knowledge and then testing students on it is exactly the kind of instruction that skills model teachers engage in and that leads to the kind of isolated bits of information and fragmented curriculum that Hirsch deplores. Further, such instruction completely ignores schema theory research. Children do not come to school as little blank slates. They come to school with fairly well-developed schemata (world knowledge/ cultural literacy) that, when taken into account in reading instruction, not only enhance their comprehension but, also, enable them to become independent learners who can think critically. Hirsch is right in suggesting that more content is needed in reading instruction, but his proposed dispensing and testing of the knowledge on his list will only lead to an even more fragmented curriculum filled with isolated bits and pieces of information.

Hirsch does understand that comprehension is possible only when readers have developed a schema that enables them to fit new information into a previously developed framework. The problem lies in the way he thinks teachers should help students to develop that framework/background information/ world knowledge, that he calls cultural literacy. Hirsch thinks that this kind of framework can be "given" to students and he thinks that it should be standardized across the nation, not necessarily in the form of a national core curriculum; but, at least, in what he calls "an extensive curriculum based on the national vocabulary and arranged in a definite sequence."27 And even though Hirsch says that he allows for diversity in textbooks and teaching methods, the very fact that he has published a list of what should be learned and that he wants school materials to be more based in "factual information and traditional lore"28 already mitigate against diversity in either textbooks or teaching. Finally, the dispensing of this knowledge creates the most significant problem. What happens after the students leave the class? How will they achieve, on their own, the cultural literacy they need to comprehend the "texts" they will encounter, whether those "texts" are newspaper accounts of daily events, directions for filing tax returns, television special reports, job-related instructions, professional journal articles, or reading-for-pleasure materials?

Hirsch's model makes students teacher-dependent and robs them of the opportunity to become self-sufficient, independent learners. And, it virtually guarantees that students taught under this model of instruction will become the "deprofessionalized," white collar, assembly-line workers that Coe warns against. Hirsch plays right into the hands of the corporate leaders of America who desire workers who are literate enough to function at the middle level of management without being too literate to be overqualified.

The lessons of the past to be learned for the future need to start with learning that the past restructuring of schools based on the models suggested by the business community have proven inadequate; imposition of business models on the schools —consolidation and centralization for the sake of efficiency and the imposition of the assembly line model — have destroyed what Cheney calls the original purpose of schools: the transmission of our culture in order to reaffirm our humanity. In short, the business community, not the educational community, has been responsible for the failure of our schools; and, yet, in the latest decade of business-sponsored reform, few dare to put the blame where it belongs. We seem to have forgotten that America needs citizens educated to participate in a democracy as much as, maybe even more so, than we need education for economic superiority. Our hope for the future does not lie in accepting a narrowly based definition of literacy nor does it lie in another round of what-business-can-do-for-the-schools. Our hope lies with those teachers, professors, educators, and researchers who have learned the lessons of the past and, in addition, not only understand the phenomenal insights into literacy that recent research has produced but who use this knowledge to challenge their students and themselves to contemplate and understand the larger business of America, to create a society in which there is liberty and justice for all — and not just that constricted arena in which the business of America is only business and the teaching of humanities is driven by skills, tests, and the memorization of facts.

References

1. Lynne V. Cheney, *American Memory: A Report on the Humanities in the Nation's Public Schools*. Washington D.C.: National Endowment for the Humanities, 1987, p.5.
2. *Ibid.*, p. 6.
3. *Ibid.*, pp. 16-17.
4. *Learning in America*, narrated by Roger Mudd, PBS, Washington D.C., 27 March, 1989.
5. Cheney, *op. cit.*, p.19.
6. Personal Communication, March, 1989.
7. Clarence Karier, "Testing in the Corporate Liberal State," in Clarence J. Karier, Paul Violas, and Joel Spring, eds., *Roots of Crisis: American Education in the Twentieth Century*. Chicago: Rand McNally and Company, 1973, p. 135.
8. David Owen, *None of the Above: Behind the Myth of Scholastic Aptitude*. Boston: Houghton, 1985.
9. Ellen Graham, "Retooling the Schools," *The Wall Street Journal*, March 31, 1989, pp. R1-R36. Nancy J. Perry, "The Education Crisis: What Business Can Do," *Fortune*, July 4, 1988, pp. 71-73. Manuel J. Justiz and Marilyn C. Kameen, "Business Offers a Hand to Education," *Phi Delta Kappan*, January, 1987, pp. 379-33.
10. David Nasaw, *Schooled to Order*. New York: Oxford University Press, 1979.
11. *Ibid.*, pp. 105-113.
12. Robert L. Church and Michael W. Sedlak, *Education in the United States*. New York: The Free Press, 1976, p. 305.
13. Nasaw, *op. cit.*, pp. 121-123.
14. Barbara Z. Presseisen, *Unlearned Lessons: Current and Past Reforms for School Improvement*. Philadelphia: The Falmer Press, 1985.
15. David T. Kearns and Denis P. Doyle, *Winning the Brain Race: A Bold Plan to Make Our Schools Competitive*. San Francisco: Institute for Contemporary Studies, 1988.
16. "You wouldn't organize your office this way...so why do we do it in our schools?" *Teacher*, September/October, 1989, p. 3.
17. Bruce Nussbaun et al., "Human Capital: The Decline of America's Work Force," *Business Week*, September 19, 1988.
18. *Ibid.*, p. 135.
19. *Ibid.*, pp. 26-27.
20. *Ibid.*, p. 105.
21. Richard Coe, "The Restructuring of the 'White Collar' Worker and the Restructuring of the Curriculum," unpublished paper, International Federation for the Teaching of English, East Lansing, Michigan, November 11-14, 1984.

22. *Ibid.*, p. 5.
23. *Ibid.*, p. 5.
24. E. D. Hirsch, *Cultural Literacy: What Every American Needs to Know* New York: Random House, 1988, p. 1.
25. *Ibid.*, p. 17.
26. *Ibid.,* pp. 140-215.
27. *Ibid.*, p. 27.
28. *Ibid.*, p. 28.

The Neoconservative Backlash against Feminism in the the 1970s and 1980s: The Case of *Commentary*

Nina Roth
Odense University

From its beginnings, the development of an American consumption-oriented society implied fundamental changes in the relationsjiop betwen the sexes. As the home increasingly lost is significance as a center of production, most men began to engage in paid labor outside the home and women had to define new roles for themselves within the domestic sphere. In theory, at least, the new consumer goods such as ready-made clothing, canned goods, and bakery bread relieved middle-class women from most housework, and as the birth rate dropped sharply in the same period, urban middle-class women found themselves with a great deal of leaisure time on their hands. This time was spent on various consumer activities in the new department stores, and on a variety of cultural activities such as world fairs, amusement parks, and movie theaters. In addition, women were told how to consume "correctly" in the new home economics programs at the universities. Women´s expanding role as consumers in the early twentieth century cemented a nuclear family model, in which married women were overwhelmingly homemakers and consumers.

In the consumption boom that followed in the wake of World War II this family model reached its peak of cultural acceptance. Yet as the socioeconomic conditiuons and the cultural environment changed, this family type became less viable and less prevalent. Yet it has continued to hold a powerful ideological attraction; politicians and intellectuals alike often refer to "traditional" family values and morality when they try to explain the ills of the modern American welfare state. To the great resentment and dismay of large parts of the American population, the counter-culture of hte 1960s and especially the second wave of feminists vociferously attacked the ideal of the nuclear family. Part of the political and intellectual establishment opposed these attacks vigorously, and a good deal of the heated debate took place in the pages of the intellectual journal *Commentary,* which has consistently opposed the feminist movement, and which even today advocates a return to "traditional" family life. One characteristic passage suggests the journal's editorial stance:

Seen from the perspective of today, the 60's were like a tidal wave that swept over America. The wave has begun to roll back, but in its wake the shore is revealed to be littered with broken glass, burned-out fires, dead animals, and all kinds of garbage. A lengthy period will be required before the beach is cleaned up and put back into use.[1]

Commentary continues to view itself as a bastion against the destructive cultural *Zeitgeist* that lingers on from the 1960s, as the quotation from Joseph Epstein's "It's Only Culture" so poignantly demonstrates. Even in the 1980s, *Commentary* and the intellectuals associated with this New York-based journal seem obsessed with the 1960s and the damage that the cultural and social upheavals of this period wrought on American society and the American way of life.

This was not always so. Under Norman Podhoretz's editorship in the early 1960s, the magazine published a good deal of reform liberal and left-leaning articles that called for a more activist political stand and were critical of the status quo of American intellectual, social and political life. In 1960 Paul Goodman published parts of *Growing Up Absurd* [2] indicting the American system for not providing enough worthy jobs for the young because American politicians are more interested in expanding production and maintaining full employment. The journal fully endorsed the aims of the early Civil Right's Movement, and the editor himself stated that America needed to find a way to cope with the revolutionary problems of affluence and that there was a hunger for a new far-reaching idealistic political movement. All in all, *Commentary* was characterized by a fairly progressive and critical outlook on the contemporary American scene.

Furthermore, one should not forget that many of the intellectuals who constituted the core group around *Commentary* in the 1960s had flirted with radicalism and socialism in their youth. Although they had always belonged to the firmly anti-Stalinist wing, by the 1950s most of them were more traditional liberals and definitely anti-Communist. (I am thinking of intellectuals such as Irving Kristol, Daniel Bell, Irving Howe, Sidney Hook and Nathan Glazer).[3]

But by 1970 *Commentary*'s image had changed markedly, and the journal had started its turn to what has been labeled neoconservatism. Many spokesmen of neoconservatism were old-style liberals who felt uncomfortable with the new reform liberalism epitomized by the McGovern campaign of 1972, and they were turned off by the cultural antagonism of the New Left and the Counter Culture. The cultural issue is central to the disenchantement of these liberals with the New Left and the Counter Culture, and neoconservatives are to a great extent characterized by their cultural traditionalism as well as their notion of a minimalist welfare state. Their politics, however, usually turn out to be more diverse than their cultural outlook on issues such as feminism, sexuality, family life, art and literature. In short, these intellectuals believe that the Counter Culture has subverted liberalism in America. Tellingly, Podhoretz labels the Counter Culture a "spiritual plague."4

Some of these intellectuals have even called their conversion from a left-liberal political stance to a more cautious conservative liberalism a "deradicalization" process.5 Norman Podhoretz has written at great length about his own deradicalization although it is questionable whether he was ever a political radical in any sense of the word. However, he did see himself as undergoing such a process and in his autobiography *Breaking Ranks: A Political Memoir*(1979), he explains his political transformation to his son in the form of a pseudo-letter. His self-righteous tone does not help explicate his argument, but it does demonstrate the never-ending concern which he shares with other intellectuals about the future of liberalism in America and their sense that bourgeois culture is being undermined by radical intellectuals and by the popularized version of the culture and ideology of the 1960s and early 1970s.6

At the political level, neoconservatives are not easily identifiable as they have no fully articulated or coherent agenda, but they do converge around a number of cultural and political issues and share a particular style: an inclination to complex, rational intellectual discourse and theories and an appreciation of high culture; a distrust of populist sentiments and a dislike for the narcissistic, nihilistic, irrational and irresponsible impulses which they felt emanated from the Counter Culture and the New Left; a strong commitment to anti-Communism and anti-socialism in any form and to the view that America should serve as the bulwark of the free world; and a belief in the freedom of the individual as opposed to federal affirmative action programs that enforce group rights.

However, neoconservative intellectuals unite almost unanimously on the issue of the importance of the preservation of traditional family values and structures as a way of counteracting the undermining of liberal bourgeois values and questionable government intervention in private life. Another theme that unites neoconservatives is the conviction that the feminist movement and the dissemination of its ideas, even in a diluted version, is a regrettable development. More "rightist" conservatives and many liberals would undoubtedly agree with this view.

For two decades *Commentary* and the intellectuals associated with the journal have sounded the theme that radical feminism is an expression of self-hatred and nihilism. Only rarely do *Commentary*'s contributors distinguish between different kinds of feminism, and they apparently take the most radical feminism of the early 1970s to be the only feminist currency around. Podhoretz makes the link between nihilism and feminism explicit in the "letter" to his son: "But if the plague seems for the moment to have run its course among [the young, the blacks, and intellectuals], it rages as fiercely as ever among others: among the kind of women who do not wish to be women.This identification of sterility with vitality is what links the new narcissism of the Me Decade to Women's Lib and the gay-rights movement, and it is what links all of them to the radicalism of the sixties."7

In the early 1960s before the second-wave of feminism had gained either the imagination of the American people or the attention of legislators, intellectuals of all political persuasions were mostly silent on issues of women's rights and family policies although there was a new concern with the growing number of divorces and the decline of a "traditional" family structure 1950s style: breadwinner father, housewife mother, and dependent children. The concern about the first signs of the decline of this family model was most obvious in connection with the black family in the inner-city ghettos. The controversial "Moynihan Report" is a case in point.8

That the American family has undergone some changes since 1950 is undeniable. In 1960, over 60 percent of all American households conformed to this ideal family model. In the 1980s, less than 15 percent of the nation's households account for such a family structure.9 The massive entrance of women into the labor market, especially women with young children; the drop in the birthrate; and the rise in the divorce rate accompanied by a new feminist consciousness and the women's movement have all contributed to the erosion of the reality as well as the ideology of the traditional nuclear family.10 (This should not obscure the fact that a majority of Americans eventually marry, have children and prefer to live in some kind of family context, that most children grow up with two parents present and that most divorcés and divorcées remarry.)

Intellectuals writing in *Commentary* in the 1970s and 1980s have never ceased to regret these changes but only rarely do they view them as part of larger social and economic transformations in American society. These neo-conservatives usually insist on seeing the rise and continuing influence of feminism as a cultural conspiracy and the women and men who participate or sympathize with the movement as morally deficient.

In the 1960s *Commentary* was a fairly typical example of an intellectual journal in so far as women both as subjects and as contributors were largely absent. And the comments that *Commentary* did make on the issues of family life and women's role were quite conventional. For example in 1961, Midge Decter wrote an article on women's work, commenting on the new phenomenon of married women with children working even though they were not economically forced to do so. Decter realized that this social change had come to stay but she believed that the tension between the obligations of married life — such as the bearing and rearing of children — and paid work outside the home potentially could plunge the country into a domestic crisis of major proportions. This, of course, turned out to be an exaggeration although she correctly predicted the double burden that working mothers would have to undertake and which today is very real for a large number of women.

Although she acknowledged that women suffer discrimination in the labor market, she believed that they would always have one undeniable privilege compared to men: "Women always have a place of retreat when failure threatens...this is not what they really are, what they really do."[11] Decter clearly thinks that a woman's first responsibility is to her family although that does not exclude some kind of career or paid work. The matter of course way in which she assumes that all women really have such a retreat is partly due to the social realities of the early 1960s where most women married young as much as to the pervasive ideology that women could only realize themselves through becoming wives and mothers.

Significantly, Decter believes that family life should ideally remain a private concern and that the difficulties of balancing work and family life must ultimately rest with the individual woman. In the best liberal tradition, she advocates formal equality of opportunities in the labor market but without an increase in publicly funded institutions to ease women's labor force participation.

However, one should bear in mind that the view of family life as a private sphere outside politics and as a kind of refuge from the public sphere of work and competition in no way is particular to a specific political standpoint. The old Left voiced its concern over the breakdown of the "traditional" family, and especially the undermining of fathers' authority in the family. When the New Left considered the question of family at all, they saw it as maintaining the bourgeois values they were rebelling against and usually advocated its dissolution.

Liberals and conservatives alike reacted against what they saw as a threat to the moral order and social stability of American society. Christopher Lasch's book *Haven in a Heartless World* is a good example of a reaction by a left-liberal intellectual against the New Left's attack on family life and the Counter Culture's experiments with alternative family arrangements. Lasch sees the youth rebellions of the 1960s and 1970s as a sign of "massive cultural and psychological regression" and as a rejection of adulthood and maturity."[12] He interprets the instability of the modern family to be precisely a result of the collapse of distinct boundaries between the public and private realm as well as the growing intervention of the so-called helping professions. Most of the *Commentary* intellectuals would agree with Lasch on all points.

From 1970 and onward *Commentary* changed its former editorial policy of being rather uninvolved in issues concerning women's rights and family issues and launched a series of articles about the women's movement; men's and women's different sexuality and psyche; and the values of "traditional" family life. Midge Decter published her controversial article "The Liberated Woman" in the October issue 1970, and she expanded on her argument in her book *The New Chastity and Other Arguments against Women's Liberation*(1972). Decter argues that the women's movement is ultimately destructive because it advocates freedom without responsibility; because it claims that women are sexually oppressed when they are not and thus the movement seems to indicate that women should reclaim their right to remain chaste and should forego motherhood. Much like Lasch, Decter reacts against what she interprets as the immaturity and irresponsibility of the baby boom generation. She concludes her article:

> To judge from what [the liberated woman] says and does, however — finding only others at fault for her predicament, speaking always of herself as a means of stating the general case, shedding tears as a means of negotiation — the freedom she truly seeks is of a rather different kind. It is a freedom demanded by children and enjoyed by no one: the freedom from all difficulty. If in the end her society is at fault for anything, it is for allowing her to grow up with the impression that this is something possible to ask.[13]

But Decter's most serious objection to Women's Lib is its nihilism and self-denial. In her book *The New Chastity and Other Arguments Against Women's Liberation,* she states this point quite clearly:

> Such an expression of self-hatred is indeed, exactly the primary motion that informs Women's Liberation's diatribes against the impositions of motherhood. Neither society nor the current organization of the family but the womb itself...is ultimately the object of this movement's will to correct, to alter, to extirpate. There is no more radical nor desperately nihilistic statement to issue forth from the lips of humans than that there are no necessary differences between the sexes. For such differences both issue in and do in themselves constitute the most fundamental principle of the continuation of life on earth...it becomes the denial of life itself.[14]

Decter's article is actually rather moderate compared to an article published in March, 1971 by Arlene Croce, "Sexism in the Head." She absolutely vilifies the women's movement, while, at the same time, she exposes some of its real weaknesses and demonstrates the lack of appeal that the more radical fringe of the women's movement holds for most people regardless of sex or political convictions. As for feminism as a way of illuminating life, she has only this to say: "To a healthy woman it becomes a burden...but to the less fortunate — those who can't expel the poisons of self-pity or sexual jealousy or utopian greed — feminism is a solipsistic haven, a place in the psyche where all the bad and bitter feelings unite, where unbearable personal failures are rationalized by a belief in organic failures in society."[15] The women's movement is diagnosed as a disease which afflicts those narcissistic women who lack self-control or a sense of social responsibility and morality and who want to blame society and not their own shortcomings for their failures in love and work.

Croce bases her article on three of the radical and provocative feminist books, all published in 1970: Shulamith Firestone's *The Dialectic of Sex,*the anthology *Sisterhood is Powerful* edited by Robin Morgan, and Kate Millet's *Sexual Politics*. That these texts (especially the first two) shocked and offended most people is not surprising. They represent the early radical feminist movement's undisguised hostility to men and to a patriarchal family structure which they believe is oppressive. Firestone even goes as far as disavowing biological motherhood all together. She locates the oppression of women in their biology and the patriarchal family which controls and exploits her ability to bear and rear children.16 This negative view of female biology and the implicit misogyny is problematic, especially since it casts women and children solely in the role of victims. However, Firestone represents a radical fringe of the women's movement whose mainstream participants and sympathizers have endorsed motherhood and, indeed, have often celebrated it.17 Certainly today the women's movement does not show hostility to motherhood but tries to find ways in which motherhood and work can be balanced through agendas for child care and maternity benefits.

Croce expressed her disbelief and disgust at the media's willing and rapid incorporation of the most sensational feminist ideas and their apparent easy acceptance among young students, the radicalized protest movements and even among traditional liberals, especially in academia. She placed feminism in line with other cultural excesses of the New Left and the Counter Culture and did so precisely at the time when both were on the decline. However, feminism and the gay-rights movement became the visible remnants of the culture of the sixties and thus an appropriate target for the uneasiness of a great deal of intellectuals with the new moral and cultural climate as well as with the new liberal welfare agenda.

Ultimately, Croce's article fails because it never seriously tries to grapple with the political and economic implications of the women's movement. This is a failure her exposition shares with practically all other *Commentary* articles published on the subject for twenty years. They argue that because women have now achieved formal equality through the Civil Right's Act of 1964, the Equal Pay Act, the Women's Educational Equity Act and other legislation, and indeed sometimes have achieved even more than that through affirmative action programs, the women's movement is both obsolete and an expression of the demands of spoiled, neurotic women.

In this sense, Croce's article distills the neoconservative view of feminism; namely, that it is a result of a loosening of morality and an erosion of traditional values and manners since the 1960s, and that the socioeconomic changes over the past two decades are only a secondary contributing factor to the institutionalization of feminism. When neoconservatives deplore the breakdown of traditional family patterns and values, they are in fact indicting the consequences of modernity without at the same time coming to terms with the role that both the development of the capitalist market place and the Constitution's political potential for individual equality or gender neutrality have played in this process.

After its initial broadside against feminism in the early 1970s, *Commen-*

tary continued to express unequivocal support for marriage and family in a traditional sense and to deplore the harmful effects of the integration of formal feminist demands into the educational and political system. Neoconservatives do not usually resist formal equality in the labor market, in politics or in the educational system, but they object to demands that are built on the assumption that the biological differences between the sexes do not matter. Consequently, they object to affirmative action programs for women. In the same vein, they object to liberal and feminist agendas for family policies in so far as these policies actually precipitate the breakdown of the nuclear family. Thus *Commentary*'s contributors have devoted energy to explicating the inherent biological and psychological differences between men and women and to defending some version of a traditional nuclear family where the responsibilities of parenting are primary. This is usually interpreted as the mother being the primary caretaker and the father the protector of his wife and children.

Feminists, on the other hand, are seen as upsetting the delicate balance between the sexes in the family and are in fact liberating men from their traditional responsibility toward their families thus leaving a lot of women and children in the lurch. Women comply in undermining their own social and economic position by rejecting male protection; and by refusing to civilize the aggressive male sexuality through monogamous marriage, women are threatening the foundation of Western civilization. This line of argumentation is advanced by the political scientist and Republican activist George Gilder in his two books *Sexual Suicide* (1973) and *Men and Marriage* (1987) and in a 1974 *Commentary* article "In Defense of Monogamy."[18]

Sexual Suicide and Steven Goldberg's *The Inevitability of Patriarchy* (1973) were reviewed by the psychology professor David Gutmann, who shared a deep concern with the two authors over the inversions of sex roles taking place in America. Gutmann sees both books as long awaited masculine counterattacks against the claims of the women's liberation movement that all men are male chauvinist pigs. These "masculine" books try to prove that men's and women's differential social positions and roles are firmly rooted in biology. Since men have a larger biological endowment of aggressive energy in their reproductive years, men's drive for dominance over females and other males is not part of a patriarchal conspiracy but part of the inevitable male imperative. Gutmann believes that Gilder's insights are the most lucid because he realizes that male sexuality and aggression are not only inflexible biological forces but that they respond to the reciprocal sexuality of women and the need to provide a stable and protective environment for children.

This is close to Gutmann's own life cycle argument which he develops at some length. Young married men need to be competitive in order to provide for their families and aggressive in order to protect them. He argues that: "Men, the providers of physical security, give up the sensual dependency that might inhibit their courage and endurance; and women, the providers of emotional security, give up the aggression that might frighten or hurt a vulnerable and needful child"[19] However, in later life when the children are provided for and grown up, male and female sex roles seem to reverse themselves somewhat. Men reclaim a more passive and tender "femininity," and women tend to become more aggressive and domineering thus breaking down the sharp sexual distinctions of the child-bearing years. Gutmann clearly believes this to be a sensible arrangement of nature that ensures the survival of the species and that interference in this process may have irrevocable consequences. So Gutmann joins Gilder and Goldberg in their disapproval of the feminist project, as they interpret it, of creating a unisex society that purports to "liberate" humanity. All three authors fear that the consequences for the psychic health of the future generation of children will be severe and already see damages in the present young generation. Gutmann claims:

> For these are precisely the families – characterized by the domineering mother and the "weak or absent" father – that have generated such a high proportion of today's psychiatric casualties, the drop-outs, drug-heads, and religious freaks. Too many of these families, in which the normal family life cycle has been inverted, send forth their children, full of need, to turn to chemicals, liquor, anonymous sex, and charismatic but totalitarian leaders for the kind of psychic supplies they never found in their parents – or in themselves.[20]

Again the blame is put squarely in a private realm of morality and on a permissive liberal education that fails to provide highly differentiated sexual role models for the children.[21] How Gutmann manages to prove that drug addiction, alcoholism, promiscuity and participation in various religious cults are the results of inverted sex roles in the middle class family remains at best unclear. Furthermore, the family dynamic he criticizes is not characterized by an actual inversion of roles as exactly a "weak and absent" mother was not typical of the traditional family model he apparently has in mind. It seems that the family structure that he, perhaps involuntarily, indicts is the modern urban middle class family in which the father is absent most of the time due to his work and the mother manages the household responsibilities and the raising of the children.

Today sex roles may seem more blurred due to the fact that most married women with children are engaged in paid labor and because the relations between spouses and between parents and children have become more egalitarian. However, I think that he greatly exaggerates the blurring of sex roles (perhaps this is understandable as the article was written at the height of the feminist movement), and secondly he misses the historical dimension of the development of the middle class family. Anxiety over the decline of parental and especially patriarchal authority is evident already in the 19th century and is, at least partly, due to other large-scale social and economic changes.[22] Yet, Gutmann focuses on the educational failures of parents without considering factors outside the psychological realm and one-sidedly represents families that have raised their children in the 1960s and 1970s under the influence of liberal and feminist ideas as emotionally crippled and the cause of much misery.

Although neither George Gilder nor David Gutmann can substantiate their claims convincingly, they nevertheless serve as a reminder of the continued resistance to feminist ideas when these ideas are directed against the institutions of family and motherhood. But more importantly, the authors also remind us of the often troubled and painful emotional state of the relationship between the sexes and between parents and children who are groping for new guidelines and directions in the 1980s.

Feminists today have not been able to provide concrete viable solutions either and the debate among feminists themselves has intensified. The 1980s have witnessed a neoconservative backlash against the liberal family agenda and the feminist movement but part of the reaction comes from deradicalized feminists as well as from "pro-family" conservative women who feel that their traditional roles as mothers and housewives are being threatened and devalued by feminist consciousness and liberal welfare legislation. The feminist movement today then faces a serious crisis as self-conscious feminists and other vocal groups of women turn against the idea of sexual equality as epitomized in the struggle over the Equal Rights Amendment and in the struggle over sexual and reproductive freedom. A number of prominent feminists of both liberal and radical feminist persuasions have abandoned or modified their original concern with creating a sexual egalitarian society and instead they focus on women's need for formal equality in politics and in the labor market and their special need for protection as working mothers, as potential victims of violence and abuse, and as especially vulnerable to trade cycles and unemployment.

This group of deradicalized and conservative feminists do by no means share the same assumptions about human nature or politics but they agree on a number of points concerning family policies and sexual equality. These feminists unite in an attack against the goals and politics of the women's movement of the 1970s and its supposedly excessive demand for sexual equality interpreted as "sameness" between men and women. These feminists have retreated from sexual politics and the original concern of the women's movement to uncover the political aspect of private life and sexuality which had been obscured by the liberal political ideology. These feminists want to reconstitute a private realm of family life and sexuality while pursuing equality of opportunity and protection in the economic and political realm. However, clearly government regulations and legislation are necessary to protect women and to give them the possibilities to freely choose motherhood, housewifery , wage work and perhaps a professional career.[23]

One of the issues that is foremost in the debate over the future of the modern American family among all intellectuals and politicians is child care. Who is going to look after the young children when the mother works outside the home? Both mainstream feminist and liberal agendas have called for a more aggressive public family policy that would include more public child-care arrangements, flexible working hours, maternity leave and better benefits for single mothers on welfare. In general, neoconservatives do not want totally to dispense with public involvement in family life (like some social conservatives and right-to-lifers would) as they realize that the well-being of families is dependent on a whole array of government activities such as housing, education, health, welfare and tax policies. However, neoconservatives argue that too much government interference in family life may actually break up families, for example by giving mothers more benefits as a right, and they argue that public child care may cause psychological damage to children.

In a March, 1978 article "The Rediscovery of the Family," Nathan Glazer thoughtfully evaluates the present state of the American family and the possibilities for a better public policy concerning families. He expresses his concern over: 1) the state of the black family in America with its high proportion of poor children who are raised by single mothers 2) the radical attack of segments of the women's movement on the traditional family 3) the anxiety of middle-class parents over their parental responsibilities and authority 4) the expansion of state interference in the private life of the family. In spite of these areas of concern, Glazer is heartened by the current trends in the debate over the family coming from disparate quarters. In reviewing the intellectual and social science literature on the contemporary family, he finds that all agree that massive publicly subsidized child-care is not the answer. If funds should be employed for the care of children, then the money should be given directly to mothers to enable them to take care of their children within the family and not to public agencies.

Glazer is in particular delighted by the Freudian analyst Selma Fraiberg's book *Every Child's Birthright: In Defense of Mothering* (1977) because she is not afraid to claim without a shadow of a doubt that infants and toddlers need constant mothering in order to develop properly and that the biological mother is usually the most suitable person for this job. She points out that the lack of qualified and devoted "mother substitutes" means that it is not feasible for mothers to find people whom they can trust with their children. Instead of subsidized public day care which is almost guaranteed to harm the psychological development of children, she suggests that federal money should be appropriated to those mothers on welfare who want to take care of their own children.

Although Glazer joins in the celebration of the traditional family, he realizes soberly that in the contemporary highly complex social reality it is impossible to envision a blanket family policy that would solve all the social and economic problems of the diverse manifestations of the American family. In the end, he falls back on the assumption that all things considered the traditional family provides the best framework for raising children and works pretty well. In view of this, social policies should be designed to support this model.

Commentary reviewed several other books dealing with the family in the 1980s: *In Defense of the Family* (1983) by Rita Kramer and *The War Over the Family: Capturing the Middle Ground*(1983) by Brigitte and Peter L. Berger.24 The latter is appropriately reviewed by Rita Kramer. Both books and reviewers reiterate the concerns voiced by Nathan Glazer in his 1978 article over growing government involvement and institutionalized day care. Rita Kramer claims in her review that "[e]ver-increasing areas of publicly-funded social-welfare programs, for instance, have resulted in a disenfranchisement of the family by professionals and government bureaucrats pledged to protect it. The family has grown steadily weaker in precisely the period in which professionals have been most involved with it."23 Once again the theme of harmful state intervention is sounded and the traditional middle-class family upheld as the model that most effectively ensures the development of mentally healthy individuals and useful citizens.

It would actually be hard to know what the liberal and feminist family agenda was all about if one had to rely on *Commentary* since they have not published articles explaining any of these positions. The journal does occasionally review a book by a feminist author but then they choose a book that is as far removed from mainstream liberal feminism as possible. The choice of Germaine Greer's *Sex and Destiny*(1984) testifies to this editorial policy.26 Obviously, Greer's latest book is not a feminist manifesto but almost a reversal of her earlier radical feminism and cry for sexual freedom as a means of women's liberation. *Sex and Destiny* is about the conditions of modern family life in the Western world but it turns out to be an erratic celebration of Third World "primitive" patriarchal extended family structure which presumably enables women and children to bond in meaningful ways. Greer indicts the whole of Western civilization and accuses the Western population (women) of being utterly hostile to children and fertility. Greer's disgust with radical feminism is of course an interesting phenomenon in itself but finally the book review serves as a stepping board for yet another round of anti-feminism. The reviewer Carol Iannone argues:

> For what *Sex and Destiny* most clearly reveals is that feminism — at least in its messianic, world-transforming manifestations — was less a rational program with fixed goals than an irrational shriek of hatred against the human condition itself, one that will not be silenced until every aspect of life, with its attendant irregularity, imperfection, and inequality, has been eradicated. This book is a reversal of feminism only if one assumes that feminism is the humane movement it purports to be. In fact the book is no reversal at all, but a logical, if absurd, conclusion.27

Most neoconservatives and social conservatives remain convinced that the pernicious influence of feminist ideas has not been halted even in the generally more conservative political climate of the 1980s. Firstly, because

Washington has thrown its support behind educational programs and hiring practices that favor women and feminist ideology,28 and secondly because of the changing relationship between the sexes that feminism has fueled and maintained. Ultimately the new sex roles and the "liberation" of women have consequences for the future of the American family and this development is deeply troubling to many of these intellectuals and indeed to most people as the contemporary situation is, to say the least, still unsettled.

The liberation of women from their traditional roles as mothers and wives is deplored by neoconservatives because it in a sense leaves women and their children more vulnerable than before. The women's movement has perhaps unwittingly released men from their former responsibility of protecting and sustaining their families and the easy access to divorce and the lack of social pressure to make married couples stay together has made the sexual competition for a mate all the more fierce and difficult especially for older women and sexually unattractive women and men. In "Liberating Women: Who Benefits?"29 — the sequel to "The Liberated Woman" — Midge Decter argues that at first glance the great beneficiaries of the women's movement have been men who have been cut loose from demanding familiar responsibilities and that the modern liberated middle class woman who wants to have it all — a career, children and a loving husband/partner — complains about male withdrawal. The withdrawal of men and the liberation of women is in the end harmful to both sexes as they are relieved of the necessity of negotiating with the other sex in order to create viable family settings for themselves and for their children.30

Likewise George Gilder argues from a male perspective in "In Defense of Monogamy"31 that a traditional monogamous family structure protects women from being deserted when they grow less sexually attractive and ensures that the largest number of men and women will be able to find a marriage partner and set up a family. And Allan Bloom picks up the argument in "Liberty, Equality, Sexuality."32 He believes that as a result of the sexual liberation movement and the feminist demands for equality, the modern middle class family consists of two equal wills but without any inclination to mediate between the two and to create a harmonious alternative to the traditional family structure. This situation has generated a spiritual crisis and ultimately it has placed women in a disadvantaged position. He says: "All our reforms have helped to do is to strip the teeth of our gears, which can therefore no longer mesh. They spin idly, side by side, unable to set the social machine in motion. It is at this exercise in futility that young people must look when thinking about their future."

These authors all point to some of the most troubling aspects of the contemporary relationship between the sexes. However, it should be equally clear that no amount of nostalgic longing will bring back the unusual situation of the 1950s or the reconstitution of the earlier rural self-sustaining family. The most pressing concern today is to construct social policies and encourage private initiatives that will provide the best possible socioeconomic conditions for parenting in modern America for a variety of family types.

References

1. Joseph Epstein, "It's Only Culture,"*Commentary*, Vol. 75, (Nov. 1983), p. 61.
2. Paul Goodman, *Growing Up Absurd*. New York: Vintage Books,1960.
3. For a history of their background, see Peter Steinfels, *The Neoconservatives: The Men Who Are Changing America's Politics*. New York: Simon and Schuster, 1979.
4. Norman Podhoretz, *Breaking Ranks: A Political Memoir*. New York: Harper & Row, 1979, p. 362.
5. Nathan Glazer, "On Being Deradicalized," *Commentary*, Vol. 50, Oct. 1970.
6. Podhoretz does not fully accept the political label "neoconservative" which others have given him. In *Breaking Ranks: A Political Memoir*,he says: "Others might call us conservatives or neoconservatives, and we certainly had no desire to be identified with the views of many of the people usually known as liberals today. In looking for convenient alternatives to use in public, we would say that we were 'centrists.' But privately, when we wondered what to call ourselves *to* ourselves, the invariable answer was: a liberal (p.356)."
7. *Ibid.*, pp.363-4.
8. Daniel Patrick Moynihan wrote *The Negro Family: The Case for National Action* as a policy-making document when he served as assistant secretary of labor. The report's central argument was that the breakdown of black families was a result of cyclical unemployment and the experience of slavery. The report ended up being used in an ideological warfare between white liberals, black radicals and conservatives.
9. Steven Mintz and Susan Kellogg, *Domestic Revolutions: A Social History of American Family Life*. New York: Free Press, 1988, p.203. The make-up of American households varies considerably according to race and ethnic origin. Black and hispanic households have a much larger percentage of single mothers than white households. In 1985, 53.3 percent of all black children lived only with their mother as compared to 15.4 percent of white children and 25.6 percent of hispanic children. Sara E. Rix, *The American Woman 1987-88* . New York: W.W. Norton & Co., 1987, p.298.
10. In 1950, the female/male employment ratio was 34.0/96.0 in the prime

child-bearing years 25-34. In 1986, the ratio was 71.3/94.1. About 48 percent of all children under six have mothers in the labor force, and the labor force participation rate of women between the ages 18 and 44 who had had a child in the last year was 48.4 percent in 1985 (Rix, pp. 302, 305, and 307). Needless to say that working mothers and women have become a crucial part of the labor force. The average number of children per family fell from 3.8 at the peak of the baby boom to less than 2 today. The number of divorces have tripled since 1950 (Mintz, p. 203).

11. Midge Decter, "Women at Work," *Commentary*, Vol. 31, (March, 1961), p. 250.
12. Christopher Lasch, *Haven in a Heartless World: The Family Besieged.* New York: Basic Books, 1977, p.129.
13. "The Liberated Woman," *Commentary*, Vol. 50, (Oct. 1970), p.44.
14. Midge Decter, *The New Chastity and Other Arguments Against Women's Liberation.* New York: Coward, McCann & Geoghegan, 1972, p.180.
15. "Sexism in the Head," *Commentary,* Vol. 52, (March 1971), p.63.
16. Shulamith Firestone, *The Dialectic of Sex: The Case for Feminist Revolution* New York: Doubleday, 1970, p.81.
17. A good example of this approach is Adrienne Rich's book *Of Woman Born: Motherhood as Experience and Institution.* New York: W. W. Norton, 1976.
18. "In Defense of Monogamy," *Commentary,* Vol. 58, (Nov. 1974), pp. 31–36.
19. David Gutmann, "Men, Women, and the Parental Imperative," *Commentary,* Vol. 56, (Dec.1973), p.62.
20. *Ibid.*, p. 64.
21. In her book *Liberal Parents, Radical Children.* New York: Coward, McCann & Geoghegan, 1975, Midge Decter too blames the permissive liberal education for the social and cultural troubles of the 1960s and early 1970s.
22. See for example Richard Sennett, *Families against the City: Middle Class Homes of Industrial Chicago, 1872-1890.* Cambridge, Mass.:Harvard University Press, 1970.
23. For two good discussions of feminist revisionism see, Judith Stacey, "Are Feminists Afraid to Leave Home? The Challenge of Conservative Pro-Family Feminism," in Juliet Mitchell and Ann Oakley, eds., *What Is Feminism?* Oxford: Basil Blackwell, 1986, and Zillah Eisenstein, *Feminism and Sexual Equality: Crisis in Liberal America.* New York: Monthly Review Press, 1984.
24. *In Defense of the Family* is reviewed by Chester E. Finn, Jr., in *Commentary*, Vol. 74, (May 1983), pp. 78-80: *The War Over the Family* is reviewed by Rita Kramer in *Commentary* vol 75, (Nov. 1983), pp. 73-75.
25. "Holding the Center," *Commentary,* Vol. 75, Nov. 1983, p.73.

26. *Sex and Destiny* is reviewed by Carol Iannone in *Commentary*, Vol. 77, (Aug. 1984), pp. 71–72.

27. *Commentary*, Vol. 77, Aug. 1984, p. 72.

28. Michael Levin's "Feminism and Thought Control" in *Commentary*, Vol. 73, (June 1982), pp.40-44, is an instructive article on some of the absurdities that the implementation of feminist ideology has resulted in — in this case in the guidelines for "sex fairness" in textbooks which demand distortions of reality in the name of a representation of an abstract sameness and complete equality between men and women. Nevertheless, Levin overestimates the extent to which these guidelines have been carried through and the actual influence of feminist ideology in any wider sense especially beyond academia and certain public sector jobs.

29. "Liberating Women, Who Benefits?" *Commentary*, Vol. 76, (March 1984), pp.31-36.

30. In an autobigraphical and personal article Ruth R. Wisse in "Living With Women's Lib," *Commentary*, Vol. 85, (Aug. 1988), pp.40-45, makes similar points about the unfortunate influence of feminism on family life and the relations between the sexes.

31. "In Defense of Monogany," *Commentary,* Vol. 58, (Nov. 1974), pp.31-36.

32. "Liberty, Equality, Sexuality," *Commentary,* Vol. 82, (April 1987), pp.24-30.The essay is adapted from Bloom's book, *The Closing of the American Mind.* New York: Simon & Schuster, 1987, p. 30.

Emily Dickinson:
Poetic Consumption, or the Poet as Reader

Lis Møller
University of Copenhagen.

I

Father . . . buys me many Books — but begs me not to read them—
because he fears they joggle the Mind.   — Emily Dickinson

One of the persistent myths in American literary history is the legend of Emily
Dickinson as "Queen Recluse": the image of the superbly isolated poet who
had sealed herself off from the world. In keeping with this image, we have
read Dickinson's poems as expressions of her tormented inner life rather than
responses to her intellectual and cultural environment. It has been assumed
that her enigmatic, elusive, and strikingly original poetry remained largely
uninfluenced by the works of her contemporaries as well as by the literature
of previous ages.

Lately, however, Dickinson's cultural isolation has been called in
question. "The Soul selects her own Society — / . . . / Then — close the
Valves of her attention — / Like Stone —" claimed Dickinson in one of her
famous poems (P 303). Yet, in *Beneath the American Renaissance*, David
Reynolds has convincingly argued that Dickinson's work shows the poet's
remarkable openness and "unique responsiveness"[1] to a wide spectrum of
voices in her literary culture. And Reynolds is only one of several Dickinson
scholars to remind us that Dickinson's separation from her culture may be a
"spurious assumption."[2] These critics and literary historians point out that
Dickinson participated in the literary culture of her day through her reading.
Physical insulation reinforced the importance of the printed word, and the poet
consumed with avidity a vast quantity of novels and verses, essays and
articles. Moreover, it is maintained that one cannot fully understand
Dickinson's poetic achievements unless one takes into account the range of
her readings and attempts to resituate her poetry in its cultural context.

But what did Dickinson actually read? And how can we chart the literary
and cultural context of her poetry? Biographers have drawn up lists of books

owned by the Dickinson family.3 Not surprisingly, these lists tend to foreground the works of Shakespeare and Milton as well as Romantic and Victorian poets: Wordsworth, Coleridge, Shelley, Byron, Tennyson, the Brownings, Longfellow, and Emerson. Important as the works of these poets may be (I shall presently discuss the influence of Mrs. Browning), they merely represent a selection of the texts available to Dickinson. For a broader and less prejudiced view of the poet's reading, one should include the journals, magazines, and newspapers which she hungrily devoured. The Dickinson household subscribed to influential journals such as the *Atlantic Monthly*, *Scribner's Monthly*, and *Harper's Monthly Magazine* as well as to several daily newspapers, of which the *Springfield Republican* was the most important. All of these journals and papers printed fiction and poetry. *Harper's* featured literature and literary criticism, together with reprints from English newspapers, fashion, and humor, for instance. *Scribner's* (founded in 1870 by J.G. Holland, a friend of the Dickinsons) and the *Atlantic* were more explicitly "literary" periodicals, featuring literary essays and original poetry of fairly high quality such as poems by Emerson, but also less demanding literature. Thus the *Atlantic* serialized a number of the most popular novels of the day. And it was the *Atlantic* which, in 1860, printed "Circumstance," a gothic tale by Harriet Prescott Spofford whose writings deeply impressed Dickinson. "Circumstance" tells about a woman who, walking through the woods at night, is caught by a half-human beast, the "Indian Devil."4 About to be devoured, she finds that the monster will not harm her as long as she sings; singing all night, she saves her life. Having read this story, Dickinson sent her sister-in-law, Susan Dickinson, the following note: "This is the only thing I ever saw in my life I did not think I could have written myself. You stand nearer the world than I do. Send me everything she writes."5 Two years later she would mention "Circumstance" in a letter to Higginson, her literary "preceptor": "I read Miss Prescott's 'Circumstance,' but it followed me, in the Dark — so I avoided her —." In the same letter, however, Dickinson speaks of herself as poet in terms evocative of this gothic narrative: "I had a terror — since September — I could tell no one — and so I sing, as the Boy does by the Burying Ground — because I am afraid —" (L 261).

In the literary magazines poems by Emerson, for instance, gothic tales like Prescott Spofford's, and sentimental verses would appear side by side. This heterogeneity reflected Dickinson's reading. The works which she consumed were not only those written "for immortality," but also those written for the market. Dickinson's biographers have pointed out that the poet — whose own work was deemed too unconventional for publication — had a wholly conventional literary taste, or even an embarrassingly bad taste.6 As Capps diplomatically puts it, she did not presume to criticize. Dickinson once said that Shakespeare was the only true poet. But "true" was also the word which she applied to pious banalities:

I have just read three little books, not great, not thrilling — but sweet and true. "The Light in the Valley," "Only," and "A House upon a Rock" — I know you would love them all — yet they don't *bewitch* me any. There are no walks in the wood — no low and earnest voices, no moonlight, nor stolen love, but pure little lives, loving God, and their parents, and obeying the laws of the land; yet read, if you meet them, Susie, for they will do one good. (L 85)

Dickinson was twenty-two when she wrote this letter; she was forty-one when she referred to George Parson Lathrop's sentimental consolation verse "The Child's Wish Granted" as "piteously sweet" (L 737). As Richard Sewall remarks, Dickinson's "capacity for absorbing what we would consider banalities was apparently lifelong."[7] In fact, her last letter, written from the death-bed, was a reference to Hugh Conway's best-seller Called Back — according to Sewall "a novel in the sentimental-melodramatic mode at its worst."[8]

Dickinson was a large-scale consumer of many different kinds of literature, from Isaac Watts's hymns, to Shakespeare and the English metaphysical poets, to gothic tales and saccharine verses. And she did not merely read for relaxation; she read as a poet, that is, she read for inspiration. The critics and literary historians who inquire into Dickinson's reading generally agree on this point, although they disagree on the question of the extent to which her poems derive from external sources. According to Richard Sewall, "the references are usually fleeting and peripheral."[9] Others say that she liberally incorporated that which she read into her own work. And, in the opinion of John Evangelist Walsh, Dickinson borrowed so heavily from other writers that her poetry, in sober truth, was not entirely her own. Dickinson, Walsh contends, was little but a literary "scavenger" who managed, quite literally, "to steal . . . into the company of the immortals."[10] Outrageous as this description would seem, there may nevertheless be pertinent truth in the observation that Dickinson's themes and images are less "original" than we have been inclined to believe. Both Reynolds and Cheryl Walker point out numerous thematic parallels between Dickinson's poetry and, for instance, the works of American nineteenth-century women writers: Lydia H. Sigourney, Sara Willis Parton, Alice Cary, Elizabeth Stoddard, Harriet Prescott Spofford, Louise Chandler Moulton, and others. Death was one of the themes which all of these women writers explored with an almost necrophilous interest. As Sigourney had remarked, "the death-bed" was a female topic *par excellence*.[11] In the case of Sigourney herself, the death-bed gave rise to poems of pious sentiment (the death of a child being a repeated theme) as well as of gothic horror. Death is the Fatal Lover:

To beauty's shaded room,
The spoiler's step of gloom
Hath darkly stole;

Her lips are ghastly white,
A film is o'er her sight —
Pray for her soul.

And Death is the Great Ennobler:

The pauper layeth down
Gaunt penury's galling crown
Of scorn and dread;
Great as a king he goes
Unto his long repose —
Toll for the dead.[12]

Quite similar figurations of Death occur in Dickinson's poetry. "Death is a supple Suitor / That wins at last — / It is a stealthy Wooing," she wrote (P 1445). And: "Wait till the Majesty of Death / Invests so mean a brow!" (P 171).

In a period which, according to Cheryl Walker, seems a relatively optimistic and "sane" one for American male poets, women writers were preoccupied with subjects such as forbidden love, secret sorrow, renunciation, deprivation, pain, and madness.[13] As is well known, Dickinson dealt with all of these themes. In addition, she made use of specific images characteristic of the female tradition, for instance the volcano image which Reynolds discusses, as well as the image of the prison or the cage: confinement and restraint versus inward explosiveness and passion. "Dickinson's topics and sentiments are often indistinguishable from those of her sister poets,"[14] concludes Christanne Miller. But while Dickinson was obviously indebted to a female tradition, she also responded to male voices of her culture — just as she borrowed from "elite" as well as from "popular" literature. In fact, it is the diversity of the literary and cultural material that inspired Dickinson which indicates the limitations of a traditional source-study approach to her poetry. In *Emily Dickinson's Poetry* Ruth Miller suggests that it was the reading of an epitaph, reprinted in Thomas Bridgam's *Inscriptions on the Grave Stones in the Grave Yards of Northampton, and of the other Towns in the Valley of the Connecticut*, commemorating a young man "who was instantly killed by the / upsetting of a load of wood,"[15] which prompted Dickinson to write "In falling Timbers buried —" (P 614). And Walsh argues that "Upon the gallows hung a wretch" (P 1757) is a condensed version of a story about a hanging from Maria Lydia Child's *Letters from New York*. In the case of a poet who was capable of drawing inspiration from such offbeat material, it would not only be an impossible and endless task to compile lists of possible sources for her poems; it would also be a futile one. To gain a better understanding of Dickinson's poetry, one must not just show *what* she read and what she used, but also *how* she read, and how she used that which she

102

consumed. This 'how' will be my main concern in the following.

II. Reading as a Poet

.. the ideas of the time are in the air, and infect all who breathe it.
—Ralph Waldo Emerson, *Representative Men* (1850)

A Word dropped careless on a Page
May stimulate an eye
When folded in perpetual seam
The Wrinkled Maker lie

Infection in the sentence breeds
We may inhale Despair
At distances of Centuries
From the Malaria —
—Emily Dickinson (P 1261, c. 1873)

Commenting on Dickinson's well-known poem "A Word dropped careless on a Page," Sandra Gilbert and Susan Gubar point out that the poet's observation about "infection in the sentence" indicates her "keen consciousness that, in the purest Bloomian or Millerian sense, pernicious 'guests' and 'ghosts' inhabit all literary texts."[16] "Bloomian" means, of course, Harold Bloomian. Since the publication in 1973 of Harold Bloom's *The Anxiety of Influence*, words like "tradition," "influence," and "source" have lost their innocence. Poets, Bloom contends, do not simply "inherit" their precursors; poetic influence is a life and death struggle with Oedipal overtones. According to Bloom's theory, the basic experience of the modern (romantic and post-romantic) poet is the anxiety of influence. The (strong) poet desires more than anything else to be "self-begotten," to be his own "Great Original." Yet he realizes that he is hopelessly belated, hopelessly influenced: His language does not belong to himself, but to a powerful Precursor. Minor poets content themselves with imitating their precursor, says Bloom. The stong poet, on the other hand, tries to defend himself against the influence of the precursor, and this defense can only take the form of a poetic mis-reading of the precursor's work. A strong mis-reading is in fact an act of violence directed towards the precursor-text, a "perverse, wilful revisionism."[17] Ultimately, the poet desires to take the precursor's place; he wants to commit a symbolic parricide.

In *Beneath the American Renaissance*, Reynolds proposes a supplement to Bloom's theory. According to Reynolds, American nineteenth-century poets defended themselves against their (British) precursors by opening their texts to the influence of popular modes and stereotypes. It "has not been recognized," he says, "that one of the main weapons wielded by the American writers against oppressive literary influence was a native idiom learned from their own popular culture."[18] While key-terms in Bloom's theory are *belatedness, anxiety,* and *defense,* cues to Reynolds' supplementary theory could be: *textual fluidity, responsiveness,* and *openness.* Taking as his point of departure the lines by Emerson quoted in my epigraph, Reynolds introduces his study of the American Renaissance with these words:

> The present book describes the socioliterary 'air' surrounding the major writers and explores the process by which this air seeped through the pores of their skin. . . . It studies literary texts as products of a sudden fluidity of textual modes and strategies perceived and recorded by certain authors . . . It suggests that certain writers . . . produced literary texts precisely because of their keen responsiveness to their social and literary environment.[19]

Thus the writers of the American Renaissance were engaged in revisionary work at two fronts. On the one hand, they had to defend themselves against the influence of their (British) "Fathers" through wilfully distortive misreadings. On the other hand, they absorbed and thus transformed their own popular culture.

How does this model apply to American mid-nineteenth century women writers; do female poets read differently? *Beneath the American Renaissance* fails to distinguish, theoretically and methodologically, between the "openness" and "responsiveness" of, for instance, Hawthorne and Dickinson. Nor does gender appear to be of any consequence to Bloom's theory of poetic influence. But, as feminist critics have pointed out, Bloom's theory is indissolubly bound up with Freud's concept of the *boy's* Oedipus complex — the woman writer does simply not fit in, say Gilbert and Gubar. Studying female poets of the nineteenth century, the authors of *The Madwoman in the Attic* postulate a more primary "anxiety of authorship" which compelled the woman writer to seek out "foremothers who could help them find their distinctive female power."[20] Cheryl Walker makes a similar observation: "Unlike American men who were preoccupied during this period with establishing a national literature distinct from British traditions, American women poets in the nineteenth century were perfectly willing to acknowledge solidarity with their English sisters."[21] But Walker is here referring to minor — or, in Bloom's Nietzschean terminology, "weak" — poets; what about Dickinson?

In his paraphrase of Emerson's statement about ideas "in the air," Reynolds ignores the notion of disease implicit in the term "infect." It is precisely this connotation, Dickinson explores in her poetic elaboration of Emerson's metaphor: Words and texts may be germs, bacteria. Thus Dickinson's poem deals with that which Bloom calls "influenza." Furthermore, it is itself inhabited by a sort of precursor-text: Emerson. Emerson's metaphor, I think, was the "germ" from which Dickinson's poem grew. Yet Dickinson is haunted by no sense of "belatedness"; her poetry in general betrays little Bloomian "anxiety of influence." She had no great precursor in the Bloomian sense of the term — no literary forefather or foremother whom she wished to annihilate, and whose place she wanted to take. What is so striking about Dickinson is rather her capacity, as a poet, to import and absorb multiple and very different cultural voices. In this respect, it appears, she made *no distinction* between male or female literature, or between popular and "elite" culture. Her poems show no sign of the "double" strategy — defensiveness towards British elite literature; responsiveness towards American popular culture — which Reynolds has postulated. I have already mentioned that Dickinson, according to her biographers, read uncritically; it seems, they say, that she was lacking in judgement. But I think that it was this lack of judgement which made her poetic assimilation of her literary culture so unique. Reading *as a poet,* Dickinson broke down literary hierarchies. She took from everybody *indiscriminately,* and made quite similar use of very disparate texts.

In *The Life of Emily Dickinson* Sewall quotes a poem by a certain Charles Mackay which was printed in the *Springfield Republican* in 1858. "Little Nobody" is the title of the poem which consists of two stanzas, ending with the lines: "I'm but little Nobody — Nobody am I" and "Who would be a Somebody? — Nobody am I." No doubt, this trivial poem was the source of Dickinson's brief poem on the same theme:

> I'm Nobody! Who are you?
> Are you — Nobody — Too?
> Then there's a pair of us!
> Don't tell! they'd advertise — you know!
>
> How dreary — to be — Somebody!
> How public — like a Frog —
> To tell one's name — the livelong June —
> To an admiring Bog!
> (P 288, c. 1861)

Sewall, half apologetically, refers to this poem as an "early exercise."[22] However, if Johnson's chronology of poems is to be trusted, Dickinson had at that point written almost 300 poems, among these one of her most famous: "I felt a Funeral, in my Brain." According to other critics, this poem, too, derives from a clearly identifiable source, not another poem, but Nathaniel Hawthorne's gothic tale "The Hollow of the Three Hills." Hawthorne's narrative is about a woman who, through the medium of a old witch, experiences the terrible fate of the dear ones whom she has abandoned.

Lastly, she learns that her child is dead and is about to be buried. What is in this connection so interesting about Hawthorne's story is that the funeral is internalized — enacted in the woman's mind — as pure sound-experience. The lady "heard that boding sound. Stronger it grew and sadder, and deepened into the tone of a death-bell, knolling dolefully from some ivy-mantled tower. . ." Hawthorne's language captures the cadence of the funeral train: "Then came a measured tread, passing slowly, slowly on, as of mourners with a coffin, their garments trailing on the ground, so that the ear could measure the length of their melancholy array."[23] These features — the internalized funeral, the sound of the death-bell, the mourner's measured tread — reappear in intensified form in Dickinson's poem from which I quote the first stanza:

I felt a Funeral, in my Brain,
And Mourners to and fro
Kept treading — treading — till it seemed
That sense was breaking through —
(from P 280)

Given such examples, an apt expression from Capp's study of Dickinson's reading comes to mind: The poet, he says, "was shopping in the literary market place,"[24] taking what she found useful. Sewall suggests that she regularly read (and wrote) for competition: "See how *I* can do it!" However, it should be noted that one seldom detects a one-to-one relationship between a Dickinson poem and another text; in this respect, "I'm Nobody!" is exceptional. Nor does she revel in explicit citations and references. What we hear are numerous echoes, some clear, some faint. Her poetry depends on a complex textual web of allusions and relations. To describe this web we may turn to the chapter on the dream-work in *The Interpretation of Dreams*, more precisely to Freud's concept of condensation or overdetermination. I evoke this term not just because Dickinson, in the examples quoted above, did indeed seem to compress or condense. Freud's description of how particular elements of the manifest dream are related to the latent dream-thoughts is also an apt description of the relationship between a poem by Dickinson and its "raw material." "Not only are the elements of a dream determined by the dream-thoughts many times over, but the individual dream-thoughts are represented in the dream by several elements," says Freud. "Associative paths lead from one element of the dream to several dream-thoughts, and from one dream-thought to several elements of the dream."[25] Applied to Dickinson's poetry: A particular poem or a single image may fuse, or may be determined by, passages from several different sources. But it is equally true that a particular passage from her reading may recur in several different poems.

"I died for Beauty" — another well-known Dickinson poem — may, I think, be read as an example of the fact that one brief poem may derive from several different (male/female; popular/"elitist") sources:

> I died for Beauty — but was scarce
> Adjusted in the Tomb
> When One who died for Truth, was lain
> In an adjoining Room —
>
> He questioned softly "Why I failed"?
> "For Beauty", I replied —
> "And I — for Truth — Themselves are One —
> We Brethren, are", he said —
>
> And so, as Kinsmen, met a Night —
> We talked between the Rooms —
> Until the Moss had reached our lips —
> And covered up — our names —
> (P 449)

The most obvious reference in this poem is of course John Keats's famous line "Beauty is truth, truth beauty" — in a letter to Higginson from the same year Dickinson referred to Keats as one of "her" poets. But presumably Keats's words came to Dickinson via Elizabeth Barrett Browning's poem "A Vision of Poets" where we encounter the following lines: ". . . these were poets true, / Who died for Beauty as martyrs do / For Truth — the ends being scarcely two."[26] However, the setting of Dickinson's poem is closer to the gothic death-and-graveyard verses of the American Women's Renaissance. Compare, for instance, the following poem "Fantasia" by Harriet Prescott Spofford (the author of "Circumstance") which, like Dickinson's, explores the theme of "the Extension of Consciousness, after Death" (L 650):

> We're all alone, we're all alone!
> The moon and stars are dead and gone;
> The night's at deep, the wind asleep,
> And thou and I are all alone!
>
> What care have we though life there be?
> Tumult and life are not for me!
> Silence and sleep about us creep;
> Tumult and life are not for thee!
>
> How late it is since such as this
> Had topped the height of breathing bliss!
> And now we keep an iron sleep, —
> In that grave thou, and I in this![27]

But Dickinson's poetic strategy was not simply to fuse several different texts. For a more thorough understanding of how she was reading "as a poet," let me briefly compare Dickinson's "It sifts from Leaden Sieves" with a poem, entitled "The First Snow-Fall," by James Russell Lowell, whose poetry and literary essays Dickinson often referred to in her correspondance.[28] Here is his poem which first appeared in 1849:

The snow had begun in the gloaming,
And busily all the night
Had been heaping field and highway
With a silence deep and white.

Every pine and fir and hemlock
Wore ermine too dear for an earl,
And the poorest twig on the elm-tree
Was ridged inch deep with pearl.

From sheds new-roofed with Carrara
Came Chanticleers's muffled crow,
The stiff rails were softened to swan's-down,
And still fluttered down the snow.

I stood and watched by the window
The noiseless work of the sky,
And the sudden flurries of snow-birds,
Like brown leaves whirling by.

I thought of a mound in sweet Auburn
Where a little headstone stood;
How the flakes were folding it gently,
As did robins the babes in the wood.

Up spoke our own little Mabel,
Saying, "Father, who makes it snow?"
And I told of the good All-father
Who cares for us here below.

Again I looked at the snow-fall,
And thought of the leaden sky
That arched o'er our first great sorrow,
When that mound was heaped so high.

I remembered the gradual patience
That fell from that cloud like snow,

Flake by flake, healing and hiding
The scar of our deep-plunged woe.

And again to the child I whispered,
"The snow that husheth all,
Darling, the merciful Father
Alone can make it fall!"

Then, with eyes that saw not, I kissed her;
And she, kissing back, could not know
That *my* kiss was given to her sister,
Folded close under deepening snow. 29

And here is Dickinson's "Snow" poem:

It sifts from Leaden Sieves —
It powders all the Wood.
It fills with Alabaster Wool
The Wrinkles of the Road —

It makes an Even Face
Of Mountain, and of Plain —
Unbroken Forehead from the East
Unto the East again —

It reaches to the Fence —
It wraps it Rail by Rail
Till it is lost in Fleeces —
It deals Celestial Vail

To Stump, and Stack — and Stem —
A Summer's empty Room —
Acres of Joints, were Harvests were,
Recordless, but for them —

It Ruffles Wrists of Posts
As Ankles of a Queen —
Then stills its Artisans — like Ghosts —
Denying they have been —
(P. 311)

Lowell's "leaden sky" in stanza seven recurs as "Leaden Sieves" in
Dickinson's poem, but this far from the only affinity between these two

poetical treatments of the snow-fall. In both poems, snowing is a noiseless work; snow covers "field" and "highway" (Lowell), "wood" and "road" (Dickinson), and wraps the stiff rails in soft material: "Swan's down" (Lowell) or "fleece" (Dickinson). Snow dresses the ordinary landscape in royal gowns: "ermine to dear for an earl" and "pearl" in Lowell's poem. In Dickinson's words, "It Ruffles Wrists of Posts / As Ankles of a Queen —." Thus snow ennobles, distinguishes. But, at the same time, snow smoothes out, levels — "it makes an Even Face." Snow hides and heals the scars of absence and loss. In Lowell's poem: "the scar of our deep-plunged woe." In Dickinson, the scars of loss are the more ambiguous stumps and stems, the empty room "where Harvests were." Thus death is present in both poems. Literally in "The First Snow-Fall" — the small grave and the memory of the dead child — and symbolically in Dickinson's poem, by virtue of the connotations of "Harvests" and "Celestial Vail." But Dickinson — wisely — ignored the sentimental story of the kiss given to the dead child which concludes Lowell's poem. Instead, she derived her conclusion from another source, namely Emerson's "The Snow-Storm":

> And when his hours are numbered, and the world
> Is all his own, retiring, as he were not,
> Leaves, when the sun appears, astonished Art
> To mimic in slow structures, stone by stone,
> Built in an age, the mad wind's night-work,
> The frolic architecture of the snow. [30]

Apparently, Dickinson observed her New England snowfalls through the filter of New England poetry! "It sifts from Leaden Sieves" was obviously written in response to another text. But it was in a way Dickinson herself who constructed the text which she transcribed: The source of her poem is Lowell's "First Snow-Fall" — torn apart, and grafted upon the last lines of Emerson's poem. Thus Dickinson dismembered the texts which she used. She did not simply "import" and "absorb"; in so doing, she dissolved and cut to pieces. With a reference to Harold Bloom's concept of poetic mis-reading as an act of violent distortion, one might say that reading, in the case of Dickinson, implied mutilation as well as appropriation, or rather appropriation through mutilation. Reading as a poet, she shattered the texts which she consumed, extracting fragments which had been disengaged from their original context. We know that Dickinson from time to time quite literally mutilated the books which she read: She cut out passages from her father's copy of *The Old Curiosity Shop,* for instance. Recently, St. Armand has advanced the thesis that Dickinson—like many other nineteenth century middle-class women—kept a scrapbook or a file of clippings from newspapers, journals, and books, and that she used this file for her own poetical work.[31] St. Armand's hypothesis throws new light on Dickinson's working method. But we do not need actual scrapbooks in order to show that Dickinson was a poet of fragments or fragmentation. Take for example her poetic use of Emerson's essays: From "Circles" (1841), for instance, she took out the phrase "there is no end in nature . . . under every deep a lower deep opens"[32] and turned it into a brief poem, "As if the Sea should part" (P 695). She felt no need or obligation to consider Emerson's transcendentalist philosophy; what she found was simply an intriguing image. Her reading of Elizabeth Barrett Browning's romance in verse, *Aurora Leigh,* is yet another apt example of her characteristic approach.

Aurora Leigh which first appeared in 1857 enjoyed immense popularity in its time, in America as well as in England. Dickinson was one of many enthusiastic readers, and, according to Walsh, it was the reading of Barrett Browning's epic poem which launched her as a poet. But although Dickinson in her letters quite frequently appears to be posing as Barrett Browning's poet-heroine Aurora Leigh, she resisted the temptation to imitate or to try to write a rival *Aurora Leigh.* Instead, she extracted images and short passages; disregarding the overall structure of Barrett Browning's work, she constructed entire poems or parts of poems on the basis of these fragments. Walsh lists 69 passages from *Aurora Leigh* which Dickinson appropriated. The following example is taken from Walsh's list. In Book Four Aurora Leigh compares herself and her cousin Romney Leigh to two ticking clocks:

> . . . leave two clocks, they say,
> Wound up to different hours, upon the shelf,
> And slowly, through the interior wheels of each,
> The blind mechanic motion sets itself
> A-throb to feel out for the mutual time.[33]

The poem which Dickinson based on this fragment is far from being one of her best:

> The Rose did caper on her cheek —
> Her Bodice rose and fell —
> Her pretty speech - like drunken men —
> Did stagger pitiful —
>
> Her fingers fumbled at her work —
> Her needle would not go —
> What ailed so smart a little Maid —
> It puzzled me to know —
>
> Till opposite — I spied a cheek
> That bore *another* Rose —
> *Just* opposite — Another speech

That like the Drunkard goes —

A Vest that like her Bodice, danced —
To the immortal tune —
Till those two troubled — little Clocks
Ticked softly into one.
(P 208)

In this way, Dickinson broke up Barrett Browning's text in search of striking phrases, images, and words. I shall give but one more example. In Dickinson's *poetry, royal, queen, crown,* and *white* are recurrent but rather enigmatic key-words or -symbols. Of course, these words belong to the vocabulary of Dickinson's Calvinist culture. But they are also part of the vocabulary of *Aurora Leigh.* In Barrett Browning's poem—which is both a romance and an art-novel in verse— *royal, queen, crown,* and *white* are overdetermined, associated with the title of "poet" and with "poetic inspiration" as well as with "love," "bride," and "wifehood." Am I a poet? asks Aurora in Book First: "The name / Is royal, and to sign it like a queen / Is what I dare not" (I, ll. 934 -36). In Second Book, she proceeds to crown herself: "The worthiest poets have remained uncrowned / Till death has bleached their foreheads to the bone / . . . / What, therefore, if I crown myself to-day" (II, ll. 29-33). Later, *crown* is associated with love and marriage: "This perhaps was love — / . . . / Who crowned her? — it sufficed that she was crowned" (IV, ll. 176-86) and "Small business has a castaway / Like Marian with that crown of prosperous wives" (VI, ll. 347-48). Dickinson discarded the narrative pattern of *Aurora Leigh,* but she retained the meanings which Barrett Browning read into *royal, queen,* and *crown,* and she explored these connotations in poems such as "Her 'last Poems'—" (P 312), "Ourselves were wed one summer — dear —" (P 631), and "Title divine — is mine!" (P 1072). Similarly, she lifted out Barrett Browning's "white heats" of poetic imagination (I, l. 986 and VII, l. 568) as she wrote "Dare you see a Soul *at the White Heat?*" (P 365). And Barrett Browning's ironic description of the five miss Ganvilles "dressed in white / To show they're ready to be married" (IV, ll. 634-35) is echoed in Dickinson's far more ambiguous lines: "A solemn thing — it was — I said — / A woman — white — to be —" (P 271) and "Dressed to meet you — / See — in White!" (P 388).

Dickinson was no plagiarist, as Walsh would have it: She re-wrote; she did not imitate. Nor was she, strictly speaking, a revisionist in the Bloomian sense of the word. She fragmented and mutilated the texts which she used. But she did not seek to annihilate an Oedipal father- (or mother-) poet. Remaining within the framework of psychoanalytic theory, one could perhaps claim that she decomposed into pre-oedipal part-objects. At any rate, she read — as a poet — without any sense of wholeness. What characterizes Dickinson as a reader is precisely the fact that she saw literature — all kinds

112

of literature — in terms of parts, phrases, images, and words, rather than in terms of narrative, thematic, or rhetorical wholes. Richard Sewall has made this point. Dickinson, he writes, "seems constantly to have been on the the lookout for the nugget, the germ, some striking word or phrase that would set her mind going. . . . 'In the beginning was the Word' has been said of her, and rightly."[34] Indeed, poems such as "A Word dropped careless on a Page" which is quoted in my epigraph express an intense and peculiar sensitivity to words. Words breed independently of their maker. Words are potential carriers of fatal diseases; the reader may be consumed from within by the words which she consumes. Words may be poisoned nourishment (Dickinson quite consistently associated the act of reading with eating and drinking: "He ate and drank the precious Words —" (P 1587)). But words may also be "balsam" (L 281). Words may be "bad" or "good" objects; they may heal as well as hurt. It appears that Dickinson's poetical project — to put it bluntly — had to do with language and words rather than with thought and ideas. This may explain her "unique responsiveness," as Reynolds puts it, to different voices of her literary culture: To a poet who concerned herself with words rather than with meanings, with *signifiers* rather than with signifieds, *any* text was potentially useable.

III. The Quilt and the Puzzle

I felt a Cleaving in my Mind —
As if my Brain had split —
I tried to match it — Seam by Seam -
But could not make them fit.

The thought behind, I strove to join
Unto the thought before—
But Sequence ravelled out of Sound
Like Balls — upon a Floor.
(P 937)

Dickinson is a poet of fragments. She based her own poetical work on bits and pieces from a large variety of very different texts. Reading as a poet, she mutilated and decomposed; figuratively and perhaps also quite literally speaking, she cut out what she wanted to retain. She read for parts rather than for wholes. And she did not seek to create a new whole. On the level of the individual poem, Dickinson's poetic strategy appears to be compression or condensation. But her *oeuvre* spells dispersion. The poems do not add up, but go off in different directions. Dickinson's poetical work remains an assembly of disparate fragments; it consists of parts which do not match or even contradict each other. Walsh's description is unkind, but not entirely untrue. Dickinson, he writes, created "an artistic anomaly unparalleled in the province of great literature, a true literary Sphinx, whose head does not belong to its body, yet which is implacably *there*."[35] What Walsh does not understand, however, is that the fragmentary nature of Dickinson's poetry does not invalidate her work. On the contrary, fragmentation may be a clue to Dickinson's unique poetic strength, a clue to the specific modernity of her poetry.

It is interesting to compare Dickinson's poetical work to *Aurora Leigh*. For Barrett Browning's poem — from which Dickinson took out numerous passages—is itself a text that has borrowed heavily from other literary works. Among the works which *Aurora Leigh* is indebted to are Mme de Stael's *Corinne*, Charlotte Bronte's *Jane Eyre*, and William Wordsworth's poems, including his great epic poem on the growth of the poet's mind, *The Prelude*. In her "Introduction" to Barrett Browning's poem, Cora Kaplan describes it as "a collage of Romantic and Victorian texts reworked from a woman's perspective."[36] Thus both Dickinson and Barrett Browning cut out "blocks" from their literary culture which they used as raw-material for their own poetical work; writing was a kind of *bricolage* in the sense that they constructed their poems from the available textual material. One wonders if this procedure is characteristic of the nineteenth century woman poet — just as the keeping of scrapbooks appears to have been a typically feminine activity? The poetical works of both Dickinson and Barrett Browning are based on bits and pieces cut from other texts. But, at the same time, it is precisely this fact which sets off the essential difference between these two female poets. *Aurora Leigh* "is, to use another 'woman's figure,' a vast quilt, made up of other garments,"[37] says Kaplan. The metaphor of the quilt is apt. It suggests that Barrett Browning failed to achieve the organic synthesis, cherished by Romantic aesthetics. However, a quilt is nevertheless a whole, although a whole made up of parts with the seams showing. But Dickinson's poetic work is no "quilt." She never sewed up her parts. She insisted on the fragmentary — from deliberate poetic strategy, or because she "tried to match it — Seam by Seam — / But could not make them fit."

Readers of Dickinson's poetry have continued to ask themselves how the individual poem relates to the total corpus of poems. What kind of totality do the poems form? Only recently, Dickinson scholars have begun to realize that there may not be any hidden organizing pattern — no overall thematic unity and no cumulative wholeness. Dickinson's poetic work has no sustaining philosophy or idea, says David Porter [38]; indeed it has no structuring center. Individual poems are fragments, but, Miller adds, "the cumulative fragments never make a single whole: there are too many for any single arrangement or pattern to account for. However one solves the puzzle of her work, pieces will remain."[39] Gilles Deleuze and Felix Guattari's metaphor of the "schizoid jig-saw puzzle" comes to mind: Dickinson's poems are "pieces of a puzzle belonging not to any one puzzle but to many" — pieces which may be assembled only "by forcing them into a certain place where they may or may not belong, their unmatched edges violently bent out of shape, forcibly made to fit together, to interlock, with a number of pieces always left over."[40]

The "quilt" and the "schizoid puzzle": As women writers, Barrett Browning and Dickinson responded to their literary culture in very different ways. With *Aurora Leigh*, the longest poem of the decade, Barrett Browning asserted herself as an epic poet; she reworked the epic poem, a male genre *par excellence*, from the perspective of the female poet. Dickinson, on the other hand, not only created the largest body of short lyrics in the English language. She refrained from trying to unite the parts to a narrative and thematic whole. Thus insisting on the fragmentary, the broken, and the disjunctive, Dickinson created a poetic language that, in Miller's words, "could almost have been designed as a model for several twentieth-century theories of what a woman's language might be."[41]

References

Quotations are from Thomas H. Johnson's standard editions of Emily Dickinson's poems and letters, Cambridge, Mass.: The Belknap Press of Harvard University Press, 1955 and 1958. The numbers follow the numerical order of the poems and letters in these editions. The poems are marked by a preceding P and the letters by L.

1. David Reynolds, *Beneath the American Renaissance. The Subversive Imagination in the Age of Emerson and Melville*. New York: Alfred A. Knopf, 1988, p. 437.
2. Barton Levi St. Armand, *Emily Dickinson and Her Culture*. Cambridge: Cambridge University Press, 1984, p. 19. See also Jack L. Capps, *Emily Dickinson's Reading 1836-1886* Cambridge, Mass.: Harvard University Press, 1966, John Evangelist Walsh, *The Hidden Life of Emily Dickinson*. New York: Simon and Schuster, 1971, Cheryl Walker, *The Nightingale's Burden. Women Poets and American Culture before 1900*. Bloomington: Indiana University Press, 1982, and the chapter on "Books and Reading" in Richard B. Sewall, *The Life of Emily Dickinson*. New York: Farrar, Straus and Giroux, 1980.
3. See for example Ruth Miller, *The Poetry of Emily Dickinson*. Middletown, Conn.: Wesleyan University Press, 1968, Appendix III, pp. 385-92.
4. "Circumstance" is reprinted in *A Library of American Literature,* eds. Edmund Clarence Stedman and Ellen Mackay Hutchinson. New York: Charles L. Webster & Company, 1889, Vol. IX, pp. 273-83.

5. Quoted from St. Armand, *op. cit.*, p. 173.

6. On one of the few occasions where Dickinson expressed her literary taste, she wrote (in a letter to Higginson, December 1879): " -of Poe, I know too little to think - Hawthorne appalls, entices - Mrs. Helen Hunt Jackson soars to your estimate lawfully as a bird, but of Howell and Henry James, one hesitates -" (L 622).

7. Sewall, *op. cit.*, p. 671.

8. *Ibid.,* p. 673.

9. *Ibid.,* p. 669.

10. Walsh, *op. cit.*, p. 154.

11. Quoted from Walker, *op. cit.*, p. 24.

12. From "The Passing Bell" in *Poems by Lydia H. Sigourney*. New York: Allen Brothers, 1869, p. 217.

13. Walker, *op. cit.*, p. 84.

14. Christanne Miller, *Emily Dickinson. A Poet's Grammar*. Cambridge, Mass.: Harvard University Press, 1987, p. 158.

15. *Emily Dickinson's Poetry*, p. 614. The Dickinson family owned a copy of Bridgam's book.

16. Sandra Gilbert and Susan Gubar, *The Madwoman in the Attic: The Woman Writer and the Nineteenth-Century Literary Imagination*.New Haven: Yale University Press, 1979, p. 52.

17. Harold Bloom, *The Anxiety of Influence. A Theory of Poetry*. London: Oxford University Press, 1975, p. 30.

18. Reynolds, *op. cit.*, p. 5.

19. *Ibid.*, p. 6.

20. Gilbert and Gubar, *op. cit.*, p. 20.

21. Walker, *op. cit.*, p. 27.

22. Sewall, *op. cit.*, p. 674.

23. Nathaniel Hawthorne, *Selected Tales and Sketches*. Harmondsworth: Penguin Books Ltd., 1987, pp. 5-6.

24. Capps, *op. cit.*, p. 25.

25. Sigmund Freud, *The Interpretation of Dreams*, Standard Edition of the Complete Psychological Works of Sigmund Freud, trans. James Strachey . London: The Hogarth Press, Vol. IV, p. 284.

26. Elizabeth Barrett Browning, *Poetical Works*. London: Smith, Elder & Co., 1890, Vol. I, p. 239.

27. *A Library of American Literature*, Vol. IX, p. 285.

28. See for instance: L 337 - where Dickinson praises Lowell's essay "A Good Word for Winter" with the words: "one does not often meet anything so perfect" - and L 622 which includes a poem (P 1464) apparently written in response to Lowell's "After the Burial." Lowell was the editor of the Atlantic Monthly from 1857 to -61 and a frequent contributor to the journal.

29. *The Poetical Works of James Russell Lowell in Four Volumes*. Boston and New York: Houghton, Mifflin and Company, Vol. III, pp. 166-67.

30. Ralph Waldo Emerson, *Poems*. Boston and New York: Houghton, Mifflin and Company, p. 42.
31. "There is ample evidence from her published letters that Emily Dickinson herself kept a scrapbook of clippings from national magazines, local newspapers, and illustrated books," writes St. Armand. "Jay Leyda reproduces an illustration clipped from the August, 1876 issue of *Scribner's Magazine* . . . Of Dickinson's use of a tombstone illustration cut from the *Hampshire and Franklin Express* to embellish a copy of 'She laid her docile Crescent Down' (J 1396), Thomas H. Johnson writes that Dickinson 'enclosed funerary scraps in messages from time to time, and thus suggested clue to the inspiration for certain verses. The disparity in the date of the clipping (1856) and the poem (1877) leads one to conjecture that she kept a scrapbook or a file of items which to her were meaningful' (J, note to 1396)." St. Armand, *op. cit.,* p. 26.
32. Ralph Waldo Emerson, *Selected Essays,* ed. Larzer Ziff. Harmondsworth: Penguin Books Ltd., 1982, p. 225.
33. Aurora Leigh, Book IV, ll. 422-25. Quotations are drawn from *Aurora Leigh and other Poems,* ed. Cora Kaplan. London: The Women's Press Ltd., 1978. Subsequent references to *Aurora Leigh* are included in the text.
34. Sewall, *op. cit.,* p. 675.
35. Walsh, *op. cit.,* p. 156.
36. *Aurora Leigh and other Poems,* p. 5.
37. *Ibid.*
38. David Porter, *Emily Dickinson: The Modern Idiom.* Cambridge, Mass.: Harvard University Press, 1981.
39. Miller, *op. cit.,* p. 180.
40. Gilles Deleuze and Felix Guattari, *Anti-Oedipus: Capitalism and Schizofrenia*, trans. Robert Hurley, Mark Seem, and Helen R. Lane. New York: Viking Press, 1982.
41. Miller, *op. cit.,* p. 161.

Naturalism, Revitalization, and The Novels of Frank Norris

William J. Clark
University of Wyoming

In his most widely known essay "Zola as a Romantic Writer," Frank Norris (1870—1902) vividly summarized the credo of the Naturalist: "Terrible things must happen to the characters of the naturalistic tale. They must be twisted from the ordinary, wrenched out from the quiet, uneventful round of everyday life, and flung into the throes of a vast and terrible drama that works itself out in unleashed passions, in blood and in sudden death."[1] Such statements of purpose as well as the flourishes of Naturalistic rhetoric in Norris' novels, with their images of life as a vast machine grinding humanity "to dust beneath its myriad iron wheels" and tropes of an enfeebled and uncomprehending humankind being overwhelmed by vast cosmic and social "forces," have understandably led critics to dwell on Norris' debt to European Naturalistic theory. He is seen borrowing idea and method from Emile Zola and mirroring the impact of the Darwinian revolution in science on his generation of American writers, including Crane, Dreiser, and Garland, who came of age in the 1890s.[2] Norris did read Zola during his four years at the University of California at Berkeley, 1890—94, did borrow both technique and specific incidents and characters from the Frenchman, was instructed in evolutionary theory by his favorite professor, Joseph LeConte, even half-jokingly signed letters to friends "The boy Zola." Yet this critical tradition, helpful as it is in elucidating the literary environment of the young novelist, has served to detach the intellectual influences on Norris from the cultural context in which he lived and worked as a writer.

Norris' essay on Zola is a response to both the literary and cultural climate of the nineties in America. Consciously setting his fiction against that of his friend and supporter William Dean Howells, Norris rejected the elder writer's "dramas of the reception-room, tragedies of an afternoon call, crises involving cups of tea," calling for a fiction closer to the disturbing truth of his time.[3] Howells' novels, in Norris' judgment, dealt with surfaces only, with the conventional and thus the trite; most importantly, they supported the *status quo*, the bourgeois conception of the world. It is a commonplace of attacks on the Naturalists that they were drawn to the low, the "seamier side of life," and this aspect of the fiction of this group of writers has been considered an indulgence in the grosser, more *outré* elements of their society. In Norris' work (as in that of Crane and the young Dreiser), however, this turning toward the underclasses and outcasts of society represents a pointed criticism of late-nineteenth century bourgeois culture, and an attempt to critique that culture from a point of view outside the mainstream values and explanatory frameworks represented by Howells and his disciples. "We, the bourgeois, the commonplace, the ordinary," Norris brashly asserts in this essay, "have no part nor lot in the *Rougon-Macquart*, in *Lourdes*, or in *Rome*."[4] Of course, the bourgeois world does "have a part" in the novels of Zola as in his own; what Norris is searching for here and what he found in the works of his French master was a perspective, an authorial stance outside what he conceived to be the too-narrow point of view of a Howellsian realism that confined itself to, in Norris' wonderful phrase, "the drama of a broken teacup."[5] The essay in which he delivers this swipe goes on to outline his search for a fiction that can instruct, can change attitudes and culture. Naturalism, he writes, calls to the reader "from the squalor of a dive, or the awful degradation of a disorderly house, crying: 'Look! Listen! This, too, is life. These, too are my children, look at them, know them and, knowing, help!'"[6]

The modernist aesthetic of our day may cause us to cringe at the sentimental excesses of Norris' statements, but an understanding of the Naturalist moment at the end of the last century and the beginning of this one, of the cultural impulse shared by Jacob Riis, Jane Addams, the Ashcan School of painters and others, however various their forms and expressions, requires an appreciation of the depth and sincerity of the response shared by these critics to a period of rapid change, to the dislocations and conflicts that characterized their generation. To Naturalism, Norris believed, "belongs the wide world for range, and the unplumbed depths of the human heart, and the mystery of sex, and the problems of life"—the last a rare example of understatement in his writings on the subject.[7] Zola provided him with a lens through which to observe the tensions of his time and a narrative framework outside the conventional realist mode to structure the early novels, but the culture of Gilded Age America provided the material, the characters and conflicts, the symbols and landscapes of these disturbing tales. The Naturalism of Crane's *Maggie,* of Dreiser's *Sister Carrie* and of Norris' novels of the nineties was a product and expression of a crisis of values in late-nineteenth century America, of the conflict between inherited American dreams and the confusing imperatives of an emerging urban-industrial society. The terms in which Norris and his fellow Naturalists depict their time—"terrible," "twisted," "wretched," and "unleashed passions...blood...and sudden death," to extract a few examples from the passage cited at the beginning of this paper—express this sense of crisis, as do the characters, plots, signification systems, the very style of these tales of disintegration and "degeneration."

The anthropologist Anthony F.C. Wallace has provided an explanatory model for cultural change that he and other scholars have applied to periods of sudden transformation in both pre-modern and modern societies.[8] The "Revitalization Movements" model not only charts the process of change as a culture moves into such a critical period, but offers an explanation of the motives driving attempts to save the society from entropy, even collapse. Wallace's model, typically applied to social and religious efforts at revitalization, also charts Frank Norris' attempts as a writer to analyze the crisis of the 1890s in his first two novels, *Vandover and the Brute* and *McTeague*, to define its perameters and register its shocks; and, in those books written after the turn of the century, *The Octopus* and *The Pit*, to act as a prophet of revitalization, calling Americans back to their fundamental beliefs and modes of behavior.

Critics have found it difficult to explain why Norris dropped the extreme Naturalism of the early novels so quickly after 1899. The revitalization movements model helps us understand Naturalism as a set of assumptions and techniques especially well suited to investigate cultural declension. Its reversal of conventional plots, its troubled, apathetic, even psychotic characters, its urgency of tone and extremity of incident, its investigation of the dark underside of the social surface and what Norris called "the black, unsearched penetralia of the soul of man": these elements of the Naturalistic story focus and dramatize the plight of a people in crisis. When, however, by the turn of the century, Norris sought in planning and writing what was to be the epic trilogy of the Wheat, to offer solutions to the dilemmas of American society, many, though not all of the elements of the earlier Naturalistic mode could no longer serve him. In the manner of other prophets of revitalization, he must then try to bring forward ideas, beliefs, novelistic approaches from the past and reshape them to accommodate the changed social situation of the present. His two completed novels of the Wheat trilogy (he died while planning the final volume, to be called *The Wolf*) are—to the dismay of critics who respond to the new notes of stridency and grotesquerie in the earlier books—more conventional, hopeful and didactic. This is the case not because the author had lost his edge as a writer, nor because, as has been suggested, he "sold out" to commercial interests and the best-seller mentality emerging in his day, but rather because he felt obliged to fulfill in the novel a social purpose "such as inspires the great teachers, the great divines, the great philosophers, a well-defined, well-seen, courageously defined purpose,"— that purpose to rescue his culture from the conflicts and contradictions that he had experienced in his own life and had embodied in his fiction through the late nineties.

The process of revitalization, according to Wallace, begins with a culture in "steady state," during which period there is a congruence, a harmony between dominant attitudes and values, a people's "mental image" of its world and its place in that world, on the one hand, and, on the other, the external social reality with its institutions and modes of behavior, so that "chronic stress within the system varies within tolerable limits."[9] As the culture moves into crisis, a significant number of individuals in the population "experience increasingly severe stress as a result of the decreasing efficiency of certain stress-reduction techniques" which are provided by the prevailing ideology. Profound changes in the political, economic or social spheres, such as the rapid growth of Industrialization in nineteenth-century America, erodes confidence in the older value system. As this erosion of a coherent world view spreads to more and more people, especially among the dominant groups within the society, this Period of Individual Stress becomes a broadly-based Period of Cultural Distortion, during which the culture becomes "internally distorted." Major elements of the cultural system are not only in conflict with external developments and behavior patterns, but these elements become "mutually inconsistent and interfering" among themselves. Especially apropos of Norris' early Naturalistic novels, Wallace notes that during this phase of the revitalization process an increasing number of individuals turn to "psychodynamically regressive innovations" in an attempt to escape their sense of anxiety and of the loss of a meaningful world; these regressive patterns can include "alcoholism, extreme passivity and indolence, the development of highly ambivalent dependency relationships, intragroup violence, disregard of kinship and sexual mores...states of depression and self-reproach, and a variety of psychosomatic and neurotic disorders."10

A people, of course, will resist the continued disintegration of their sense of a meaningful way of life. This attempt to forestall the mounting anxieties and destructive behaviors that, if they continue, are perceived to result in the possible collapse of the culture is, for Wallace, a revitalization movement. During the periods of declension, various prophets arise, secular as well as sacred in a complex modern society. They seek to reestablish traditions, project the past onto the future, renew the fundamental ideology and demonstrate that it can be reshaped to meet the exigencies of the new world in which the people find themselves. In Wallace's delineation, such movements are culturally conservative: they "depend on the restructuring of elements and subsystems which have already attained currency in the society."11 Revolutionary elements may be a part of the revitalization process, but to serve the aims of revitalization, they must be made to appear compatible with a people's visionary conception of itself since the primary mode of revitalization is accommodation. The backward-looking/forward-looking character of the revitalization effort assumes that a culture resists radical change; in fact, the purpose of prophecy (as was true, for instance, of the Puritan jeremiads) is to transcend the present conceived as a declension from past harmony and security by projecting the traditional cultural system onto the future. In doing so, the revitalization effort supports the status quo and reinforces the hegemony of dominant groups within the culture. This is an important reason why Norris' later novels return to more conventional fictional methods than he employed during his Naturalistic phase, and to mythic American values.

If one or more such prophets is successful—probably in a populous modern society a number of like-minded revitalizers will reinforce one another's approach to ideological reorientation—a cultural transformation occurs "signalized by the reduction of the personal deterioration symptoms of individuals, by extensive cultural changes and by an enthusiastic embarkation on organized programs of group action."[12] If the prophecy can gather adherents who can channel the widespread desire for change and communicate their vision of a stable society to enough of their fellows, then the values and behaviors proposed by the movement will become the norm in various economic, social, and political institutions and customs, and the culture will return to a NEW steady state in which the society's traditional conception of itself informs and valorizes the changes.

Frank Norris was prepared by temperament and experience to become a prophet of revitalization by 1900. He was born Benjamin Franklin Norris, Jr., the son of one of the most successful jewelers in Chicago. By 1882 the self-made senior Norris was able to move his family into a mansion on Michigan Avenue,[13] and by 1885 the Norrises were living in the Henry Scott mansion on fashionable Sacramento Street in San Francisco. Frank and his younger brother Charles, who was also to become a novelist, were indulged by a mother of romantic temperament who read to them from the novels of Walter Scott and encouraged their artistic talents. At the same time their father was trying to push them (especially the older Frank) into a life of entrepreneurial action. Though his father reputedly insisted that he prepare for a career in business, Frank was allowed to enter the San Francisco Art Association, and then to enroll in the fashionable Bouguereau studio of the Atelier Julien in Paris. During his two-year stay on the continent, he indulged the romantic sensibility fostered by his mother, reading in medieval history, becoming something of an expert on armor and composing juvenile narratives of brave knights and fair damsels. When Frank's father, so the story goes, learned of the nature of his son's "pursuits" abroad, he angrily insisted that the boy come home at once.

Returning to San Francisco dressed in the foppish attire of a continental esthete, Frank must have experienced a shock of unfamiliarity. He acquiesed to his father's demands by entering the University of California at Berkeley to train for the business world, but he subverted his father's intention by determining to become a writer, by taking courses in philosophy and languages, and by wandering the streets of San Francisco, notebook in hand, observing the life of its markets and mansions, tenements, bars and docks. Significantly, it was during these years at Berkeley, not while he was in France when *La Terre* was published and the Naturalists were "at the peak of their influence," that he read Zola.[14]

A confluence of events and influences in the early nineties shook Norris' romantic illusions. His idealism was undermined by the conditions of life that he observed in the poorer quarters of the city at a time when the nation's newspapers carried (often sensationalized) reports of the living conditions and activities of the lower classes. The wealthy young man who would be a writer was struck by the gap between the rich and the poor who, in San

Francisco at the time, might live within blocks of one another. At the same time the debate over the applications of the theory of evolution in the realms of morals and society that were the subjects of a number of his classes and were in the intellectual air at Berkeley combined with Zola's novelistic format to provide a set of ideas and techniques to tell the story of his time and place.

And then, in 1892, Frank's father left the family, filed for divorce in Chicago, and never returned to his wife and sons again. In what became a long and apparently acrimonious divorce proceeding, Mrs. Norris filed a counter-suit and obtained a decree in 1894. The older son's fears of disinheritance, as evidenced by the near-obsessive concern with money and economic failure in his first two novels, were confirmed in 1900 when his father left his entire fortune—estimated at a million dollars—to his second wife.[15] The hypothesis that the breakup of the family and the loss of economic security that attended the father's departure had a profound effect on Norris, reinforcing the impact of an evolutionary view of life on his work, seems confirmed by the radical shift in the young writer's perspective, subject matter and style between the publication of his medieval verse romance *Yvernelle* in late 1891 and his work on *Vandover and the Brute* and *McTeague* in 1894-5. And his personal loss was accentuated by the panic that hit San Francisco, the center of Western business and finance, as well as the rest of the country by mid-1893 (of 158 bank failures during the depression, for example, 153 were in the West and South).[16]

In the fall of 1894 Norris went east to Harvard, settled into his room in Gray's Hall, and wrote the two novels in which he probed the crisis of the nineties. *Vandover and the Brute* and *McTeague* may be regarded as a single extended narrative of the fall of a young bourgeois male through the class structure of late-nineteenth century America. Separately and as an extended text, they reverse the story-line of a young man's linear rise to success exemplified in Norris' day by the Horatio Alger rags-to-respectability tales, and thus challenge the gospel of progress that supported the Franklin-Alger success myth. The narrative of declension, far from being simply a self-consciously adopted Naturalistic strategy used to tell a story of "degeneration," calls into question deeply-held cultural expectations and the values upon which these are based. In these novels Norris creates a central character singularly at odds with the dominant culture of his time, a character incapable of controlling, or even understanding, the changing forms and modes of action of the emerging urban-industrial society in which he must live—or die. And this society is an interlocking web of confusions and conflicts, the root causes of which, in Norris' judgment, were to be found in the heightened spirit of acquisition and the emerging ethos of consumption that were the defining paradigms of America in the Gilded Age.

The double structure of *Vandover* embodies Norris' fear and condemnation of the acquisition-consumption nexus. The young anti-hero of the novel returns to San Francisco with a Harvard education and dreams of studying art in Paris. These hopes are dashed when his father suffers reverses in the real estate market in the first shocks of the depression of 1893. When Vandover loses his chance for a genteel career in art, when his father, who is his financial support, dies (here one of the more overt expressions of the fear of the loss of a father's support in the wake of Norris' own father's abandonment of the family), and when he loses the love of a "good woman," he is thrown upon the business world of the nineties to find his way. Norris peppers the early chapters with details of rents, mortgages, investments and credit. The sensual, congenial and naive young Vandover is unfit for survival in this environment of single-minded striving and deal-making. He lacks the Franklinian, by the 1890s the employee virtues of self-reliance, initiative, industry and asceticism and drifts from part-time work to bar, and from elegantly furnished apartment to cheap hotel to flophouse.

Vandover's fall into idleness, dissipation and ultimately despair is charted against the rise to wealth and power of his friend and former classmate, Charlie Geary, the new driven businessman of the period, an emblem for Norris of the venality of the Robber Baron mentality. Geary's success is a parody of the Alger hero's rise in the world: "You bet I've been working," he tells his friends, "working like a dog. A man's got to hustle if he's going to make a success....I'll make my way in this town and my pile. There's money to be made here and I might just as well make it as the next man. Every man for himself that's what I say; that's the way to get along."[17] Geary repeats this statement so often in the text that it becomes a refrain accompanying the rise and fall of these two characters. Alan Trachtenberg, among others, has elaborated the unresolved tensions in the image of the captains of industry during the period: beneath the surface consensus that business was a field of just rewards and the apotheosis of the businessman as rugged individualist, there was a growing feeling that the robber barons were aggrandizers rather than honest producers and that "rewards flowed more often to sheer power than entrepreneurial skill."[18] The character of Geary is perhaps the 1890s sharpest condemnation of the acquisitive spirit that informed the rise of the captains of industry in the decades after the Civil War. He succeeds by taking advantage of a sick employee in the law firm in which he begins his career, lies and cheats his way through the prosecution of a law suit against Vandover, and eventually robs his former classmate of his inheritance, the money that forms the basis of Geary's growing real estate fortune. In the end the successful Geary is contemplating yet larger "fields of action" for his talents: "something to which one could sacrifice everything—friendships, fortunes, scruples, principles, life itself, no matter what, anything to be a 'success,' to 'arrive,' to 'get there.'"[19] Geary exhibits all of the qualities of the Alger hero save one: he is self-disciplined, hard-working, frugal, ambitious and very lucky; but he is, as well, completely amoral and totally devoid of human sympathy. His Faustian rage for development overwhelms the decent but non-aggressive Vandover.

This double structure, the rise to fortune of one character plotted against the fall of another, demonstrates Norris' use of Naturalistic tenets and forms to expose cultural dislocations. Trachtenberg notes that the image of warfare entered the public discourse in accounts of the careers of empire builders such as Gould, Hill and Huntington, while Herbert Spencer's Social Darwinism appeared to sanction the view of the modern city as a "scene of tumult and conflict of rising and falling fortunes."[20]

In *Vandover* this scene of tumult is caused by the unbridled release of the spirit of acquisition and the concomitant conflict between traditional moral and social values and the demands of a rapidly expanding corporate and urban nation. The spatial component of Vandover's collapse, for instance, takes him deeper into the industrial heart of the city as he moves into ever cheaper and dingier rooms. Norris' fear of the chaos and "degeneracy" of the city focuses on the most important setting in the novel, the Imperial Saloon, an emblem of the allures and dangers of the new urban nightlife. Lewis Erenberg argues that the emergence of a "cafe and cabaret society" in the nineties represented a release from Victorian constraints, "from the formal boundaries that had separated the entertainers from the respectable patrons, men from women, and upper- from lower-class culture."[21] Norris catches the appeal of the bright lights of the newly electrified fairs and bars, the clink of glasses and buzz of conversation, the camaraderie and release of sexual energy in the city. But the Imperial is, as well, a place of tragedy, of seduction (Vandover's seduction of Ida Wade in a private back room of the bar initiates the chain of events leading to his collapse) and madness. In the Imperial, traditional class and gender roles break down in what is for Norris, ever the moralist, a dangerous atmosphere of license.

In the end, the Victorian "young lady," Turner Ravis, Vandover's one-time fiancé, has retreated into her ineffectual "family traditions and usages and time-worn customs"; the "fast girl" Ida Wade has committed suicide after having been seduced and abandoned by Vandover; the corrupt speculator Geary has made "his pile" and the bewildered and apathetic Vandover is the victim of lycanthropy, a symptom of the advanced stages of v.d., and is reduced to the menial task of cleaning out the refuse from worker's cottages to earn enough money barely to keep himself alive. This melodramatic denouement glosses Norris' analysis of the tensions of his time: the growing doubts about class-based codes of behavior during a period of deepening class divisions, the simultaneous increasing rigidity and breakdown of sexual roles and standards, the challenges to traditional values of work and human worth represented by the rise of the corporation (Geary). If the emergence of the urban-industrial frontier in the closing decades of the nineteenth century was for many a threshold experience of new possibilities, for Norris and many others it figured a new and disturbing world of conflict.

McTeague deepens and focuses the cultural criticism of *Vandover*, reducing social life to a series of elemental battles that dramatize the destructiveness of the core values of the Gilded Age. In spite of general agreement among commentators that McTeague is a brute whose animalistic qualities dominate his character, Norris goes to some lengths early in the novel to make his protagonist a fairly competent dentist whose new wife Trina tries to initiate him into the customs and styles of a genteel bourgeois world hitherto unfamiliar to him.[22] For this lower-middle class couple, the stability and order represented by the society of the small shopkeepers and tradespeople of Polk Street is fragile, their economic foundation insecure. This economic and social order is broken by two events which trigger the decline of the couple into poverty, madness and death: McTeague is forbidden to practice dentistry because he has been trained in his "profession" under the older apprenticeship system at a time when occupations are being professionalized, and he does not have a certificate to practice; and Trina wins $5000 in a lottery.

As in *Vandover*, Norris again uses a double structure to heighten conflicts within the dominant value system. Having lost the ability to work at an occupation that he found meaningful and to support his wife, McTeague loses his place in family and society; Trina, clutching her lottery winnings ever more closely, becomes the power in the family. This reversal of conventional roles is, for Norris, a significant aspect of the crisis of the nineties and a theme that he would continue to explore in the three minor novels written between the completion of *McTeague* and the beginning of work on the Wheat trilogy. Here he begins, in describing the courtship of McTeague and Trina, by proposing that love is, for the male, an attempt to dominate the female; it is, for the female, submission and surrender to the stronger male force. This is "the changeless order of things—the man desiring the woman only for what she withholds, the woman worshipping the man for that which she yields up to him."[23] As soon as the conquest is complete, McTeague devalues the woman he "loves"; as soon as she is conquered, Trina devotes herself to the making of a tidy home and the social elevation of her husband. It is debatable whether or not Norris believed such a pseudo-psychological encapsulation of patriarchal mythology (the description of the couple's courtship and marriage is shot through with irony, as when the virile McTeague is reduced to a blubbering sentimental schoolboy, burying himself among his beloved's clothes in her bedroom closet), but certainly the social functionality of the myth is destroyed as the novel proceeds.

Historian Carroll Smith-Rosenberg argues that during periods of massive cultural transformation, "when the social fabric is rent in fundamental ways, bodily and familial imagery will assume ascendancy."[24] The aim of bourgeois myths of sexuality and family is to depict that which is class-specific or gender-relative as natural, timeless, and inescapable, thus rationalizing the experience of change by bringing it within the control of the imagination. Norris states the bourgeois gender myth in *McTeague* and then dismantles it by removing the mask of naturalness or universality to expose the ways in which it is shaped and sustained by economic conditions. As long as McTeague is the wage earner, he can lay claim to his role as patriarch in the family and his ego is strong; when it is Trina who literally holds the purse-strings, the roles are reversed and the bourgeois family disintegrates. "Who's the boss?" yells McTeague during one of their increasingly bitter arguments over her lottery winnings. "Who's got the money, I'd like to know," fires back the once-submissive Trina. "Answer me that McTeague, who's got the money?"

McTeague dramatizes Wallace's Period of Cultural Distortion. Acquisition becomes a mania; the lust for money destroys all personal and social relations. Virtually all of the "psychodynamically regressive innovations" that Wallace says characterize this period of unremitting stress are depicted in the novel. McTeague sinks into apathy, eventually into despair. Trina becomes psychotically attached to her treasure and her sexual drive is diverted from her husband to her money (at one point she strips off her clothes and gets into bed on top of her cold gold coins). All cultural myths of the virtue of work, of conventional gender roles and relations, of the dignity of human life and the values that bind a community together evaporate in the single-minded pursuit of wealth. The insistent gold symbolism in the novel, oppressive at best to the literary sensibility accustomed to the sophistication of a Henry James, is culturally accurate in communicating modernity's obsessive preoccupation with money: as McTeague's resources dwindle, his selfhood evaporates; Trina's ego is at once nurtured by and consumed in the increasingly intense fire of her greed. The sexual brutality, the violence of *McTeague*—the cruelties, insults, beatings, and the two murders (in both cases a husband killing a wife); more importantly, the insanity of Zerkow killing Maria for a service of gold plate that exists only in the poor woman's mind, of McTeague's murder of Trina because she refuses him a dime, and, finally, of McTeague's death chained to his mortal enemy in the middle of Death Valley with Trina's $5000 in tow, now useless to him—the unrelieved series of catastrophes that forms the storyline of fully two-thirds of this novel, as well as the violation of almost every convention of plot and character of both the elite and popular books of Norris' day suggest that *McTeague* is most profitably read as the response of an engaged observer to the unsettling dynamics of change at the end of the last century. Reversals of form and stereotype and inversions of plot, all of which challenge conventional formal elements of the novel, challenge as well the cultural premises on which the form or type is based. The anti-conventions that embody Norris' critical stance in these two novels include the apathetic male who cannot or will not work hard in the wider world; the aggressive female who holds the money, thus the power, in the family; the narrative inversions of the plot of defeat and death unredeemed by the promise of redemption or even improvement; and the mounting psychological and physical brutality, particularly the motif of sexual violence.

By about 1899, the year *McTeague* was finally published, however, Norris had begun to seek solutions, and to abandon Naturalism as an explanatory framework. Fundamentally romantic in temperament and bourgeois in outlook, he had by this time reported the Spanish-American War and been taken by the imperialist urge. He had worked for S.S. McClure in New York and returned to the east after Cuba, where he became swept up in the surge of confidence generated by such reform efforts of the Social Gospel and the emerging Progressive Movement. In his essays of 1900-1902, Norris encourages American writers to take on the task of shaping an "American epic, just as heroic, just as elemental, just as important and picturesque" as the epics of the past. Such a work would be at once sectional because "the life of one part [of the country] is very, very different from the life of another" and universal since, by penetrating deeply into the lives of the people of any one community or section, the novelist must strike the common chord and catch the vision of the nation. What he calls "the novel with a purpose" is, he unabashedly contends, "a preaching novel." "The muse," he continues, "is a teacher not a trickster. Her rightful place is with the leaders...the great teachers, the great divines."[25] Bringing forward Whitman's ideal of the poet as seer, as the voice of the people at their best, Norris conceived the Epic of the Wheat trilogy as prophecy. The two completed novels of the series, *The Octopus* (1901) and *The Pit* (1903), restate the conflicts and corruptions of the present, again attacking as the primary causes of decline the spirit of acquisition and the ethos of consumption; but each novel then moves beyond an analysis of the period of distortion to project the personal and cultural possibilities that lie ahead if only Americans can recapture their belief in the American land as a virtuous universal and can transcend their present greed to love one another.

In *The Octopus*, the Pacific and Southwestern Railroad (Norris' thinly disguised version of Collis Huntington's Southern Pacific line) defeats the farmers of California's San Joaquin Valley. The railroad—America's first giant corporation and the octopus that is strangling the economic and physical life out of the hard-working wheat growers in the novel—has corrupted politicians, manipulated rates and fees and engaged in threats and acts of violence to achieve control of the valley. The farmers' group that had been organized to fight the railroad is broken; its leader, Magnus Derrick, is defeated and demoralized; the farmers have been shot down in a last stand by the corporation's hired guns and their families have been driven from their homes that stand on land still owned by the railroad. The railroad is a sign of the corporate-technological world and the corrupt wealth of the broker-investor. The farmers signify the virtuous wealth of the Yeoman tradition. There are, however, complications in Norris' depiction of these "yeomen." They are also the agents and beneficiaries of the world that ultimately destroys them: they employ the latest developments in agricultural technology, are large landowners who seek not a "sufficiency" but a profit, and their production is inextricably linked to a national and international market economy. Thus, they cannot, in the Jeffersonian tradition that forms Norris' conceptual base here, serve as the agents of revitalization and must be defeated because they have been corrupted by the same desires for power and wealth represented by the corporate giant that kills them and takes their land.

The central tension that informs Norris' attack on the railroad and its political henchman is between the older frontier of virgin land, and the city and corporate capitalism as the threshold experience for twentieth-century Americans. The incorporation of the agricultural West means the final hegemony of industrial progress. The vision of America as a virtuous New World was lost to Norris' generation of Naturalists; their jeremiad condemned America for falling back into the chaos and corruption of Old World time. Both Vandover and McTeague are the victims of an urban society in a state of bewildering flux defined as progress. The particulars of history for the Naturalist Norris were marked by an ever more frantic scramble for wealth, the increasing stratifications of class and confusions of gender roles and behavior, and the expanding scale and might of the structures of industrial power. Presley, the young poet, is witness to the catastrophe in the San Joaquin, and serves as Norris' spokesperson in *The Octopus* on the power of corporate wealth and organization: "They swindle a nation of a hundred million and call it Financeering; they levy a blackmail and call it Commerce; they corrupt a legislature and call it politics; they bribe a judge and call it Law; they hire blacklegs to carry out their plans and call it Organization; they prostitute the honour of a State and call it Competition. And this is America."[26]

This is certainly the America in which one of the major set pieces of the novel occurs. A sumptuous dinner is in progress in the palatial home of the railroad magnate Gerard while just outside his door Mrs. Hooven and her young daughter Hilda, displaced from their farm by the railroad, are starving to death in the streets and back alleys of San Francisco. Norris' lengthy overripe description of the decor of the Gerard mansion and the dishes served the guests becomes a parody of the excesses of conspicuous consumption against which he juxtaposes the plight of the underclasses of the city. At the end of the repast, one of the guests at the Gerard table raises his glass to toast his hostess: "My compliments for a delightful dinner." The next lines, the final lines of the chapter, are: "The doctor, who had been bending over Mrs. Hooven, rose. 'It's no use,' he said; 'she has been dead some time - exhaustion from starvation.'"[27]

This is the America of the present in *The Octopus*, but it is not, as Presley thinks on the evening of the dinner, the only America. The once and future America, the "bright green breast of the New World" of Nick Carraway's musings, is communicated to Presley by a character who turns out to be Norris' other, more important voice in the novel, the visionary itinerant prophet Vanamee. In the season of the harvest, Vanamee reveals "the stupendous miracle of re-creation" to Presley, "primordial energy flung out from the hand of the Lord God himself, immortal, calm, infinitely strong."[28] Strange rhetoric for a Naturalist, but then neither Vanamee nor Norris (by 1900) is a Naturalist; both are prophets of revitalization. Though human life may come to anguish, misery and death, "*the WHEAT remained*" (caps and italics are the author's). The American land, as timeless and virtuous universal, remained as the agent of rejuvenation; and Americans could still escape the chaotic particulars of Old World time into the universal of New World space.

This projection of the transcendental promise of the American land, a conception derived from prophets and promoters of the agricultural west going back to Jefferson, as well as from antebellum philosophers of American nature such as Emerson and Thoreau, is both backward- and forward-looking, a belated attempt to reclaim American nature as the redemptive universal of American experience.

It is, then, no coincidence that Curtis and Laura Jadwin, at the conclusion of Norris' final novel, *The Pit*, leave Chicago, their mansion and his position as wheat trader, in search of a better—simpler and more virtuous—life in the West. Jadwin, like Trina and the minions of the railroad in the earlier novels, embodies the idea of acquisition as madness and chaos; Laura is an emblem of the failure of the gospel of consumption. Curtis' rapid rise to wealth and power and his precipitate fall following the collapse of his "corner" of the wheat market figures the chaos and uncertainty of the boom-bust economic world of the Gilded Age. In a larger sense, Jadwin's enormous success and financial collapse is an image of the timebound world of the international market. In *The Pit*, modern commercial culture is a web of deceits, deals and frauds in which his "corner" on the Chicago Board of Trade becomes a moral and social nightmare of increasingly convoluted and corrupt entanglements. At home, Laura is trapped, isolated in their huge elegant mansion. At the beginning of the novel, anticipating her marriage to Jadwin, she had mused, "Think of it, that beautiful house, and servants, and carriages, and paintings, and, oh, honey, how I will dress the part!"29 The pride of this dutiful conspicuous consumer in the early years of the marriage is the private museum that contains a "priceless collection" of fine art and is the centerpiece of the Jadwin estate. But the museum soon becomes, for Laura, a mausoleum of the spirit, and her role as consumer leaves her restless, bored, ultimately rebellious. The couple's marriage is saved just as Laura is about to leave home and husband by Jadwin's rejection of the market (a decision made easier, the reader notes, by the failure of his "deal in wheat") In *The Pit*, as in *The Octopus,* the values of acquisition and consumption are fundamentally inimical to the personal and cultural values that they supplant: connectedness and self-expression, affection and community. All of these latter values are linked to the American land, the ultimate source of healing and genuine progress.

The brief surge of Naturalism at the turn of the century was characterized by its tone of urgency and its preoccupation with the cultural tensions and rifts of the period. Its predominant mood of crisis was related to the pace and depth of change in the closing decades of the century, especially to the increasing hegemony of mainstream culture's ideals of acquisition and consumption. The Naturalists' troubled jeremiad, the jeremiad of *Maggie* and *Sister Carrie,* of Chopin's *The Awakening* and Norris' *Vandover* and *McTeague*, protests the rapid stratification of classes during the Gilded Age; and its nightmarish portraits of the fate of the downtrodden and destitute attack Charles Graham Sumner's brand of Social Darwinism. It exposes the gender implications of the value continuum of acquisition/consumption and the apparent failure of heroism—the decline of the possibility of individual achievement—and the emergence of conformity, standardization and control as economic and cultural imperatives.

The Naturalism of the nineties was, then, a scalpel to expose diseased cultural tissue. The healing process, the return to "steady state," however, required other instruments and strategies. For Norris, these were to be found in the mythic American values and visions of the past: a society of producers like the farmers of the San Joaquin, stable gender relations based on satisfying work for both sexes, economic self-sufficiency and personal freedom, and, most importantly, the transcendental promise of American space as spaciousness. He wanted, above all, to recapture the feeling of boundlessness (John Higham's term) that he associated with the generation before the Civil War when Jackson battled Biddle and his Bank, when Emerson and Whitman sang of the virtues of self-reliant individualism, when entrepreneurship was small-scale, and Cooper and Thoreau extolled the oneness of a people and their land.

Looking back, it all seems so visionary and impossible that such a conception of America and its people could heal the deep dislocations of the last half of the century—the stresses attending the rise of the corporation, the threats to agriculture, the class divisions and sexual repressions, the labor strife and imperialistic rumblings. In fact, of course, it not only did not effectively attack these issues but, containing as it did significant elements of racism, sexism and a roaring Anglo-Saxonism, Norris' revitalization effort could serve as much to circumscribe reform and prolong conflicts as to promote a genuine reevaluation of beliefs and priorities. This may, however, be a characteristic of revitalization efforts in America, which project an ideal past into the future in an attempt to render the present—viewed as decline—unreal and therefore illusory. Certainly Norris' ideas are consonant with those of other revitalizers in this period that witnessed a proliferation of such movements: Frederick Jackson Turner's narrative of the American past as a series of threshold experiences shaped by the virtuous space of the frontier; the Populist Movement's protest against the incorporation of the agricultural West; Progressive reform efforts based on a "redefinition of industrialism from a force creating complexity to a new frontier force leading from complexity to simplicity"; the hopeful assertion of the Social Gospel that "evil was forced upon the individual by the institutions and traditions of society...[that] if each individual were to act according to his instincts, the millennium would occur"; and the Arts and Crafts Movement's call for a return to traditional materials and folk patterns and styles in the arts.[30] When Louis Sullivan capped his modern "tall office buildings" with swirls of vine and foliage, even angels, he was expressing the same revitalization impulse derived from the desire to recapture the expansive optimism of antebellum America (Sullivan's specific debt was to Whitman) that drove Norris to "cap" *The Octopus* with his hymn to the Wheat, his "mighty world-force, wrapped in nirvanic calm." Both were attempts to rescue the culture from the throes of "the vast and terrible drama" that played itself out in the American 1890s.

References

1. Frank Norris, "Zola as a Romantic Writer," in *The Literary Criticism of Frank Norris*, ed. Donald Pizer. New York: Russell and Russell, 1964, p. 72.
2. See Lars Ahnebrink, *The Beginnings of Naturalism in American Fiction: A Study of the Works of Hamlin Garland, Stephen Crane and Frank Norris with Special Reference to Some European Influences, 1891-1903*. Cambridge: Harvard University Press, 1950, for what remains the most detailed examination of the influence of European Naturalism on Norris' generation of Naturalists. Also of interest are Richard Chase's brief discussion of Norris and the tradition of American romance-novels in *The American Novel and Its Tradition*. Garden City, New York: Doubleday and Co., 1957, and Donald Pizer's discussion of Norris' adoption of theories of ethical dualism and atavistic criminality that he learned under Joseph LeConte's tutelage at Berkeley in *The Novels of Frank Norris*. Bloomington: Indiana University Press, 1965.
3. Norris, "Zola as a Romantic Writer," in Pizer, *op. cit.,* p. 72.
4. *Ibid.,* p. 71.
5. Norris, "A Plea For Romantic Fiction," in Pizer, *op. cit.,* p. 76.
6. *Ibid.,* p. 78.
7. *Ibid.,* p. 78.
8. See Anthony F.C. Wallace, *The Death and Rebirth of the Seneca.* New York: Vintage Books, 1969, and *Rockdale.* New York: W.W. Norton & Co., 1978. For further examples of the application of the revitalization model, see William McLoughlin, *Revivals, Awakenings and Reform.* Chicago: University of Chicago Press, 1978, and Carroll Smith-Rosenberg, "The Cross and the Pedestal," in *Disorderly Conduct, Visions of Gender in Victorian America.* New York: Oxford University Press, 1985. In addition, Wallace's model opens out into the rhetorical strategy that Sacvan Bercovitch has called the American Jeremiad, as I have tried to suggest by the adoption of Bercovitch's terms "promise," "declension," and "prophecy" in the later parts of this paper. See Bercovitch, "Introduction: The Puritan Errand Reassessed," *The American Jeremiad.* Madison: University of Wisconsin Press, 1978, pp. 3-30.
9. Anthony F. C. Wallace, "Revitalization Movements," *American Anthropologist,* 58 (1956), p. 268.

10. *Ibid.,* p. 269.
11. *Ibid.,* p. 270.
12. *Ibid.,* p. 270.
13. Warren French, *Frank Norris.* New Haven, Conn.: College & University Press, 1962, p. 22.
14. *Ibid.,* p. 23.
15. *Ibid.,* p. 25.
16. Sean David Cashman, *America in the Gilded Age.* New York: New York University Press, 1984, p. 242.
17. Frank Norris, *Vandover and the Brute.* Lincoln: University of Nebraska Press, 1978, reprint of 1914 edition, ed. Warren French, pp. 95-6.
18. Alan Trachtenberg, *The Incorporation of America: Culture and Society in the Gilded Age.* New York: Hill and Wang, 1982, pp. 80-1.
19. Norris, *Vandover,* p. 328.
20. Trachtenberg, *op. cit.,* p. 81.
21. Lewis Erenberg, *Steppin' Out: New York Nightlife and the Transformation of American Culture, 1890-1930.* Chicago: University of Chicago Press, 1981, p. 113.
22. To get the details of the complex dental procedure that McTeague performs on Trina correct, Norris used Thomas Fillebrown's *A Textbook of Operative Dentistry* (1889) as well as Erasmus Wilson's *A System of Human Anatomy.* See Willard E. Martin, Jr., "Frank Norris' Reading at Harvard," *American Literature* 7 (May 1935), p. 204.
23. Frank Norris, *McTeague: A Story of San Francisco.* New York: W. W. Norton and Co., 1977, reprint of 1899 edition, p. 48.
24. Carroll Smith-Rosenberg, *Disorderly Conduct: Visions of Gender in Victorian America.* New York: Oxford University Press, 1985, p. 90.
25. The essays cited are "A Neglected Epic," *World's Work,* 5 (December, 1902), 2905; "The Great American Novelist," syndicated, January 1903; "The Novel With a 'Purpose'," *World's Work,* 4 (May, 1902), p. 219.
26. Frank Norris, *The Octopus: A Story of California.* New York: Bantam Books, 1958, reprint of 1901 edition, p. 369.
27. *Ibid.,* p. 411.
28. *Ibid.,* p. 426.
29. Frank Norris, *The Pit.* Cambridge, Mass: Robert Bentley, Inc., 1971, reprint of 1903 edition, p. 170.
30. David W. Noble, *The Progressive Mind, 1890-1917.* Minneapolis: Burgess Publishing Co., 1981, pp. 22 and 165.

Metonymy and the Promiscuous Text:
Beverly Dahlen's *A Reading*

Alan Shima
Uppsala University

"The medium is the massage" is Marshall McLuhan's inventive way of describing how art and the electronic media structure our perception of reality. One of McLuhan's convincing examples is his discussion on Renaissance art. McLuhan argues that the innovation of perspective painting organized space into a formal grid of diminishing presence. The illusion of three-dimensional space was enforced through the tyranny of the vanishing point. This effect, McLuhan observes, has had a pervasive influence on how we perceive the world. He writes that "The Vanishing Point = Self-Effacement" and that "The viewer of Renaissance art is systematically placed outside the frame of experience."[1] For McLuhan, the formal strategy of perspective painting creates a sense of detachment and non-involvement. On the other hand, the music montages of the modern composer John Cage, in their aleatory mixture of stylized and public sounds, return us to what McLuhan describes as a pre-alphabetic integration of time and space: "an acoustic, horizonless, boundless, olfactory space, rather than visual space."[2]

Cage's musical images of multiple and floating references are prime examples of Modernism's attempt to depict a reality which fluctuates between ephemeral states of precision and imaginative zones of excess. Rejecting the utopia of transcendental ideas and forms, modernist images are figured as an ensemble of histories, mythic and imaginary narratives which continuously construct and undermine the parameters of meaning. For instance, Pablo Picasso's placement of newspaper headlines, metal strips, wood and glass fragments in and around his painted images, alludes to the infinite set of relationships between things and not to some ideal or secretive meaning of things in themselves. This tendency to deconstruct and reconstruct rather than represent the stability of relationships is, I feel, a familiar characteristic of modernism.

In a similar manner, the formal innovations in contemporary feminist writing displace patriarchal representations of male and female relationships. The feminist use of fractured narratives, the abandonment of genre distinctions, and the inversion of literary conventions and symbols, collectively mark departures from the logic of the patriarchy. Efforts to rewrite the various discourses which interpret sexual difference into masculine and feminine power relations have led some women writers into experimental language projects.

In *Writing Beyond the Ending: Writing Strategies of Twentieth-Century Women Writers*, Rachel Blau DuPlessis registers some of the writing techniques used by women as they attempt to subvert masculine literary values and forms. The literary economy of meaning, DuPlessis argues, is the cultural production and exchange of images and their associations, which to a significant degree "create fictional boundaries of experience."[3] This formulation is reminiscent of McLuhan's belief that "the medium is the massage."

The aesthetic reciprocity between form and content is generally accepted. However, recognizing the reciprocity between form and content in a political context arouses deeper concerns and demands greater attention. Experiential limitations, traditionally constructed in fictional female characters, have too often been accepted as one-to-one correspondences with the "essential nature" of women. These fictional constructs, according to DuPlessis, are repeatedly internalized not solely by the female reader, but by society in general. Thus one might argue that the production and consumption of fictionalized experience become a powerful structuring force. The traditional themes of masculine power and its corresponding modes of characterization and plot have worked as a limit to the emotional and cognitive variety in women's lives.

Against this background of "writing beyond the ending" is DuPlessis' alluring description of how women writers extend the boundaries of female experience by producing a "narrative that denies or reconstructs seductive patterns of feeling that are culturally mandated, internally policed, hegemonically poised."[4] The transformation of romance plots, as in Ann Sexton's poem "Cinderella" (which transforms the Grimm fairytale into a streetwise satiric anecdote) and the recasting of mythical quests and heroes, as in H.D.'s poem "Eurydice" are among DuPlessis' numerous examples of women's "critical dissent."

A more recent American example of feminist experimentation with language and literary form can be found in Beverly Dahlen's *A Reading 1-7.5*. Not willing to choose between verse or prose, and giving up the "grandeur" and "brilliance" which Virginia Woolf felt marked a "man's sentence,"[6] Dahlen produces a pinwheel of images which rotate at different speeds and radiate various arrangements. Part analysis, part seance, *A Reading* fabulates a textual search. Like a feminist version of the Orpheus myth, it seeks its subtle and elusive other. *A Reading* mimes an endless exploration for what can never literally nor figuratively be found except as a pressure of rhythms and associations.

This expedition into the unknown is intimated in the very first line of *A*

Reading. It is a departure which is suggestive yet indeterminate: "before that and before that"[7] is a beginning which is infinitely recursive. Before what? Before the actual composition of this utterance, before grammars and language, before the invention of narrative, before the reading of *A Reading*? As soon as one possible answer surfaces it is dismissed and I am sent looking elsewhere. Without noun (name) and without verb (action) this line has no obvious referent.

Dahlen's text, unlike Ezra Pound's *ABC of Reading*, is not prescriptive or programmatic. Instead, it is inscriptive and syntagmatic. It wanders perpetually across the gap between writing and reading. It is reminiscent of the polysemic murmur of a Barthean text. Illicit and seductive, amorous yet amnesic, *A Reading* tempts chance encounters. Promiscuous, it disregards rules of literary propriety. It abandons the monogamous demands of logic. It seduces and is seduced by the misplaced, the submerged, and the forgotten; drifting inadvertently into other relationships, other chains of reference and significance.

In her essay "Forbidden Knowledge," Dahlen, by way of critical comments, re-enters *A Reading*. She describes her opening line "before that and before that" as a way of "Invoking a metonymy which is already a metaphor, the word itself, any word, a representation, a replacement, a substitution for some thing, any thing, which was not there, naming backwards, following forward, back and forth from nothing to nothing."[8] In a similar fashion, Gertrude Stein comments on the compositional method of her *Tender Buttons*. "Was there not a way," Stein asks, "of naming things that would not invent names, but mean names without naming them"? [9] By simply refusing to name an object through its standard string of signatures, Stein struggled to "put it down in writing as a thing in itself without at all necessarily using its name."[10] In her writing of things, the abundance of repetition and syntactic ellipses became Stein's way of acknowledging radical and fundamental qualities without suffering the limitation of cohesion.

However, when Dahlen talks about the shuttle between "nothing and nothing," she is not referring singularly to the modernist blueprint left by Stein. The areas of "nothingness," for Dahlen, refer to her interest in the psychoanalytic concept of the unconscious. In "Forbidden Knowledge" Dahlen cites Freud, and his French critics Jacques Lacan, Hélène Cixous, and Julia Kristeva. Following Lacan and Kristeva's reading of Freud, Dahlen textualizes an exploration of a lost origin. The "before that and before that" stage of consciousness is never detailed because it is anterior to language. According to Lacan, the appearance of consciousness coincides with our entry into language. Lacan points out that language is the symbolic system by which we can differentiate ourselves from the world around us. Prior to this moment we are unable to make such distinctions.

Keeping this in mind I sense an endless flickering between Dahlen's writing and reading strategies. Her text assumes a strangeness that oscillates between the (readable) conscious and the (unreadable) unconscious of human beings. Similar to the psychoanalytic positions of the conscious subject and the unconscious other, the readable and the unreadable aspects of Dahlen's text might be visioned as forces which are dialogically engaged. Lexical items, syntactic modifications, semantic rearrangements, and rhetorical figures are choreographed as a movement of flashes and afterglows. Emerging absences and fading presences produce valences and textual densities that demand an active awareness of what is before us:

> a new year, looking both ways, she crosses the street. the   light against me, in my eyes. looking up, squinting. taking pictures inside the womb, he said, is nothing sacred? but I   was just a child. here the thought broke off. and yet I was   aware of the connection, the father, the sun. the father, my own brother, the little sadist. I cursed him. he laughed. (p. 42)

The casual recollection of a woman stopping at a crosswalk triggers a response. What seems to be a repressed emotion surfaces. A latent anger is made manifest: "I was   aware of the connection, the father, the sun, the father, my own brother, the little sadist. I cursed him. he laughed."

The distortion and clarification of Dahlen's images seem to be "haphazardly" rehearsed. Just as Freud concluded that no dream interpretation can boast completeness, likewise, *A Reading*, strikes me as a continuous retake of obscure scenes. Rather than penetrating depths, the reader skims an endless number of surfaces. Wet fence boards, a musky voice, an ancient footprint, the playful "hey nonny nonny nonsense" of a child's rhyme slip into and across a variety of familiar and foreign references. However, unlike the mission of a modernist work such as Pound's *Cantos*, I do not think that *A Reading* wishes to immortalize an ideogrammatic series of cross-cultural and trans-historical insights. Whereas the *Cantos* attempts to reach an exactness charged with meaning, *A Reading* runs the register of possible and impossible meanings. Rather than mastering images through the meticulous overlays of conscious effort, Dahlen constructs a space of what seems to be unmediated action.

> a white space intervening, white, white. that white light, static. questioning the first draft. this is not a literary work, I told him, this is not fussy. this is not my mother dusting the daisies. this is not domestic duty. this is not the idea. a preconception. this is it. the baby. the corpse. you can take that body and cut it up forever. this is a metaphor. a something. a meaning carried over. from one thing to the next. these are my leg hairs. the short hair that grows at the edge of my lips. lips, teeth. this is my little bow mouth. you will never know what I mean. when I say you I mean me. erasing all the I's and using instead the third person. it alternates. an alternation, or alteration of generations. it changes. in other words. i.e., it changes. that is to say it alters. it becomes something else, though its original form is still visible. one can trace that. he put a mark over it, a

cross, but the word could still be read beneath it. 'the effacement of the trace.' to deface it, to cross it out, with a knife, to scar her face, his legs, that gesture, to whip the knife out, to scar it, the sign, these words do not match the thought. we will put an end to that longing. what thought there was we do not know. we will never discover it. it is not there. it is gone, or it never existed. impure. a fig leaf, someone said, of my imagination. covering it. (p. 90)

This writing/reading of a blank space strikes me as an imaginative emptying of neglect. Much of what has been previously considered marginal goes through a series of recognitions and displacements. Words migrate from one location to another. White space, the white of the page, becomes the canvas of language in action. Words hit the page, spill laterally and suggest one another into existence. These suggestions often take place in sound associations. The movement from "dusty" to "daises" to "domestic" to "duty" structure not through the interlocking logic of ideas, but through "a meaning carried over" by way of sound or by way of contiguity: leg to hair, lips to teeth to mouth, to the flippant cliché "my little bow mouth." There is no center of lexical or syntactic authority here. There is no denouement. Figures and phrases, fragments and fantasies flow into each other. The "I" in the above indented quote is not a narrative I. It is the (un)grammatical I which is under alteration, under "a fig leaf" cover, is the fig leaf cover of an "imagination covering it." In its obsession with palimpsest, Dahlen's text writes and rewrites itself in its desire to be read.

II

Tuned to the experimental forms practiced by women, Teresa de Lauretis writes: "What is emerging in feminist writings is . . . the concept of a multiple, shifting, and often self-contradictory identity, a subject that is not divided in, but is rather at odds with, language; an identity made up of heterogeneous and heteronomous representations of gender, race, and class, and often indeed across languages and cultures, an identity that one decides to reclaim from a history of multiple assimilations."[11] This notion that women are subjects at strife with language is, in part, a feminist extension of Jacques Lacan's theory on subjectivity and Louis Althusser's description of ideology. By superimposing structural linguistics onto a reading of Freud, Lacan hypothesized that human subjectivity coincides with the acquisition of language. Prior to a child's ability to participate in language, Lacan argues that the child is wholly undifferentiated from its mother. Lacan equates this pre-verbal stage with what he refers to as the Imaginary. At this time the child does not distinguish itself from its mother. It knows no interior or exterior, no "I" or "you." However, during what Lacan has termed the "mirror-phase" the child recognizes itself as a separate entity, a recognition that initiates a "grammar" of positions and a position in grammar. The child differentiates between the "I" of recognition and the "I" who is recognized. And as Catherine Belsey summarizes it, "the child learns to recognize itself in a series of subject-object positions ('he' or 'she,' 'boy' or 'girl,' and so on) which are the positions from which discourse is intelligible to itself and others."12

Subjectivity, according to Lacan, is literally inscribed by/in language and allows our entry into what he calls the Symbolic Order: the matrix of social laws, conventions, and institutions. In certain respects, Lacan's Symbolic Order could be said to coincide with Althusser's concept of ideology. "Ideology," according to Althusser, "represents the imaginary relationship of individuals to their real conditions of existence"13 and not to an obvious and public set of beliefs which correspond with real relationships. Ideology taken in this sense and translated into feminist terms, would, like Lacan's Symbolic Order, represent the values, laws, and judgements of a patriarchal society. Thus one might say that the ideology of patriarchal society constructs the "imaginary relation" of the male/female opposition experienced in the real relations in which women and men live. In this context, anatomical difference takes on an imaginary and symbolic significance. Furthermore, the management of this imaginary and symbolic significance establishes general and specific relations of power.

In various ways, *A Reading* rummages the crypt of pre-linguistic knowledge. Not knowing what the "ungrammatical I" looks like this search is vulnerable to entanglement, yet open to surprise. Relying on the clairvoyance of words, Dahlen entrusts them with maximum independence. They slide and combine, align in various configurations, and inevitably, words abandon these ephemeral arrangements.

> a star, another way to go. I noticed the fish and the turtles in the aquarium kept arranging and rearranging themselves into patterned groups. what pleases the eye. an aesthetic experience, a perfect wineglass. perfecto. to think, she said, they do it all with sand. who would have thought it? to turn sand into that? the transformations.(p. 112)

A word ignites and sends a sound or pulse adjacently: "a star, another way to go" navigates not into a metaphorical similarity but into a syntagmatic combination: (star)fish and the turtles whose aquatic calligraphy "arranging and rearranging" not only "pleases the eye," but causes another lateral movement. The aquarium and its glass encasement becomes the ground from which "a perfect wineglass. perfecto" emerges. Still proceeding in a superfluity of associations, a voice suddenly comments, "they do it all with sand. who would have thought it? to turn sand into that?" The sand in the aquarium, the sand turned to glass, the glass a transformation. Somehow there is a(n) (un)naming going on here which is never a selection and substitution for the thing or the perception of the thing. This is possible because, for Dahlen, "The materials exceed the thought, the materials of presence, and of absence as well, in the making and reading of poems."[14] She gives the poetic word maximum freedom. Ironically, this maximum freedom insists on maximum attention and maximum response. Her writing solicits a reading which is based neither on surrender nor mastery. Just as her text proposes an all inclusiveness, it prepares and encourages its reader for full and active participation. On the periphery of literary convention, and at times pre-syntactic, *A Reading* is the simultaneous production and consumption of tentative meaning.

One of Dahlen's primary concerns is to write that which has not been fully thought. It is a way to embody a future, where the very form of the writing becomes the corporeal space of that which is not fully clear. In her essay "Something/Nothing," Dahlen explains: "If I have spoken here of the form as body, I have meant the lost body, lost, as we say, in thought, lost in the poem. It seems to me that language begins with loss, with the loss of the *chora*, however that may be imagined by each of us. The inevitability of that loss is one of the boundaries of the 'speaking being.' It is just there, at the boundary, that desire is born, desire as the signified always beyond reach."[15] This referral to "the loss of the *chora*" is a direct reference to Julia Kristeva's work in linguistics and her theory which links subjectivity to language acquisition. The *chora* is Kristeva's term, which can be glossed as "anterior to any space, an economy of primary processes articulate by Freud's instinctual drives (*Triebe*) through condensation and displacement, and where social and family structures make their imprint through the mediation of the maternal body."[16] Provisional and undetermined, the *chora* belongs to what Kristeva has designated as the "semiotic," which relates to the pre-symbolic, pre-linguistic process of signification. Kristeva's theory of the "speaking-subject" is built on the hypothesis that the "speaking-subject" "is a split subject—divided between unconscious and conscious motivations"[17] which correspond to the registers of the "semiotic" and "symbolic" respectively.

Commenting on Kristeva's theories and her modification of Lacan's model of subjectivity, Toril Moi explains that like Lacan, Kristeva connects the achievement of subjectivity with entry into the Symbolic Order. "Once the subject has entered into the Symbolic Order, the *chora* will be more or less successfully repressed and can be perceived only as pulsional pressure on symbolic language: as contradictions, meaninglessness, disruption, silences and absences in the symbolic language."[18] This subversive "pressure" undermines the unity of the speaking-subject and surfaces as lexical, syntactic, and narrative disturbances and is similar to what is found in *A Reading*.

Dahlen's writing labors the "double articulation" outlined by the theories of Kristeva, Lacan, and Barthes. Working along the lode of the inexplicable, Dahlen relies on the rhythm of chance. Her words carom towards other contexts, establish other avenues of meaning. Each change in meaning exposes another possibility, another edge to examine, even if that edge borders a "terror, the first word lighted,..."19 Not posing as an articulation of an authentic and unified identity, *A Reading* is a cursive scrimmage between a social and a textual position. In this light Dahlen's experimentation with form overlaps with the textual tactics of Hélène Cixous and Luce Irigaray. If we are presently convinced by Beauvoir's inciting maxim "one is not born a woman but becomes one," and that "woman is indeed in large part man's invention,"20 Hélène Cixous now proposes a new provocation. Cixous suggests that we need "to pose the woman question to history in quite elementary forms like 'Where is she? Is there any such thing as woman?' At worst, many women wonder even if they exist, they feel they don't exist and wonder if there has ever been a place for them. I [Cixous] am speaking of woman's place, *from* woman's place, if she takes (a) place."21 These questions are not simply rhetorical ones. Cixous has no ready-made answer. In fact, the last sentence of the above quote, ironic and self-conscious in its conditional clause ending, is open and invites discussion by its side way glance at Shoshana Felman's 1975 essay "Woman and Madness: The Critical Phallacy."22

In "Woman and Madness" Felman takes the French critic Luce Irigaray's theoretical arguments to its limits. In short, Irigaray argues against the metaphysical discourse of Western philosophy. In her 1974 doctoral thesis *Speculum de l'autre femme* ("Speculum of the other woman") Irigaray expands and elaborates on Beauvoir's analysis of how philosophical discussions more often than not align the Self with the masculine and the Other with the feminine.23 She examines the metaphors which cut and stitch us into separate gender categories and concludes that woman as Other has no access to the philosophical discourse which describes woman as a vacancy, a discourse that reifies absence and silence as feminine. Sensing an obvious contradiction in Irigaray's analysis, Felman asks, "if 'the woman' is precisely the Other of any conceivable Western theoretical locus of speech, how can the woman as such be speaking in this book?" And Felman continues: "If, as Luce Irigaray suggests, the woman's silence, or the repression of her capacity to speak, are constitutive of philosophy and theoretical discourse as such, from what theoretical locus is Luce Irigaray herself speaking in order to develop her own theoretical discourse about woman's exclusion? Is she speaking in the language of men, or the silence of women? Is she speaking as woman or in the place of the (silent) woman, for the woman, in the name of the woman?"24 Returning to Cixous's statement, where she emphatically claims to speak "from woman's place, if she takes (a) place," it seems as if Cixous is attempting to respond to Felman's question. Cixous's textual exchange with Felman makes an important point about the politics of representation. Feminists have long been engaged in resisting and subverting sexist representations of women.

However, adjacent to the problem of what feminists insist are infected images of women is the problem of representations itself. If there is no such thing as a female or male essence, on what ground do our representations of women stand? A quick and common response is to say that authentic representations of women are based on women's lives. But if we accept, as contemporary French theory suggests, namely, that there are no "natural' centers of consciousness, no pure and homogeneous self, that the categories of gender are linguistic and metaphysical constructions, then we are led to assume that all subject positions are open and ultimately in flux. This type of reasoning has been powerfully argued by Barthes, Derrida, and Foucault. In combination these writers have influenced a number of other writers and critics who view the world as an undifferentiated flow of objects and events which is unintelligible until we choose to momentarily freeze this flow and attach tentative meanings which are never intrinsic, but always political, in that these tentative meanings establish a paradigm of preferences and priorities.

So when Cixous writes that she is "speaking of woman's place, from woman's place, if she takes (a) place" she is seizing a position in language which is overtly political. And her statement gains credibility not so much through her biological condition, or through her theoretical position, but through a self-effacing irony which undermines any authority based solely on biology or theory. It is as if Cixous were saying "I'm (not) here if you (don't) see me." The duplicity of the parenthetical insertions are not meant to confuse the reader, but textually compose the oscillating configurations which is often found in Cixous's writing of the "feminine." Linguistic and poetic inventiveness are often used by Cixous to subvert what has become infamously known as phallocentric thought. It is the interminable hide and seek of multiplicity and continuous surges of imaginative association, which for Cixous, mark the flight of the "feminine."

In defence of Irigaray's strategies one might mention that Irigaray, like a ventriloquist, speaks from several centers; one being in the imitated speech of a masculine scholar. Irigaray's mimicry serves as a disguise in which she hopes to invade and sabotage the inner spaces of patriarchal logic. Commenting on this particular strategy, Toril Moi writes that Irigaray "cannot pretend to be writing in some pure feminist realm outside of patriarchy: if her discourse is to be received as anything other than incomprehensible chatter, she must copy male discourse. The feminine can thus only be read in the blank spaces left between the signs and lines of her own mimicry."[25]

Some might argue that mimicry is essentially parasitic and is thus limiting in its ability to provide positive models for renewal. It is for this reason some feminists have reservations concerning Irigaray's mimicry of patriarchal discourse. Irigaray, along with other feminists who excel in the rhetoric of the academy, is sometimes accused of practicing a textual mastery that is indistinguishable from those who are her male contemporaries. It is for this reason Toril Moi finds some of Irigaray's writing less than fully satisfactory. Moi declares that "The mimicry fails because it ceases to be perceived as such:

it is no longer merely mockery of the absurdities of the male, but a perfect reproduction of the logic of the same."[26] I think this judgement is too harsh. It ignores the fact that Irigaray is operating from an informed theoretical position that exploits masculine rhetoric to undermine its fallacies. Part of the important work feminist theory and practice is laboring with is the search for ways in which a woman might give form to a consciousness that is so often distorted by the present cultural paradigms. Felman articulates this concern by asking "how can one speak from the place of the Other? How can woman be thought outside of the Masculine/Feminine framework, other than as opposed to man, without being subordinated to a primordial masculine model?"[27] Thus far there have been two principle strategies which respond to Felman's questions. And both strategies pay particular attention to, as the poet Adrienne Rich puts it, "how our language has trapped as well as liberated us."[28]

The first strategy has been dedicated to displacing the array of patriarchal images, connotations, associations, and meanings of woman. Feminists have focused on the historical conditions of women and have attempted to conceptualize female experience outside inherited norms. The second strategy concentrates more prominently on formal combinations and incongruities which present female subjectivity as a multiple, oscillating, and overflowing identity which continuously transgresses every attempt to fix or unify female subjectivity under a particular set of terms or definitions.

III

In its attempt explore this second strategy, *A Reading* ceaselessly spreads along the horizon of polyphonic images. Shreds and strips of thoughts combine with the faint projection of things remembered, written, or imagined. In this sense *A Reading* takes the shape of a textual mobius. By twisting the formal parameters of conventional writing, Dahlen's text aspires to simultaneously trace the nascent and dissolving sequences of consciousness materialized in language. The interior of introspection and the exterior of the world buckle and brace one another. Dahlen offers us a text and subject in process. Both are in motion through the convective currents of history and the atmospheric pressure of language. DuPlessis equates the expansive weather works of *A Reading* with the quality of metonymy. DuPlessis suggests that "To write metonymy is to write all margins" and that it makes "some critique of the center such that the binary distinction between text and space disappears, and so that a work bleeds, as is said of a photograph printed to the edge."[29] "Writing all margins" eventually floods formal and imaginary embankments. Dahlen's text not only spills over the space that separates center from margin, it also overflows, overwrites the division between what is known and what is hidden, lost, or repressed.

DuPlessis' reference to metonymy as a structuring strategy in a *A Reading* is prompted by what appears to be a letter in Dahlen's text. The "letter" addressed "Dear Rachel"[30] mentions Roman Jakobson and alludes to his theory on aphasia as: "language, forgotten this theory, this disease as metaphor about poetry, how it is written anyway." (p. 79) The "letter" goes on to describe the narrator's tattered childhood, the stuttering and inconsolable attempts to "say it." Saying it is a formidable task and in the case of *A Reading,* the act of saying it creates a stylistic abundance, a hypersaturation of context. DuPlessis describes Dahlen's writing as a combinatory extravagance, a metonymy which "creates the thing on the side, the thing set aside, the desire repressed, but palpable in its corrupted absence."[31] A key term, absence (along with silence) stresses the real and symbolic female conditions which feminists hope to transform. I think DuPlessis has hit upon an interesting aspect of Dahlen's writing. Her discussion of the metonymic features in *A Reading* suggestively alludes to the Modernist method of collage and the affinities between it and the experimental writing done by certain women. But before going into greater detail concerning Dahlen's metonymic writing strategy, I would like to take a detour into Roman Jakobson's theory on metonymy and its literary features.

Perhaps the most intriguing discussion on metonymy and literary form can be found in Jakobson's essay "Two Aspects of Language and Two Types of Aphasiac Disturbances."[32] Analyzing the speech of aphasics from a structuralist perspective, Jakobson observed that aphasiac disorders could be classified into two separate but related categories. Jakobson identifies the first type of disturbance as a "similarity disorder." This is characterized by an inability to select similarities (or contrasts) from the inventory of lexical items. Consequently, the ability to produce proper names or their synonyms is greatly impaired. The second type of disturbance is identified as a "contiguity disorder," and can be characterized as an inability to combine lexical items into coherent structures. For instance, Jakobson points out that "The syntactical rules organizing words into higher units are lost; . . . Word order becomes chaotic; the ties of grammatical coordination and subordination, whether concord or government, are dissolved."[33]

Jakobson makes an ingenious connection between the two forms of aphasiac disturbance and what he sees as "the two fold character of language." He argues that the distinct yet related aphasiac disorders of similarity and contiguity support the assumption that speech is orchestrated through a double movement, which he describes as "a selection of certain linguistic entities and their combination into linguistic units of a higher degree of complexity" (p. 241). Furthermore, Jakobson links metaphor with the selection operation of language and metonymy with the combinatory operation of language. The above connections may be imagined as two axes representing a selective/associative metaphoric axis, and a combinatory/ syntagmatic metonymic axis.

In discussing aphasic disturbances and the discursive qualities of metaphor and metonymy, Jakobson outlines an intriguing formula: "Metaphor is alien to the similarity disorder, and metonymy to the contiguity disorder." However, he notes that "In normal verbal behavior both processes are continually operative, but careful observation will reveal that under the influence of a cultural pattern, personality and verbal style, preference is given to one of the two processes over the other" (p. 254). This observation leads Jakobson to speculate about aphasiac symptoms and their similarities in literary genres. For instance, he proposes that heroic epics move to the metonymic pole, while Russian lyrical songs gravitate to the metaphoric pole. Jakobson also makes a convincing argument on the metonymic features of the "realistic" novel and how it is somewhat located between the "intermediary stage between the decline of romanticism and the rise of symbolism," both of which might be characterized as being shaped in the metaphoric mode (p. 255). Speaking about an author such as Tolstoy, Jakobson explains that "the realist author metonymically digresses from the plot to the atmosphere and from the characters to the setting in space and time" (p. 255). Just as the operations of "condensation" and "displacement" are considered metonymic features in Freud's interpretaion of dreams, synecdochic details (parts standing in and representing the whole) provide narrative detours and digressions. The action circulates in little eddies and side pools of mood or reflection. On the other hand Jakobson felt that Romantic and Symbolist poetry reflected a predominance of the metaphoric mode of language. The inventive pursuit of emblems and allegorical structures, or the highlighting of a particular image to replace common recognitions in Romantic and Symbolist poetry, enacts the metaphoric principle of selection and substitution.

I find Jakobson's categories perceptive and useful. They continue to maintain relevance despite Modernist experimentations in form and its tendency to blur genre distinctions. For instance, David Lodge describes the degree of metonymic-metaphoric inversion in Modernist novels.[34] His prime example is James Joyce's *Finnegans Wake*, where metaphoric relations rather than the contiguous relations of the traditional "realist" novel predominate. *Finnegans Wake*, according to Lodge, is "entirely based on the principle of similarity and substitution: structurally and thematically, in that every event is a reenactment or a premonition of a synthetic language based on the pun, which is a form of metaphor." However, he cautions that "*Finnegan's Wake* is at the extremity of modern fiction; and indeed suggests that, because the novel is inherently a metonymic form, to force it completely to the metaphoric pole entails its dissolution as a novel."[35]

In Dahlen's *A Reading* an opposite inversion is taking place. The experimental nature of Dahlen's poetic form undermines the metaphoric conventions of lyric poetry. Rather than conform to the process of selection and substitution, which creates a type of exile or repression of one term for another, Dahlen opts for contiguity and combination. Language is set adrift. *A Reading* cannot say what a woman is, for that would be a limitation, a binding of possibilities. There is an unwillingness or inability to name by selecting a single term or set of terms. Instead, *A Reading* establishes a network of dialogues, utterances, and fragments which function as verbal previews and sequels. It is at the opposite end of what has been known as "the literature of exhaustion." Rather than practicing minimalist reticence, Dahlen's writing performs with excess. It is a text of superfluity and stamina. Resisting a hierarchy of terms and relationships (whether those relationships are linguistic or interpersonal), *A Reading* is always on the move, always seeking its "lost" other. That is why Dahlen's title *A Reading* only metonymically refers to her writing. Just as an aphasiac suffering from a similarity disorder might never say the word book only, but, in connection with its context or use, might say library or *Wuthering Heights*. It is for this reason that *A Reading* does not say what it is, cannot say what it is, without syntagmatically reaching to its other(s).

Driven, inventively indeterminate, flirting with the obvious and the obscure *A Reading* is promiscuous. It does not remain "faithful" to a particular style, genre, or perspective. Neither does it pretend any loyalty to any particular coherence. Laws of propriety and the customary markers of literary identity are abandoned. Dahlen describes *A Reading* as a work "which is theoretically open-ended, which turns out to be something like a journal, at times like poetry, or prose narrative, and that it was not preconceived in terms of these or any other forms or genres originally."[36] Similar to other works of experimental writing, *A Reading* veers into a plurality of modes: "the way of the boundary the way of the flood. her face in the dark window dark how she saw it and spelled me. a fragment of an analysis: it was so easy to knock her out just like the movies she asked for it bonk on the head she was done for. but someone righteous and Spanish saw it from an upper window. we were caught. how bare-faced." (p. 17) Caught? Perhaps caught between chance and concentration, between a cliché ("like the movies she asked for it bonk on the head she was done for") and a shard of memory ("her face in the dark window dark how she saw it and spelled me"). The "spelled me" of Dahlen's image (?), figure (?), narrator (?), grammatical pronoun (?) is ambiguously lexical and literal, ambiguously figurative and fleeting. We could take this phrase to mean one who is charmed by an incantation or the letter by letter sequence which names the subject of/in speech. The subject of reading and the reading subject oscillate between ground and figure. The mirage of a unified identity is dispersed into a spread of rhetorical figures and literal references. The "primitive" syntax, progressive play of fragments, and the absence (or exaggeration) of punctuation cause a kind of leakage. Associations float in a peculiar manner. Phrases and clauses soak each other. One association stains an adjacent thought. There is a constant folding, a pleating of instances, a textual weaving and unraveling that loops through theory and praxis. Commenting on *A Reading,* Dahlen tells us that "Its method of composition throughout much, but not all of the work, aspires to be free association" but attaches an amendment: "Freud thought free association was easily learned but Lacan calls it a 'forced labor. . .so much so that some have gone so far as to say that it requires apprenticeship. . .,' that

146

'nothing could be less free'."[37]

Rather than affirm a subject as an autonomous and centered producer of speech, Dahlen seems to be in agreement with French theorists who emphasize the coextensive process of language and subjectivity. Whereas a poet like Adrienne Rich seeks a language full enough to express the previous silences of women, Dahlen explores (women's, her) silence as a continuously receding limit, a fictive space, which is the foyer to the unanticipated. One may approach, sense, or perhaps dimly glimpse the imaginary forms of original loss and absence, but one will never recover fully the primal loss which led to our own subjectivity.

Adrienne Rich also confronts the complexities of loss and desire. However, in a poem such as "Diving into the Wreck," Rich, reminiscent of the Romantics, creates an extended metaphor of subterranean depths and a blacking-out that moves from darkness to a unifying insight. Lost history is recovered and a sense of a pre-patriarchal, pre-textual female identity is affirmed. On the other hand, Dahlen's subject is constructed and tentatively discovered in the very process of writing. Dahlen's textual composition detours and hesitates. Syntactic breaks and aerial twists of "random" association avoid any facile reference to places or things outside of the text. And yet Dahlen refuses to privilege writing as a separate and superior reality: "Do we make a fetish of the poem, seduced by it, seduced by that 'something' which seems to speak meaning, embodied, or miming the condition of embodiment?" Her response is a teasing "Not I, my other, my familiar, my ghost in the woods."[38]

In a Barthean sense, Dahlen is aware that language is a process, a continuous, at times contradictory, flow of signs. To take the position of a speaking subject is to become at once a producer and product of language, a recognition which prompts Dahlen to declare: "Henceforth language in my place; it speaks me."[39] *A Reading* negotiates this double position. It suggests a loss somehow "found" in the interim between textual production and consumption. By engaging in the traffic of trivial and subliminal twitches, *A Reading* traces the leap between unarticulated thought and the instant of recognition.

Commenting on the experimental forms of writers who have been grouped under the heading of "language-centered" writing, a grouping which would certainly include Beverly Dahlen's work, Lynn Hejinian pinpoints some central concerns. Hejinian suggests that "It is useful, here, to consider the writer as the first and immediate reader of his or her own writing. The writer goes more than halfway to meet lines or sentences advancing on their own. The language itself materializes thought; the writing realizes ideas. One discovers what one thinks, sees, says, and as the words unfold the work, the work, the work directed in form, extends outward."[40] This emphasis on language as a continuous inscription of consciousness corresponds to the post-structural statements coming out of France. For instance, arguing in semiotic terms, Julia Kristeva claims that "writing is the ridge where the historical becoming of the subject is affirmed; that is, an a-psychological, a-subjective subject—an historical subject."[41] This attention to the discursive composition of "self" relocates the "self" every time it speaks or writes.

A Reading is self-critical, self-reflective. Its words rise and fall. Its syntactic units somersault, attain a tentative semantic arrangement, then move on to other points and combinations. Rather than resolving contradictions *A Reading* is a performance of contradictions. It is the aphasic mythography of contours and contexts, where the naming is done in circles and never directly. This is the duplicious writing of peripheries: "each shell splitting in the air. moreover. and came down to a valley just at twilight. it lengthened. filigree. or an afterthought. an afterimage. did she see that? head turning. we held no brief for. going down. a spin-off. a cylinder. somehow music." (p. 18)

This textual lacing is the delicate work whose form is an opening up of discursive spaces. Whether through accident or design, it moves expansively in the shade as well as in the light of desire. Or as DuPlessis claims, *A Reading* is "a continuous stream of metonymy which uncannily, the more it extends outward (writer as collector, as documentarian, as collagist), the more it seems to layer itself over and over, a texture singing through porous time and porous ego."[42] Still another comparison might take the shape of the uncensored instant, the indelible curvature of a smokey fragrance:

bitterly the coffee
a round
a round tasting that lights up the mouth with a whole definition
a creamy darkness.(p. 52)

Dahlen's "creamy darkness" is unmistakably reaching into Stein's *Tender Buttons*. Stein commented that she wrote her Tender Button pieces after "looking at anything until something that was not the name of that thing but was in a way that actual thing would come to be written."[43] Might the same be said of Dahlen's *A Reading*?

148

References

1. Marshall McLuhan, *The Medium is the Massage*. New York: Bantam Books, 1976, p. 53.
2. *Ibid.*, p. 57.
3. Rachel Blau DuPlessis, *Writing Beyond the Ending: Narrative Strategies of Twentieth-Century Women Writers*. Bloomington: Indiana University Press, 1985, p. 3.
4. *Ibid.*, p. 5.
5. Beverly Dahlen, *A Reading 1-7*. San Francisco: Momo's Press, 1985.
6. Virginia Woolf, *A Room of One's Own*. 1927; reprint London: Grafton, 1987, p. 73.
7. Dahlen, *op. cit.*, p. 15. All further references to this work appear in the text.
8. Beverly Dahlen, "Forbidden Knowledge," *Poetics Journal* 14 (1984), 23.
9. Gertrude Stein, "Poetry and Grammar" in *Gertrude Stein Lectures in America*. 1935; reprint New York: Vintage, 1975, p. 236.
10. *Ibid.*, p. 242.
11. Teresa De Lauretis, ed., *Feminist/Critical Studies*. Bloominton: Indiana University Press, 1986, p. 9.
12. Catherine Belsey, *Critical Practice*. London: Methuen, 1980, p. 61.
13. Louis Althusser, *Lenin and Philosophy and Other Essays*. New York: Monthly Review Press, 1971, p. 162.
14. Beverly Dahlen, "Something/Nothing," *Ironwood*, 27 (1985), p. 172
15. *Ibid.*, p. 172.
16. Leon S. Roudiez, Introduction, Julia Kristeva, *Desire in Language*. New York: Columbia University Press, 1980, p. 6.
17. *Ibid.*, p. 6.
18. Toril Moi, *Sexual/Textual Politics*. London: Methuen, 1985, p. 162.
19. Dahlen, *A Reading*, p. 87.
20. Simone de Beauvoir, *The Second Sex*. 1949 trans. H. Parshley, New York: Vintage Books, 1984, p. 222.
21. Hélène Cixous, "Castration or Decapitation," *Signs* 7, Autumn (1981), p. 43.
22. Shoshana Felman, "Woman and Madness: The Critical Phallacy," *Diacritics* 5, Winter (1975), p. 3.
23. Luce Irigaray, *Speculum de l'autre femme*. Paris: Minuit, 1974.
24. Felman, *op. cit.*, p. 3.
25. Moi, *op. cit.*, p. 140.
26. *Ibid.*, p. 142.
27. Felman, *op. cit.*, p. 4.
28. Adrienne Rich, "When We Dead Awaken: Writing as Re-Vision (1971)," in *On Lies, Secrets, and Silence: Selected Prose 1966-1978*. New York:

W.W. Norton, p. 35.

29. Rachel Du Plessis, "An Essay on Beverly Dahlen's A Reading," *Ironwood* 27 (1985), p. 161.

30. Both Beverly Dahlen and Rachel Du Plessis worked as *How(ever)* associate and contributing editors respectively during 1983-1985. They have also appeared together at various poetry readings. I assume that the Rachel in the letter may very well be a reference to Rachel Du Plessis.

31. Du Plessis, "An Essay on Beverly Dahlen," p. 161.

32. Roman Jakobson, "Two Aspects of Language and Two Types of Aphasiac Disturbances," in *Roman Jakobson: Selected Writings*. Hague: Mouton, 1971.

33. *Ibid.*, p. 251. All further references to this work appear in the text.

34. David Lodge, "The Language of Modernist Fiction: Metaphor and Metonymy," in *Modernism 1890-1930*, ed. Malcolm Bradbury and James McFarlane. London: Penguin, 1976, p. 481.

35. *Ibid.,* p.481.

36. Dahlen, "Forbidden Knowledge," p. 3.

37. *Ibid.* p. 3. Ellipses are Dahlen's.

38. Dahlen, "Something/Nothing," p. 172.

39. *Ibid.* p. 172.

40. Lyn Hejinian, "for CHANGE," in, *In the American Tree*, ed. Ron Silliman, Orono, Maine: The National Poetry Foundation, 1986, p. 487.

41. Julia Kristeva, *Desire in Language*. New York: Columbia University Press, 1980, pp. 97-8.

42. Du Plessis, "An Essay on Beverly Dahlen," pp. 160-1.

43. Stein, "Poetry and Grammar," p. 237.

The Value of Place:
The Redevelopment Debate over New York's Times Square

Eric J. Sandeen
University of Wyoming

New York represents the power and the threat of the modern metropolis to many Americans. Long the financial capital of the United States, New York is the place where deals are made and fortunes are accumulated. The conversion of money into electronic units of exchange, transmitted throughout the world from the glass towers of Wall Street, has made for spectacular examples of instant success, and equally horrendous cautionary tales of failure and shady dealing, in the last decade. But the buying and selling that made Wall Street the arena for cultural heroes during the Reagan years is only one indication of the capitalistic cycle — not so much of production and consumption as of investment in production and speculation on consumption — which has been driving New York for decades.

New York consumes and revalues itself even as it performs the same function for the rest of the country. This essay discusses one episode in this cycle, the redevelopment of Times Square. Because Times Square is a significant place in American culture, this debate is taking place in public: in Planning and Zoning Committee hearings, in the offices of developers, in the councils of civic organizations, in neighborhood political action groups, and behind the desks of enterprises doing business in the present Times Square. The decisions made about Times Square are to be found in the open; they are given form in the buildings and the changing ambiance of the area. Through this decade-long debate we can see how different definitions of "value" have been projected onto the cityscape. We can also measure the difficulty of maintaining an important public place in a capitalistic culture which privileges private property.

The fundamental facts of Manhattan arise from physical attributes: the geology and geography of the heart of New York City (figure 1). Manhattan is an island. Land is therefore a finite quantity and, through its scarcity, is highly valued. Except for small sandy areas such as Greenwich Village, the island offers a fine platform for the most recognizable of twentieth century building forms in New York — the skyscraper. At the turn of the century engineering innovation, architectural style, geographical possibility, and the accumulated power of corporate capital met to create the complex and sometimes overwhelmingly urban environment of present-day Manhattan.

MIDTOWN MANHATTAN

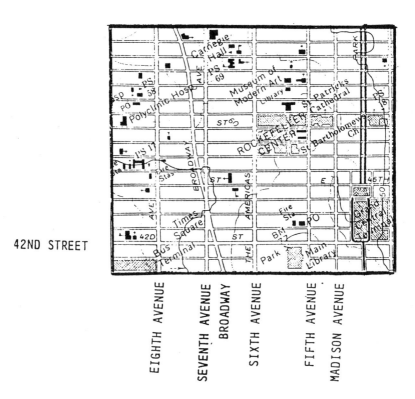

42ND STREET

EIGHTH AVENUE SEVENTH AVENUE BROADWAY SIXTH AVENUE FIFTH AVENUE MADISON AVENUE

Figure 1. This map of midtown shows an aspect of Manhattan seldom represented elsewhere: the meandering contour lines of the island's topography.   Courtesy of the U. S. Geological Survey (Central Park 7 1/2 quad.)

The scale of the buildings and the aggressive commodification of land which made the skyscrapers necessary also resulted from a conscious decision made by city leaders in 1811: to parcel Manhattan north of 14th Street into rectangular lots defined by east-west streets and north-south avenues. This grid system, the most typical way in which Anglo-Americans claimed the land during the early national period, "has remained the fundamental visual impression we have of the city and the formative structure that every architect and builder must acknowledge."[1] If architects and builders puzzled over the long, narrow sites for their structures, real estate developers have

152

reaped the advantage of parcels that are marked out in modular chunks of a Cartesian grid. Land is easily defined, divided, and exchanged in New York, driving prices up as it drives architects crazy.

One reason for the way in which the city fathers of 1811 sliced the Big Apple deserves mention, for it anticipates the modern condition of the city. New York was in financial trouble in the early 1800s and the mapping of Manhattan represented the transfer of public land to private ownership in exchange for money in the city coffers: "Thus the city surrendered control over its own destiny. As the *Regional Plan* of 1931 put it, the division of the land into salable packages made individual profit rather than 'architectural control in the interests of the community' the decisive factor in the city's growth and appearance."2

Most of Manhattan is indeed "impervious to picturesque improvement and defiant against architectural correction."3 There is one great exception in the streetscape of Cartesian Manhattan, however — Broadway. Originating in legend, if not in fact, as an Indian trail, Broadway defiantly cuts across the grid, from southeast to northwest, starting at 10th Street and ending at 72nd Street. Each time Broadway crosses the intersection of a street and an avenue a spatial anomaly in the grid is formed — a square, New Yorkers call it. These hourglass or bow-tie shaped forms create a clearing in the built environment. From Union Square at 14th Street to Columbus Circle at 59th Street these squares have been the sites of the most vigorous development action in New York City during the 1980s.

Times Square is such a clearing. Caused by the crossing of Broadway with Seventh Avenue, its open space is bounded on the south by 42nd Street and on the north by 48th Street. In the compact urban environment of Midtown Manhattan this offers New Yorkers a rare commodity — a vista, a 360-degree panorama, a truly public space. Here there is relief from the dwarfing scale of Midtown's skyscrapers. Until the late 1980s Times Square was framed mostly by two- to ten-story buildings, on the tops of which pulsated massive neon signs.

The significance of the Square has attracted, and in turn been defined by, what happens in and around it. Times Square is the heart of the theatre district. This is Broadway, The Great White Way, the greatest collection of theatres in the United States. The theatres are supported by hundreds of nearby shops, studios, and stores catering to theatre patrons. Tourists are attracted to the environment of Times Square, both for the formal entertainment of a play and for the exciting impromptu of the street. This Square is also the place where America celebrates the arrival of the New Year. Each year since 1904 a lighted ball has been lowered from the top of a building on the south end of the Square. Depending on the weather, as many as 500,000 revelers may watch this ceremony in person (figure 2). Millions more see the dropping of the ball – which became an apple in honor of New York's nickname during most of the 1980s - on television, live in the East, via tape delay in the several time zones of the United States.

Figure 2. This is New Year's Eve 1984, a clear, dry night that attracted maximum capacity. The glowing ball is visible atop the Times Tower in the center. This picture was taken from the North end of the square.

Photograph courtesy of the Municipal Art Society.

But now the environment of Times Square is rapidly changing, and 40- or 50-story office towers and up-scale hotels are replacing buildings which have sat along Broadway since the 1920s. Because of its place in the symbolic geography of the nation, during the past decade Times Square has represented the urban decay of Eastern cities. The crime, vice, dirt, and dumpiness associated with the blight of the metropolis could be found along The Great White Way. This distillate of contemporary problems bothered civic leaders, upset tourists and theatre-goers, and excited developers. Not only was Times Square a fabled address, but it was a district seemingly in need of help.

154

It was, however, not the sacrifice zone that many pro-development people seemed to see. The kaleidoscopic nature of Times Square gave even its redevelopment, or possible destruction, more verve than other discussions of development in New York City. Where some people saw loiterers others saw groups of lower class and minority individuals enjoying themselves on a tight budget. What some people saw as the unsightly activity of the street others viewed as a vibrant petty capitalism centering on the needs and desires of middle class tourists and theatre-goers. Developers saw delapidated building stock. Defenders saw an environment on a human scale thoroughly imbued with the vibrant life of the area.

Such an important area as Times Square attracts interpretation, argument, and, among many combatants that rare commodity, passion. This reading of Times Square as commodity depends, in turn, on the cultural worth of the region, for from this the transvaluation into livelihood and profit takes place.

Times Square represents the tradition of family-owned industry to the Artkraft Strauss Sign Corporation. The low scale of the area guarantees platforms for the neon signs that have been its livelihood for three generations. The life history of the founder, Jacob Starr, enacts two cherished American myths: the immigrant who makes good and the young man who heads West to find fame and fortune. Jacob arrived in New York from Russia in the early part of this century and found employment in Benjamin Strauss's metal shop. Through hard work and ingenuity he rose through the ranks of skilled workers and even put himself through Cooper Union, an educational opportunity grasped by many ambitious immigrants who wanted an academic degree to certify their knowledge of craft and materials. Engineering degree in hand, he moved West to Lima, Ohio and joined the Artkraft Company, maker of steel, porcelain-faced signs, and more importantly, the American patent-holder of the neon sign-making process. He returned to New York in the late '20s, as the Great Depression hit, and, over the next two decades, transformed the signs along The Great White Way from gas flames and ordinary incandescent light into a gallery of neon.

His son Mel, dubbed by the *New York Times* "Mr. Broadway," took over the company after the blackouts of World War II. It was under his direction that many of the most flamboyant signs were constructed. Restraint and "good taste" have never been a part of the sign maker's vocabulary, as the creation and evolution of a Budweiser beer sign on a prime Times Square location clearly shows. Most of the sign was taken up by a model of the Grand Canyon, which moved from light to dark and back to daylight on a two minute diurnal cycle. Through the Canyon rolled a train. During this last great period of American domestic train travel, it was still advantageous for train companies to have their names emblazoned in Times Square. And this could be done, provided that the train owners promised to serve only Budweiser beer in their parlor cars. Later, the Canyon was transformed by Artkraft Strauss into blocks of ice and a 30 meter-long, glowing, three-dimensional Budweiser bottle was placed on top (figure 3). The train survived this transformation but later yielded to the emerging form of transportation: in 1957 a TWA sign was placed on the same steel frame to advertise travel to Europe.

Figure 3. Budweiser beer was a consistent patron for Artkraft Strauss. This sign was located on the East side of the Square; an even more glamorous exercise in neon was located in the far northwest corner at about the same time. Photograph courtesy of the Artkraft Strauss Sign Corporation.

156

Today the company is headed by Tama Starr, the college-educated grand-daughter of the founder. She inherits a well-established family gallery in which sight lines have been commodified in dollars per month charged to a company commissioning a half-million dollar corporate coming-out in New York's most famous square. Whether flashing neon, painted surface, glowing plastic box, or computer-generated graphic overlay, messages are bought, sold, and space advertised in an endless cycle of signage that dates back six decades.

There is a close relationship between the Broadway stage and the Times Square sign industry. The language of signage clearly shows the influence of the entertainment industry. A large sign is called a "spectacular." In Mel's day this would have indicated a confection like the Budweiser sign. What goes on inside some of the theaters takes place on the rooftops as well. Many spectaculars are essentially stage sets built in public space. They are "animated" or "scored" with a series of activities. The language of the Broadway theatre and Hollywood have long since been merged with the advertising of products and the practice of a traditional craft by the signmakers of Times Square.

In effect, Tama Starr presides over an oxymoron: the neon sign, a traditional marker of modernity, is the product of traditional craft. One has only to look through her company's factory on West 57th Street to see these practices in action. In an area once devoted to light manufacturing, this is the last location in which something tangible is made. In an area controlled by media companies like the Columbia Broadcasting System and MTV, this is a place where the images of modernity are manufactured, in the true sense of the word's etymology "by hand," in shops bound by firmly-established rules of craft.[4]

The heart of the signmaking process lies in the shop of the glass benders, where four-foot lengths of coated glass tube are shaped and spliced into the many elements which will be individually wired onto the face of the neon sign. George Ylagan and Bert Vinocur are the masters of this area of the factory. They share techniques learned at opposite sides of the globe. George, who is now foreman, learned the craft of tube bending from his wife's family in the Philippines. His apprenticeship was served as Manila rebuilt after the devastation of conquest and occupation during World War II. Bert picked up the craft as an alternative to the Air Force Band, in which he at one time played trumpet. A third generation Brooklynite, he began right after the Second World War, when massive repairs on pre-War signs kept everyone busy.

Despite the different circumstances of their apprenticeships, George and Bert share the craft of the tube bender. They heat the tubes of glass over gas jets and quickly mould the pliable rods to a pattern drawn on fiberglass cloth. They view what they do as a craft, not an art. Creativity is not appreciated here; precision is the criterion. Skill is measured by the ability to stick to the pattern, to manipulate the glass through all sorts of angles and make splices without causing a crack to form, and to place the electrodes exactly in the spot indicated on the pattern.

These qualities of care and precision are prized because the functioning of the sign relies on very few characteristics, upon which there can be no compromise. There must be a tight seal within the completed element, or "unit," because the neon or argon gas must enter a stable chamber which has been evacuated and cleansed of all impurities. The electrodes mounted at either end can then ionize the gas to create the colors of the completed sign. The position of the electrode must be exact because each unit is fastened and wired to the custom-made face of the sign. More than a one centimeter mistake will cause the unit to break. If the job is done well, the sign should operate indefinitely.

The history of the craft has been passed down from master to apprentice ever since the expiration of the patent for neon signs in 1927, which released production to the public domain.[5] George's younger brother Mariano, more recently an immigrant from the Philippines, is presently learning the necessary techniques. The history of Artkraft's business is kept in the shop, too, in the scrolled patterns, stored underneath the workbenches and stuffed in pidgeon-holes in the walls, documenting all the signs produced by the company over the past several decades.

From the first artist's sketch to the final bolting of the sign on a skeleton located over Times Square, the entire signmaking process is controlled by Artkraft Strauss. The Starr family created the most spectacular of the neon signs before the War. Some of these spectaculars contained more than three kilometers of glass tubes. By stacking one layer of activity on top of another, the face of the sign could be put in motion by a complex system of motors, cams, and circuit breakers calibrated like notes in a music box. During the War Artkraft fashioned plaster versions of the Statue of Liberty and, late in the War, the raising of the flag on Iwo Jima, and transformed the Square into patriotic tableaux. During the fifties they advertised movies and plays and created the single most remembered sign in the Square — a Camel cigarette sign which blew actual smoke rings across the Square. They even survived the decline of Times Square and the invasion of plastic signs — often commissioned by new, Japanese sponsors — during the 1970s. Through all of this the Artkraft Strauss Sign Corporation blended together family history and craft traditions with the ability to capitalize on a prime location. Yet, by the time that Tama Starr entered the family business in earnest, in 1982, the nature of Times Square was beginning to change in a way which threatened this family enterprise. A new value was being projected onto the Square, one which required a different reading of the cityscape.

Cultural and financial value has been produced in Times Square ever since the place was given its name in 1904. Signified by the enormous signs which surround it, this arena of entertainment and visual excitement has come to represent the city — the freedom of the crowd and the danger of the unknown

Other. The desire to be seen at The Crossroads of the World accelerates a more conventional capitalization of land, a specific place, into rentable space within shiny, new buildings. It is important to see through the developers' eyes how a concrete entity, a potential building site, is raised to an abstraction, rentable space, and translated into monetary return on investment. In a capitalistic culture like that of the United States, in a city which was laid out in anticipation of land speculation and accumulation, this is the most powerful, transformative vision of Times Square.

The city encouraged developers to explore this part of the West, West of Sixth Avenue, through modifications to zoning laws passed in 1982. By adhering strictly to these laws, the densest buildings in Manhattan could be built around Times Square, especially on Seventh Avenue and Broadway, facing the heart of the Bow-Tie. Then, in 1984, the Urban Development Corporation, an authority invested by the city and the state of New York to encourage development in blighted areas, unveiled a huge project for the Crossroads of the World — the intersection of Broadway, Seventh Avenue, and 42nd Street. Suddenly, the Times Square area was doubly attractive. Not only was there the history of the Square and the glitz of the Broadway theatres surrounding it, but there was the promise of a state-sponsored project which would clean up an area of crime and decay with an influx of over 23,000 office workers who would inhabit four colossal buildings during the working day.

The land in Times Square was made even more valuable by the ways in which developers had become accustomed to handling building sites. Some of the vocabulary associated with the planning of a skyscraper seems to defy nature, but these words are important because they are concretely tied to the ability of a developer, who has to put together a deal worth over $250 million in order to construct an office tower in Times Square, to make a return on his massive investment. This vocabulary marks out the process through which a two-dimensional space, a building site, gets transformed into a volume of space which can be sold in cross-section, cubicle by cubicle and floor by floor, to businesses attracted not just by space, but by convenience and prestige.

The City of New York regulates the size of buildings through both height and density requirements. Of the two, the more important restriction is density, which is quantified through the Floor Area Ratio (FAR). This ratio is taken between the total size of the lot available for building and the total floor area of the building actually to be constructed. Thus, if a developer were allowed to do anything he or she wanted to in part of the city designated as FAR 14, then a building could rise which would cover the entire lot to 14 stories, or half the lot to 28, or one-quarter of the lot to 56.

There are, of course, regulations as to what can pass for architecture in the building lots of New York. But, amid the requirements for setbacks from the sidewalks and visual access for pedestrians to the sky, the developer and the architect are most concerned with the FAR allowance, for this supplies the multiplier yielding the maximum rentable space from a relatively small lot size. For years, the city has allowed developers a FAR "bonus" in return for civic improvements included in the building — a subway entrance inside the building rather than along the sidewalk, a public passageway through the building from street to street, a public sitting area within the building itself. Architects have become skilled at incorporating these amenities into designs so that taller, denser buildings can be built. Thus, for example, the 1982 density regulation in Times Square of FAR 18 could be easily turned into a more profitable FAR of 21.5.

Since the mid 1970s another way of capitalizing on space has developed, one which is especially fashionable in Times Square. This has to do with the selling of air rights over existing buildings. To see how this practice works, let us take a look at the Villard Houses, located on the East Side, on Madison Avenue, behind Saint Patrick's Cathedral, and the construction of the Palace Hotel in the Houses' air space. In 1974 the Catholic Archdiocese of New York allowed a developer, Harry Helmsley, to propose a large, 55 story hotel for the space over the Villard Houses, which the Archdiocese then owned. These Houses were by that time historic structures, having been declared so by the Landmarks Commission of the City of New York in 1968. Built in 1886 by the famous architectural firm of McKim, Mead, and White, the Houses were the last of the great nineteenth-century mansions to arise along Madison Avenue. The exterior was distinguished, the interior glamorous, especially the Gold Room, the most ornate formal ballroom in New York City.

Rather than tear down this historic structure, the Archdiocese sold the air rights to Harry Helmsley. That is, the Villard Houses were only five story buildings in an area dominated by skyscrapers. There was, consequently, a large column of unused air which could, legitimately, be occupied by a money-making building were the Villard Houses not squatting underneath. This column of air was transferred to a Helmsley property sitting just in back of the Houses, and the hotel which Helmsley built on that property thus received a part of this unused column from the Villard Houses in the form of a higher Floor Area Ratio. The signature of the "Palace" Hotel would then be the Houses themselves, which were largely to be transformed into reception rooms within the hotel. In return for extra rooms, offices, and the trappings of nineteenth-century opulence inside a $60 million building, Helmsley saved the Villard Houses, restored the Gold Room, and allowed civic organizations to inhabit one-third of the Houses at reduced rent. This was seemingly a good solution to the problem of what to do with an historic building which had become a financial liability to its owners. As the *New York Times* stated in a laudatory editorial, this was an ingenious way of creating a higher value for a property which was losing money. [6]

A smaller exercise in the capitalization of space has only recently taken place over the Museum of Modern Art, virtually around the corner from Times Square, on 53rd Street between Sixth and Fifth Avenues. The Museum

Figure 4. The Museum of Modern Art in the foreground transferred its air rights to the condominium directly behind it. Photography courtesy of the author.

of Modern Art entered the 1980s with a big problem. Although it was one of the premier institutions of its kind in the world, it could display only a small fraction of its artworks because of constricted exhibition space. Even the financial resources of a major Museum were insufficient for extensive remodeling or rebuilding, given the high costs of construction in Midtown Manhattan. Therefore, the Museum sold the air rights over its five story building so that a condominium could be built next door (figure 4). For this sale the Museum received $17 million and assistance in the $40 million remodeling of its exhibition space.

This practice of selling air rights to accumulate FAR offered both promise and peril for Times Square. Potentially, it signalled a chance to require change to occur in certain ways. The Broadway theatres, collectively one of the industries most profitable to and closely associated with New York City, could be protected through both requirements for the sale of air rights and the inducement of bonuses for new buildings sensitive to the theatre environment. However, the marketing of columns of air also guaranteed that the letter of the law would be adhered to, even prodded and transgressed, in the name of extra profit. This, in fact, was a tradition as old as the practice of selling air rights itself. For example, the construction over the Villard Houses was tolerated because it saved an historic building. The initial reaction to the proposed design of the Palace Hotel, however, was not favorable: "...this way of 'keeping' the landmark, which involves some physical destruction as well as the destruction of its integrity, and no real investment in its continued life, is a spurious trade-off. The city is being conned."7

The balance between public amenities and private speculation was not easily reached before the invasion of Times Square, as the experience with the Villard Houses showed. Certified as a cultural resource by the city, an historic building was considered a cultural commodity by the developer. During the mid- 1980s, with land prices soaring to over $2000 per square foot in the heart of Times Square, an equilibrium between the existing built environment and the wishes of developers, architects, and corporate clients was even harder to maintain. Times Square in 1984 was thus a good match for the imagination of the developer. It offered many low-rise, delapidated buildings which could be assembled into building sites. The flavor of the area was spiced by the presence of Broadway theatres, which were important both for what they were and for what they represented. That is, to the luster of a Broadway address could be added the more tangible possibility of the sale of air rights. And there was the prospect of removing some of the pungency of a visibly run-down area through the construction of public anemities which would result in FAR bonuses for the enterprising and civic-minded developer.

The easiest reading of the redevelopment of Times Square is a Marxist one.8 This allows for analysis of the stratigraphy of the canyon of Times Square and would add a narrative to account for the geologic upheavals which have taken place there in the late 1980s. The allure of space and the power of money have come together forcefully in the redevelopment of Times Square. However, the victory of multinational capital has not been complete. Taken in the context of other development frenzies in New York, it is interesting to see how the city, almost against its will, has acted on behalf of what it considers to be the public interest to control the appropriation of space through the planning and zoning process.

Capital amasses faster than the will of the public to control it. Therefore, the first developments in Times Square show the clearest examples of a class appropriation of space. In 1982 the developer-architect John Portman constructed a large hotel on the West side of Times Square. For the construction of this almost universally-reviled building, five theatres, among them two of the most famous on Broadway, were destroyed. In their place was created a phenomenon not seen before in New York. First of all, the Marriott Marquis Hotel — known colloquially as "the Portman Hotel," lest anyone forget — surrounded the column of air allotted to it with structure through the incorporation of a huge, 40-story high atrium at the center of the hotel. Second, the building sent out an "anti-urban, anti-pedestrian message"9 to the most highly-urban walking city in the country. And finally, the hotel ignored its surroundings by adding nothing to the Great White Way, the nocturnal ambiance of light (figure 5).

The effect of the hotel was startling. For the pedestrian the structure was downright forbidding. The entrance to Times Square itself consisted of a narrow, blind arcade, the kind of constricting space, beyond the vigilance of walkers on the sidewalk, in which danger could possibly lie. The functional entrance to the hotel was around the corner, on 46th Street, signalled by a lighted marquee at the bottom of a 175 meter high wall of concrete. This drive-in entrance would present the hotel adequately to a customer stepping from a cab or limousine; it did not signal welcome to a walker employing the most typical mode of transportation in New York.

Further, as one quickly discovered, the lobby for the hotel was on the 6th floor. After negotiating the entrance, one had to pass by polished mirrors framed by clear incandescent light bulbs and enter one of several gondola-shaped elevators — a signature of Portman designs — to reach a lobby which opened into the Shangri-la of the atrium. The message here was clear: the passport to this space was plastic — the vernacular for a credit card with enough line of available credit to absorb the hefty room charges. In return for money, the architecture of the hotel guaranteed a sanitized space — a middle-class haven in the aggressively heterogeneous environment of Times Square.10

Scale and money are tied together. Not only was this a tall, dense intrusion into an area dominated by two- to ten-story buildings, but the Marriott Marquis was so intent on enclosing private space rather than contributing to a public place that it offered only a large color transparency, like the snapshot of a tourist, to Times Square itself. People concerned with the environment of Times Square — the historic preservation community, the signmakers at Artkraft Strauss, not to mention the inhabitants of the nearby lower-middle-class community of Hell's Kitchen — heard clearly what the Hotel was saying. One architectural critic put the language of the building into words:

Figure 5. During 1987 the Marriot was especially visible due to all the construction in Times Square. Photograph courtesy of the author.

Here, in my sealed box is a little imitation city, in which you will be safe from the spontaneous hurly-burly outside. The air you breathe will be pure, nothing you look upon will give offense, no accident will take place more serious than the spilling of a canapé. Rather than have you waste your energy on walking, I will move you about on rotating platforms. I will provide you with a utopian Main Street, from which every urban irritant has been purged.[11]

The second major announcement for the Times Square area was the 1984 proposal for the 42nd Street Redevelopment Project, sponsored by the Urban Development Corporation (UDC). Right at the Crossroads of the World, the intersection of Seventh Avenue, Broadway, and 42nd Street, the UDC proposed four of the densest buildings in New York. Even with the generous allowances of the 1982 zoning for Times Square, buildings could only achieve an FAR of 21.5. The four UDC sanctioned buildings, designed by the famous architect Philip Johnson, topped out at FAR 46. While the Portman Hotel attempted to control space by enclosing it, the Johnson towers threatened to conquer the area by overwhelming it with an army of office workers.

The fight over the 42nd Street Redevelopment project is long, complicated, and incomplete. Because of the density of the buildings an Environmental Impact Statement had to be filed. Americans associate these statements with the public lands of the West — how the "harvesting" of large quantities of trees in a National Forest would affect both wildlife and the recreational use of a specific area, for example. In the case of the 42nd Street project, the study had to anticipate the physical effect that the buildings would have (the change in the air currents, the shadows thrown by the buildings at various times of year), the impact that the buildings would have on the infrastructure of the area (how street use, commuter patterns, and subway travel would be changed), and the change that would be felt in the economy of the Times Square district (not only what the office workers would buy during the day but what would happen to nearby neighborhoods should they decide to move closer to their work).

The sponsor of the project, a public authority, had responsibilities to both the city and the state. The machinery of the Environmental Impact Statement mandated public comment. Thus, a $2 billion project, favored by city and state officials, lost momentum during the years of public comment, innumerable lawsuits, and expressions of professional outrage among architects, civic groups, and sociologists. The Project has yet to be built, although the buildings have been redesigned more than once.

The fundamental problem faced by the Project is lodged in an irony more complicated than any of the lawsuits which occupied so much time from 1984 to 1987: if the Project was designed to clean up an area of blight and thereby encourage developers into nearby Times Square, then it had succeeded without having been built. The *Wall Street Journal* voiced the unutterable: "Should government carry out massive public projects after economic conditions, and perhaps the very reasons for doing a project, have changed?"[12] Pondering this conundrum, the Project remains ·a prospect rather than a reality.

The reality of the new Times Square has taken shape since 1984. Taking advantage of the 1982 zoning allowance of FAR 18, five sites were assembled in the heart of Times Square between the middle of 1984 and the end of 1987. Although more recent zoning requirements have reduced the bulk of buildings to FAR 14, these five sites were "grandfathered" in — that is, because these buildings were begun before the enforcement of the new rules, on Friday, May 13, 1988, they were allowed to conform to the older, more generous rules. Since 1986 there has been regulation of the visual aspect of Times Square: signs are now required on new buildings and the skyscrapers must step back from the street to maintain the bowl effect of Times Square. Finally, since 1987 there have been new use requirements for the structures now being finished in Times Square. That is, 5% of the total space of the skyscrapers must be devoted to "entertainment-related uses." The last of these regulations created the most vociferous opposition, even though several of the development sites contained existing Broadway theatres, which had surrendered their air rights, and these theatres could be counted in that small percentage.

What are we to make of this continuing story of the commodification and consumption of Times Square? First of all, it is interesting to note how architecture at this scale ceases to be either art or design but is transformed by the power of capital into social engineering. As Ada Louise Huxtable, one of the most perceptive critics of the building boom in New York, points out: "one must come to the reluctant conclusion that at this level of overbuilding and its attendant problems, aesthetics cancel out. Architecture simply doesn't count."[13] Thomas Bender, one of the most insightful commentators on New York culture, has written about an earlier conquest of the city by commercialism at the beginning of the twentieth century in terms of the transformation from the horizontal to the vertical.[14] Taken in these terms, New York may now be entering the apotheosis of this phase — the emergence of a conglomerate aesthetic. When one looks at the most famous skyscrapers on the pre-1980 New York skyline, one can associate the buildings with the products of the corporations inhabiting them: dry goods, gasoline, magazines. The new Times Square is being sold to corporations one step removed from actual goods: brokerage houses, banks, law firms. This appropriation of space is symbolized by the battle over signs. A family tradition produced these spectaculars, and real goods are being advertised: Canon, Coke, Panasonic. The new inhabitants want a quiet place to work. Like the sign maker, the developer, on behalf of his client, looks for a node of activitiy within the city. The sign maker, however, seeks flamboyantly to have his or her product seen within a vital place that must be lively both day and night. The developer and

166

his architect desire bulk and an attractive space to market.

The irony is that the sort of sedimented capitalism one sees in Times Square — individual entrepeneurs (both legal and illicit), family-run operations, and corporate ventures of all sorts — cannot be reproduced in a designed environment. As Paul Goldberger, the present architecture critic for the *New York Times*, says:

> It is not really possible to have a place that is at once both a formal, dignified office environment and a lively entertainment district; some side of this equation has to give....There are, after all, numerous other parts of town in which office buildings can be erected, but nowhere else in which Times Square's particular characteristics can be reproduced. The honky-tonk vitality of Times Square and its incomparable visual energy have no equal in New York, and if they are to be lost in the current wave of office construction, they will be lost forever.[15]

It is important to note that the theatre-owners have wavered through this whole period of development. They rely on the vitality of the Times Square scene, which their defenders often visualize in ecological terms. On the other hand, they are the biggest property owners in the area and they can make more money from the sale of a theatre or its air rights than any production could yield.

How one describes a culturally significant place in which very few people actually live is a particular problem in Times Square. In the debate over Times Square, the representative figure is the tourist.[16] This is a fine touristic space. One can acquire things at every turn from sellers both legal and shady. The middle-class culture of Broadway can be obtained, most ritually by standing in line at the TKTS booth,[17] congenially braving the cabs, smog, and pan-handlers in search of half-price, same-day tickets. And, from that triangular vantage point, there are countless opportunities for visual appropriation: the signs, buildings, and vistas of which slide shows are made. By placing themselves in the center of the action, this mob of tourists becomes a part of the attraction.

The tourist and the office worker have in common a middle-class canon of tastes.[18] In fact, if one sees these two groups as nearly identical, an interesting dialectic appears between the outsides and the insides of these new buildings. Times Square can retain its value as a cultural node only if the new environment simulates The Great White Way of legend. It is no surprise, therefore, that signage requirements were met with grumbling, but little real resistance; everyone should feel the wonder and excitement that the tourist so sedulously seeks. However, once inside the buildings, one has entered a machine, indistinguishable from any corporate headquarters or monument to real estate development anywhere. Tinkering under the skin of the building threatens profitability.

The struggle over design requirements for the new buildings enacts the search for an authenticity which will be all surfaces and will re-commodify the thoroughly encrusted surroundings of Times Square. That is, those signs which remain will become important as metonymic decorations which remind viewers that they are standing in an area which was once a special environment. There are interesting systems of exchange here: tourists and office workers become part of the spectacle and are themselves the subjects of observation; buildings simulate an environment which by their scale and use they destroy.19

The sustainability of family businesses and craft traditions in the face of an incorporated America; the maintenance of public space; the design of both space and structure for the complex needs of an urban culture; the nature of the American theatre as an art form or business; the definition of "district" and "neighborhood" — all of these issues are being addressed, in public, by city agencies, artists, designers and architects, civic groups, and even sundry academics. Space and culture are being contested in Times Square. The power of capital has procured space within the Square; the ability of the city to mould the space to its use is still being tested.

References

1. M. Christine Boyer, *Manhattan Manners: Architecture and Style, 1850-1900*. New York: Rizzoli, 1985, p. 8.
2. Alan Trachtenberg, *Brooklyn Bridge: Fact and Symbol*. Chicago: University of Chicago Press, 1965, p. 32.
3. Boyer, *op. cit.*, p. 8.
4. Information on the signmaking process is the product of observations and interviews I conducted at the Artkraft factory during 1987 and 1988. I wish to thank Tama Starr, George Ylagan, and Bert Vinocur for their generosity.
5. See Rudi Stern, *The New Let There Be Neon*. New York: H. N. Abrams, 1988.
6. *New York Times*, September 18, 1975.
7. *New York Times*, June 22, 1975. This article was written by Ada Louise Huxtable, the newspaper's influential architecture critic.
8. The most persuasive urban geographer who speaks from a Marxist perspective is David Harvey. See especially *The Urban Experience*. Baltimore: Johns Hopkins University Press, 1989, which condenses two of his previous works.
9. Susan Woldenberg, "The Future of Times Square," *New Criterion* V (February 1987), p. 28.
10. For a reading of Portman hotels which places the atrium and the gondola elevator within the Postmodern period, see Frederic Jameson, "Post-

modernism, or the Cultural Logic of Late Capitalism," *New Left Review* 146 (1984), pp. 53-92, reprinted in condensed form as "Postmodernism and Consumer Society," in *Postmodern Culture*, Hal Foster, ed. Port Townsend, Washington: Bay Press, 1983.

11. Woldenberg, *op. cit.*, p. 36.
12. *Wall Street Journal*, June 30, 1987.
13. Ada Louise Huxtable, *The Tall Building Artistically Reconsidered: The Search for a Skyscraper Style*. New York: Pantheon Books, 1984, p. 105.
14. See especially his essay "Culture and Architecture: Some Aesthetic Tensions in the Shaping of Modern New York City" in William Sharpe and Leonard Wallock, eds., *Visions of the Modern City*. New York: Columbia University Press, 1983.
15. *New York Times*, January 30, 1987.
16. See Dean McCannell, *The Tourist: A New Theory of the Leisure Class*. New York: Schocken Books, 1976.
17. TKTS is an abbreviation for "tickets." The booth, designed by a famous architectural firm, literally puts in the foreground the central activity of the area — Broadway plays. With the top price for Broadway plays now at $46, the booth is a popular place.
18. See Lyn Lofland, *A World of Strangers: Order and Action in Urban Public Space*.New York: Basic Books, 1973, especially p. 90 ff.
19. As of spring 1990 the five new structures are virtually complete and promise quick inhabitation, even in a rental market which has turned down with the economy of the city. The four towers of the 42nd Street project were redesigned in late 1989 and continued to be promised – by 1994. They remain for the present only in the drawings of the firm of Johnson & Burgee and in the models of the Urban Development Corporation. The Artkraft Strauss Sign Corporation is awash in orders for decorative neon. The drama of the capitalist metropolis continues.

Not For Sale:
Some American Poets' Perspectives on the American Dream

F. Richard Thomas
Michigan State University

The World is too much with us; late and soon,
Getting and spending, we lay waste our powers;
Little we see in Nature that is ours,
We have given our hearts away, a sordid boon!
William Wordsworth, "The World Is Too Much with Us," 1807.

Like most teachers, if I want to learn about something, I decide to teach about
it. Thus, I picked the American Dream as my focus for a course in American
Thought & Language—an interdisciplinary writing course for undergraduate
students. The first day of class, I asked my students to write a page that
defined and exemplified their version of the American Dream. Seventy-nine
of my eighty-one students indicated that they viewed the American Dream as
the opportunity for individual gain—for individual economic success and
therefore power—to be happy, to be secure, to rule others, to buy and
consume desired goods. Only two of the eighty-one students referred to the
"liberty and justice" ideals of the Pledge of Allegiance or the egalitarian ideals
of the Declaration of Independence and exemplified their dreams in ways that
could be construed to show their concern and desire for a community of
people working toward the happiness and well-being of everyone. Needless
to say, I was disturbed by my impromptu survey, and glad that I had chosen
the American Dream as a focus for the course, for I believed the American
Dream to be much more profound, and this idea is what I wanted to teach.
The books I used included Robert Bellah, et al. *Habits of the Heart*,[1] Marvin
Harris's *America Now*,[2] Studs Terkel's *American Dreams: Lost and
Found*,[3] and a number of shorter articles in a course packet.
    While I was teaching the class, I began to see that what I was learning had
relevance for one of my main interests—American poetry. Having read,
studied, and even written poetry myself for more than thirty years, I recognized the pervasiveness of a theme that runs through a number of contemporary

American poets. That theme is as follows: At one time we knew our place in nature and community, and we strived for liberty and equality and happiness, not only for ourselves but for others in our community and in our nation; now, we seem to be "one dimensional" (to borrow terminology from Herbert Marcuse [4]) and strive only for individual wealth in order to buy the goods that will make us individually happy.

Walt Whitman of course is the spiritual father of many contemporary American poets, and the American Dream he announces has inspired poets for almost a century and a half. Through him, the idea that nature is the primal source of political equality and therefore American democracy sings. We are all, literally, brothers and sisters in Whitman's political ideology, which is grounded in the natural, sexual procreative urge to life. We are all literally brothers and sisters not only with the rest of humanity, but also with animals, plants, trees, the "leaves of grass." Our American Dream is guided by natural divine law that requires commitment not only to the individual but also to the community and nature in which the individual lives. If we fulfill the commitment we will achieve, as Whitman says in "Song of Myself," form, union, plan, eternal life, happiness (verse 50).

The American Dream as it is revealed in Whitman is wondrous because it evokes the possibility of radical equality, of wholeness—of oneness with all people, all nature. To experience Whitman is to experience the form, union, equality, liberty, community, democracy, and happiness that constitutes his American Dream of 1855. Many poets writing today, while appreciating and often accepting the Whitmanian American Dream, also recognize that it has all but disappeared in contemporary society. Their poems, therefore, are 1) observations of an America that has lost its inspirational Dream, 2) pleas for the revitalization of the Whitmanian American Dream, and 3) expressions of despair over the passing of this American Dream. Sometimes all of these ideas come together in one poem.

Perhaps the most famous of our contemporary poets, who also clearly acknowledge their debt to Whitman, are the Beats. Allen Ginsberg in his notorious *Howl* condemns Moloch, his symbol of the forces destructive of individuals in American society, the "sphinx of cement and aluminum [who] bashed open their skulls and ate up their brains and imagination. . .whose blood is running money!"[5] In fact an anthology of poems — observations, pleas, and expressions of despair — by Ginsberg alone could be collected on a debased American Dream. Hayden Carruth, poet, former editor of *Poetry* magazine, and editor of the excellent anthology of American poetry titled *The Voice That Is Great Within Us*,[6] says "We live in an age in which the collapse of all previous standards coincides with the perfection in technique for the centralized distribution of ideas; some kind of revolution is inevitable and will as inevitably be imposed from above by a minority." These words, he says, were written in 1933. "In the half-century since then," Carruth continues with words that might also be used to describe Ginsberg's Moloch, "we have experienced its truth; the revolution has occurred. The minority from above is clearly the corporate will of our commercial megalosaurians; the technique for centralized distribution is clearly electronics; and the 'ideas' are our own conditioned responses."7 William Stafford's short poem "Being an American" observes the debasement of the American Dream by the individual's substitution of reality with the acceptance of and consumption of electronic images and the idea that happiness can be bought by consuming.

> Some network has bought history, all the rights
> for wars and games. At home the rest of us
> wait. Nothing happens, of course.
> We know that somewhere our times are
> alive and flashing, for real. We sigh.
> If we had been rich we could have lived
> like that. Maybe even yet we could buy
> a little bit of today and see how it is.8

Randall Jarrell (1914-1965) begins his poem "Next Day" with the image of the shopper who has learned to ignore the human community and focus on her purchases.

> Moving from Cheer to Joy, from Joy to All,
> I take a box
> And add it to my wild rice, my Cornish game hens.
> The slacked or shorted, basketed, identical
> Food-gathering flocks
> Are selves I overlook. Wisdom, said William James,
> Is learning what to overlook. And I am wise
> If that is wisdom. Yet somehow, as I buy
> All from these shelves
> And the boy takes it to my station wagon,
> What I've become
> Troubles me even if I shut my eyes. . . .9

Howard Nemerov satirizes the degraded American Dream in "Boom!: Sees Boom in Religion, Too" a poem that is a reaction to a printed statement by President Eisenhower's pastor, Edward L.R. Elson of the National Presbyterian Church in Washington, who said, "These fruits of material progress have provided the leisure, the energy, and the means for a level of human and spiritual values never before reached." Nemerov's poem ends like this:

> But now the gears mesh and the tires burn
> and the ice chatters in the shaker and the priest
> in the pulpit, and Thy Name, O Lord,
> is kept before the public, while the fruits

172

ripen and religion booms and the level rises
and every modern convenience runneth over,
that it may never be with us as it hath been
with Athens and Karnak and Nagasaki,
nor Thy sun for one instant refrain from shining
on the rainbow Buick by the breezeway
or the Chris Craft with the uplift life raft;
that we may continue to be the just folks we are,
plain people with ordinary superliners and
disposable diaperliners, people of the stop'n'shop
'n'pray as you go, of hotel, motel, boatel,
the humble pilgrims of no deposit no return
and please adjust thy clothing, who will give to
                                        Thee,
if Thee will keep us going, our annual
Miss Universe, for Thy Name's Sake, Amen.[10]

Andrei Codrescu, poet-comentator on National Public Radio's "All Things Considered" and editor of *Exquisite Corpse* review has edited a poetry anthology entitled *American Poetry Since 1970: Up Late*, which is a plea for change.[11] "It has become increasingly difficult," says Codrescu in his Introduction, "to distinguish reality from the illusions of commodity culture . . . . The making of community against anti-social technology is the chief object of poetry gathered here. [The poems in this anthology are] an incantation against the organized forgetting of capitalism. The purging of the commodity church is an agonizing process and it is not ironic, though it is often hilarious. Demystifying in order to believe is steady work. Sometimes black, most often purgative, humor is one of the ritual constants of this generation, whose poetic physiognomy is shaped by an erotic and sometimes unstoppably gruesome laughter" (*Late*, xxxviii).

An exemplification of this demystifying, purgative black humor is the poem by Anselm Hollo, "manifest destiny."

to arrive in front of a large video screen,
in pleasantly air-conditioned home with big duck pond in back
some nice soft drinks by elbow, some good american snacks as well,
at least four hundred grand in the bank, & that's for checking,
an undisclosed amount in investments, & a copacetic evening
watching the latest military *techne*
wipe out poverty everywhere in the world
in its most obvious form, the poor (Late, 60)

And another by Hollo:

t.v. (1)

"for he is ishi the last of his tribe"
"couldn't help noticing your aftershave"
the brain which takes that in its stride
is yours & mine & it is late (Late, 64)

Two further examples—not in the Codrescu anthology, but by poets who are
active today, reveal that the poems of purgative humor, by the very fact of
their being written and requesting an audience, are pleas to change the values
of consumer culture. Marge Piercy's "Barbie Doll" reads:

This girlchild was born as usual
and presented dolls that did pee-pee
and miniature GE stoves and irons
and wee lipsticks the color of cherry candy.
Then in the magic of puberty, a classmate said:
You have a great big nose and fat legs.

She was healthy, tested intelligent,
possessed strong arms and back,
abundant sexual drive and manual dexterity.
She went to and fro apologizing.
Everyone saw a fat nose on thick legs.

She was advised to play coy,
exhorted to come on hearty,
exercise, diet, smile and wheedle.
Her good nature wore out
like a fan belt.
So she cut off her nose and her legs
and offered them up.

In the casket displayed on satin she lay
with the undertaker's cosmetics painted on,
a turned-up putty nose,
dressed in a pink and white nightie.
Doesn't she look pretty? everyone said.
Consummation at last.
To every woman a happy ending. (CAP, 409)

Every American at one time or another has received a magazine-sweep-
stakes-advertisement in which, as a result of computer technology, the name
and address of the addressee appear as a personal touch to the come-on letter.

174

Donald Kummings reveals this degradation of the American Dream in the
following poem entitled "Letter for Henry: *Poeme Trouve*."

This notification of eligibility
has been specially prepared for:

H.D.Thoreau
Thoreau Lyceum
156 Belknap Street
Concord, Massachusetts 01742

Yes, MR. HENRY DAVID THOREAU, you *already* may have won
the grand prize
in this year's *Reader's Digest* Sweepstakes.
Just think of it!
Walking to your mailbox
in CONCORD
and finding there made out to YOU
a certified check
for $1,000,000.
YOU could pay off all your bills,
invest for the future,
and still have plenty left
to treat the THOREAU family
to some pretty fancy luxuries.

Or: How about one of these colossal prizes?
A G.E. 1000 Giant-Screen TV!
A sumptuous Bourbon-Toned Mink Coat!
A 33' Morgan Sailing Yacht!
A European Holiday for Two!
A Customized Cobra Motorhome!

If you roll down BELKNAP STREET
in a brand new Cadillac Seville,
loaded with options,
or in a sporty Corvette—
a car you pay for in cash—
imagine the look on the faces of your neighbors! 12

Louis Simpson uses his poetry primarily as a vehicle for social criticism.
Editor and critic A. Poulin, Jr. says that "Simpson's quarrel is more specifically with America. It is an ongoing struggle to come to grips with the
pathetic or tragic failure of the American dream and myth—especially as

announced by Whitman. 'Where are you, Walt?/ The Open Road goes to the used-car lot,' [Simpson] says in 'Walt Whitman at Bear Mountain'" (CAP, 664). Two short poems reveal Simpson's despair:

In The Suburbs

There's no way out.
You were born to waste your life.
You were born to this middleclass life

As others before you
Were born to walk in procession
To the temple, singing. (CAP, 466)

American Poetry

Whatever it is, it must have
A stomach that can digest
Rubber, coal, uranium, moons, poems.

Like the shark, it contains a shoe.
It must swim for miles through the desert
Uttering cries that are almost human. (CAP, 468)

David Ignatow reluctantly and with a great deal of anxiety became involved in his father's bindery business. Perhaps more than any other poet represented here, he has wrestled with the American Dream as announced by Whitman. Whitman, he says, "remains the important factor to whom we must address ourselves. We address ourselves as sons to a father who finds his sons no longer believing in what he has to say, but who are taking, point for point, everything he had to say and showing how it is the opposite of what he thought or hoped for. . . . How do we console ourselves in a world that can no longer be motivated by the ideals of the nineteenth century? We haven't any ideals to speak of now and the spirituality is the sense of defeat."[13]

Ignatow's poem, "For One Moment" reveals a life of "quiet desperation," to use Thoreau's words, in a society that has no ideals apart from business and the dollar:

You take the dollar
and hand it to the fellow beside you
who turns and gives it to the next one
down the line. The world being round,

you stand waiting, smoking, and lifting
a cup of coffee to your lips, talking
of seasonal weather and hinting
at problems. The dollar returns,
the coffee spills to the ground
in your hurry. You have the money
in one hand, a cup in the other,
a cigarette in your mouth,
and for one moment have forgotten
what it is you have to do,
your hair grey, your legs weakened
from long standing.[14]

Ignatow's poem, "The Dream," reveals the despair of attempts to empathize with the victims of consumer culture and despair at the loss of communal values:

Someone approaches to say his life is ruined
and to fall down at your feet
and pound his head upon the sidewalk.
Blood spreads in a puddle.
And you, in a weak voice, plead
with those nearby for help;
your life takes on his desperation.
He keeps pounding his head.
It is you who are fated;
and you fall down beside him.
It is then you are awakened,
the body gone, the blood washed from the ground,
the stores lit up with their goods.[15]

How total does Ignatow find the loss of communal values in the face of what is—the material items of consumer culture, "the stores lit up with their goods." Fortunately, poems of despair, like the pleas and less desperate observations of other poets, are signs of hope. As long as a poet can evoke the despair within us, there is a chance that we might feel strongly enough to take action. The poem itself is an act against hopelessness.

Contemporary American poet, farmer, and social critic Wendell Berry is an example of the poet who has spent a great part of his life writing poetry and essays and living the life by which he hopes to instruct us in the possibility of a revitalized American Dream even in the face of apparently hopeless odds. Berry defines the human condition as one in which the individual lives within a "system of systems": "This system might be suggested by a sketch of five concentric circles, with the innermost representing the individual human, the second representing the family, the third the community, the fourth agriculture, and the outermost and largest representing nature. So long as the smaller systems are enclosed within the larger, and so long as all are connected by complex patterns of interdependency, as we know they are, then whatever affects one system will affect the others. It seems that this system of systems is safe so long as each system is controlled by the next larger one. If at any one point the hierarchy is reversed, the destruction of the entire system begins."

Berry implies, of course, that this is exactly what consumer society does; it reverses the hierarchy by presuming the individual can become the larger circle that encloses nature. It ignores the fact that "humans have a place in Creation and that this place is limited by responsibility on the one hand and by humility on the other." Consumer society makes us one-dimensional, it specializes our thinking, it abstracts our intellect, it separates us from nature, from the living earth, from the responsibility and the humility that comes with the recognition of our interdependence in the system of systems. The "looking out for number one" mentality that appears to dominate the minds of college students today, the abrogation of the interdependent consciousness, and the one-dimensional consciousness that assumes that happiness can be realized by the consumption of material goods and electronic imagery — these exemplify the way in which the hierarchy of the systems is reversed in contemporary thought. [16]

"Man will perish," says poet Stanley Kunitz, echoing not only Berry but also Whitman, "unless he learns that the web of the universe is a continuous tissue. Touch it an any point, and the whole web shudders."[17] "Poets, as few others," says poet Gary Snyder, "must live close to the world that primitive men are in: the world in its nakedness, which is fundamental for all of us—birth, love, death; the sheer fact of being alive."[18] Most of Snyder's poetry celebrates his intimate connection with the natural world and he attempts to divorce himself, like Berry, from the one-dimensional, the consumerist American dream, in his poetry, in his essays, and in his life.

Despite the great number of excellent poets who write poems on the "world in its nakedness, which is fundamental for all of us," there are an extraordinary number of people who call themselves poets who never write on anything that comes close to touching on the human condition. In fact, there are disturbing signs that the increase in the number of people who call themselves poets may in fact be a consequence of consumer culture. Poet-essayist Donald Hall in *Poetry and Ambition* explains that,

> Today the American industrial corporation provides the template, and the university models itself on General Motors. Corporations exist to create or discover consumers' desires and fulfill them with something that satisfies briefly and needs frequent repetition. . .
> Thus: Our poems, in their charming and interchangeable quantity, do not presume to the status of "Lycidas"—for that would be elitist and un-

American. We write and publish the McPoem—ten billion served—which becomes our contribution to the history of literature as the Model T is our contribution to a history which runs from bare feet past elephant and rickshaw to the vehicles of space. Pull in any time day or night, park by the busload, and the McPoem waits on the steam shelf for us, wrapped and protected, indistinguishable, indistinguished, and reliable—the good old McPoem identical from coast to coast and in all the little towns between, subject to the quality control of the least common denominator.

And every year, Ronald McDonald takes the Pulitzer.

To produce the McPoem, institutions must enforce patterns, institutions within institutions, all subject to the same glorious dominance of unconscious economic determinism, template and formula of consumerism.

"The McPoem is the product of the workshops of Hamburger University."[19]

While it is true that we seem to have a surfeit of poets who write McPoems—pleasant, lightweight, predictable poems that 1) do not make connections with the fundamentals of existence, 2) are uninformed by purpose, history, or nature, 3) do not "by [their] language make art's new object,"[20] and therefore, 4) seem to be written solely for their marketability—it is also true that we still have a number of poets who are able, like Whitman, whose vision was profound, to see through the veneer of consumerism and recognize our essential interdependence with nature and humanity. Some of these are the poets I have quoted here who recognize what poet Lewis Hyde so convincingly shows to be the nature of their works of art. "A work of art," says Hyde in *The Gift: Imagination and the Erotic Life of Property* "is a gift, not a commodity. Or to state the modern case with more precision . . . works of art exist simultaneously in two 'economies,' a market and a gift economy. Only one of these is essential, however: a work of art can survive without the market, but where there is no gift there is no art."[21] "If I am right," he continues, "to say that where there is no gift there is no art, then it may be possible to destroy a work of art by converting it into a pure commodity." This may already be the case with the McPoems and the plethora of McPoets who are writing them. Not only are McPoets unable to see their place in history and nature, they do not perceive their works as gifts, but as items that will advance their image or fame or salability as university professors (for example) teaching creative writing courses in consumer culture.

Poet-fiction writer George Garrett in "How It Is; How It Was; How It Will Be," which explores the writer's relationship with business, says "It is a fact that no serious writer of fiction or poetry has or will have even a ghost of a percentage of a chance of earning a living by and from writing alone. (Most of the pop writers don't either.) Maybe John Updike is an exception of a kind, but the only serious writer in this century to create and leave a real estate, worthy, say, of a doctor or a lawyer or a reasonably successful corporate executive, was John O'Hara. . . . All of which means that any sane and reasonable writer must be able to disregard almost completely the economic aspects of the craft. These not only can, but also should, be ignored. . . . The art and craft of writing is not trivial. It is not a business at all and has not been so for most of this century. . . . Serious writing, the absence of which would be a national disaster and a national shame, is outside of the network of the economy. By definition, then, serious writing is not a matter of dollars and cents. Forget about dollars and cents."[22]

Do the writers of poems and McPoems find it impossible to forget about dollars and cents in the United States? I don't see how any American poets can completely forget about dollars and cents, when they know that it is up to each one of them, individually, to be sure that they have enough money to buy health, dental, and retirement care. Most poets try not to think of the other potential purchases—that seem to have become needs—like straight teeth for daughter Jennifer and running and walking and tennis and golf and soccer and gym and basketball and dress shoes for son Tony. But if the American poets do think about these items of status and sometimes apparent need, they are likely also to think about the possibility, with their gift for words, of writing Hallmark greeting cards or TV ads. This is the constant dilemma of the poet in consumer society (especially U.S. consumer society, where there are no comprehensive national health, dental, or retirement plans).

An American poet and fiction writer told me of his change of jobs from college professor to ad-man. "When I was a teacher," he said, "I worked hard, but I was not appreciated by my bosses, and that showed in my low salary. Now, as an adman, I work hard and I'm appreciated by my boss and he rewards me with lots of money. Unfortunately, I knew that teaching was worthwhile; it meant something. What I'm doing now is totally meaningless, so I use my money to buy toys to make me feel good."[23]

"Every culture," says Hyde, "offers its citizens an image of what it is to be a man or woman of substance. There have been times and places in which a person came into his or her social being through the dispersal of gifts, the 'big man' or 'big woman' being that one through whom the most gifts flowed. The mythology of a market society reverses the picture: getting rather than giving is the mark of a substantial person, and the hero is 'self-possessed,' 'self-made.' So long as these assumptions rule, a disquieting sense of triviality, of worthlessness even, will nag the man or woman who labors in the service of a gift and whose products are not adequately described as commodities. Where we reckon our substance by acquisitions, the gifts of the gifted man are powerless to make him substantial." Another difficulty of the contemporary artist is living in "a land which feels no reciprocity toward nature, in an age in which the rich imagine themselves to be 'self-made'. . ." Nevertheless, our gift-givers remain. The poets quoted here — Wordsworth,

Whitman, Berry, Carruth, Garrett, Ginsberg, Hall, Hollo, Hyde, Ignatow, Jarrell, Kummings, Kunitz, Nemerov, Piercy, Simpson, and Snyder — are but a very, very few of those gift-givers.

American Indian tribes of the Pacific coast returned the intact bones of the first salmon caught back to the sea, believing, as Hyde says, "if they were not, the salmon would be offended and might not return the following year with their gift of winter food. . . .The first salmon ceremony establishes a gift relationship with nature, a formal give-and-take that acknowledges our participation in, and dependence upon, natural increase. And where we have established such a relationship we tend to respond to nature as part of ourselves, not as a stranger or alien available for exploitation. Gift exchange brings with it, therefore, a built-in check upon the destruction of its objects; with it we will not destroy nature's renewable wealth except where we also consciously destroy ourselves. Where we wish to preserve natural increase, therefore, gift exchange is the commerce of choice, for it is a commerce that harmonizes with, or participates in, the process of that increase."

I can personally vouch for the power of the gift. In 1974 when I left Denmark with my family after a one year stay, I had no idea that I would ever return. I expressed some of my sadness about the finality of my leave in a poem that was dedicated and given to a friend who taught at the University of Copenhagen. It goes like this:

Friends

That cold fall day
when we were first together
walking across an empty field,
we saw a wave of sparrows
crash against the grass.
That was beautiful, we said;
and final: the field stood
dead still again
except for our walking.

Yesterday
I was thinking:
now that we must say goodbye,
I would like to leave you as slowly
as a grey winter day.
But I wouldn't
know what to say
sitting there
thinking I should say something
about parting,
my throat corked,

181

my mind stuck,
the passing time
tearing words
from the corners of my mouth.

I would like to say:
Today
I saw a wave of sparrows
crash against the grass.
But they leapt up again
above the houses and trees
and for an instant
in the upper air
caught fire.[24]

I believe that this poem, as a gift, and others like it have participated in the process of increase. They have played a part in my returning to Denmark for two more years and they have, both literally and metaphorically, introduced me to new friends here in Denmark. These poems are partly responsible for the fact that both of my children are bi-lingual — able to speak both Danish and English. And there is no doubt in my mind that they have something to do with my being in Denmark today, 18 August 1989. The experiences that I and my family have had as a result of our life in Denmark have come about because of a mutual dream that both my wife and I had when we were very young—to try to become citizens of the world, and to give something to that world through poetry, study, scholarship, and teaching. This, of course, we have only meagerly accomplished. Clearly we have not escaped the pressures nor the allure of consumer society, but I believe we have been able to modify our perceptions of what goods and comforts are "necessary" in order to pursue our communitarian dream that requires active giving and sharing. Without denying some hardship and pain, the happiness we have received in pursuit of this dream has been immeasurable.

Although Studs Terkel in *American Dreams* laments the loss of our connections with nature and our apparent loss of the ideals of liberty and equality, he also suggests that the gifts of poetry and art may help salvage the American Dream. This hope, that the banal, one dimensional, consumerist ideology can be overcome is expressed in the introduction to his book through one of his respondents, who says, "It's amazing, even in the back woods of Alabama there's a classic tucked away in some country school. There's a buried beauty. . . . Gray's 'Elegy' changed my life. Who knows who's buried, who could have been what. The men in power should get all the poetry out of schools, anything that touches on real beauty. It's dangerous" (Terkel, xxii). "Something's happening," Terkel says, "as yet unrecorded on the social seismography. There are signs, unmistakable, of an astonishing increase in the airing of grievances: of private wrongs and public rights. . . . A long-buried American tradition may be springing back to life. In a society and time with changes so stunning and landscapes so suddenly estranged, the last communiques are not yet in" (Terkel, xxv-xxvi).

The last communiques from serious poets have never been in, for they have never felt themselves as integral participants in consumer culture. Furthermore, our gift-givers are not only the poets and writers, but they are also the teachers and scholars whose primary thought is not for profit or personal gain through their creations. They express gratitude and humility for the miracle of being able to participate in the birth, life, death cycle of nature. They frequently express frustration at the getting and spending mentality that pervades the American consciousness. They express pain at seeing those of us who have given our hearts away, who see little, if anything, in nature that is ours. And sometimes they become tired and cynical. But their *dreams* and *values* (derived from their, perhaps utopian, belief that the individual is one with nature and community in which equality and liberty and justice for all might prevail)—these dreams and values are not for sale and, therefore, their artistic *works* are not created for the purpose of being sold.

References

1. Robert Bellah et al., *Habits of the Heart: Individualism and Commitment in American Life*. New York: Harper and Row, 1985.
2. Marvin Harris, *America Now: The Anthropology of a Changing Culture*. New York: Simon and Schuster, 1981.
3. Studs Terkel, *American Dreams: Lost and Found*. New York: Ballantine Books, 1980. Subsequent citations indicated in text by "Terkel."
4. Herbert Marcuse, *One-Dimensional Man: Studies in the Ideology of Advanced Industrial Society*. Boston: Beacon Press, 1964.
5. Quoted in A. Poulin, Jr. ed., *Contemporary American Poetry* 4th Ed. Boston: Houghton Mifflin, 1985, p. 166. I have quoted poetry from popular anthologies wherever possible. Subsequent citations indicated in the text by "CAP."
6. Hayden Carruth, ed., *The Voice That Is Great within Us: American Poetry of the Twentieth Century*. New York: Bantam, 1970.
7. Hayden Carruth, "A Chaconnade for Everyone Named Rebecca (1983)," in Richard Jones, ed., *Poetry and Politics* .New York: Quill, 1985, p.289.
8. William Stafford, *An Oregon Message*. New York: Harper: 1987, p. 47.
9. Quoted in Richard Ellman and Robert O'Clair, eds. *The Norton Anthology of Modern Poetry*. New York: Norton, 1973, p. 884.
10. Quoted in George McMichael, et al., eds. *Anthology of American*

Literature: Realism to the Present, 2nd Ed. New York: MacMillan, 1980, p. 1633.

11. Codrescu, Andrei, ed. *American Poetry Since 1970: Up Late.* New York: Four Walls Eight Windows, 1987. Subsequent citations indicated in the text by "Late."

12. Donald Kummings, *The Open Road Trip.* New York: Geryon Press, 1989, p. 27.

13. David Ignatow, *Open Between Us.* Ann Arbor: The University of Michigan Press, 1980, p. 25.

14. Quoted in Stephen Berg and Robert Mezey eds. *The New Naked Poetry.* Indianapolis: The Bobbs-Merrill Co., 1976, pp. 101-102.

15. *Ibid.,* p. 99.

16. Wendell Berry, "Standing by Words (1981)," in Richard Jones ed., *op. cit.,* pp. 229, 235, 237.

17. Stanley Kunitz, "Poet and State (1970)," in Richard Jones ed., *op. cit.,* p. 124.

18. Gary Snyder, "Poetry and the Primitive: Notes on Poetry as an Ecological Survival Technique (1968)," in Richard Jones ed., *op. cit.,* p. 74.

19. Donald Hall, *Poetry and Ambition.* Ann Arbor: University of Michigan Press, 1988, pp. 7-8.

20. *Ibid.,* p. 19.

21. Lewis Hyde, *The Gift: Imagination and the Erotic Life of Property.* New York: Vintage, 1983, quotations from pp. xi, xiv, 280, 27.

22. George Garrett, "How It Is; How It Was; How It Will Be," *Intro 8* (1976), pp. 179-181.

23. Jack Helder, Adwriter, Williamston, Mich. Interview with the author, 4 July 1989.

24. F. Richard Thomas, *Frog Praises Night: Poems with Commentary.* Carbondale, Ill.: Southern Illinois University Press, 1980, p. 19.

Consumption as an Act of *Bicolage*

Gertrude Øllgaard
Århus University

This representation of suburban American culture is based on six months of ethnographic fieldwork in New Jersey. Through the method of participant observation I have been addressing my informants as composers of expressions in and of their culture. In experiences, observations and interviews with inhabitants of the suburban homes I have been seeking an understanding of what goes into making a home. This means tracing the constructions of the consumers who do not produce their own objects but rather manifest themselves as users who combine available products. Claude Lévi Strauss named this activity *bricolage*. It consists in adapting oneself to the circumstances and the available means, while assembling these heterogeneous elements in a collage of one's own. In such projects means as well as ends will be saturated with the character of the *bricoleur* and his or her culture.

It is as elements in the *bricolage* which makes a home that three kinds of objects will be considered below. These elements – the TV, the fireplace and general appliances – are quite ordinary in the white middle class homes visited; for that very reason they will serve to illustrate general aspects of this American bricolage.1

I

One need not be a very keen observer to bee able to detect TV-sets in the homes visited. They are scattered in sleeping rooms, in kitchens, in the children's rooms, by the exercise bike, and in a lot of other places from where they transmit images and sounds in the presence of these various activities. These TV's can be seen in almost every part of the home where they accompany the family in their doings and go with the members to their private areas. The placing of these numerous and mobile TV's is transitory like the media itself. Everywhere they appear as small boxes referring to their function as carriers for an omnipresent media – as long as they stay within a reasonable range of vision, they can function from any place in a room.

During interviews when informants were asked to tell about their home and it's furnishing, the treatment of the TV-set was just as transient. The presence of the TV was sometimes explained away – for example by stressing that actually the TV ought not to be in the kitchen where it disturbs the family during mealtime – but not explained. And why should one make an effort to explain the presence of an object which is taken for granted because it brings something other than itself into the home. However, an informant's description of a different type of furniture provides some information about how TV's are placed in the home. Mrs. explains that an "armoire" is a kind of closet which people once used when they did not have built-in closets. She continues, "and now what I would like to do is to put one in the living room. I put the stereo in you know, you close the doors and it is a nice piece of antique furniture, but yet you open it, you have your modern stereo equipment in there you can put a TV in there, too. Except, we don't watch much TV, this is a very un-American house: We have a 25 year-old black and white TV, yes, only one."

Mrs. establishes it just as much as she is proud. It is unusual just to have one old TV in the home, and not even a color TV at that. But both her general ideas about accommodating the TV in the home, and the way her own family actually accommodates one reveals more than the un-Americanness of the home. The old black-and-white is put in the family room, which is organized as an extension of the kitchen. The furniture in this room, Mrs. tells me, is Mr.'s bachelor furniture. It is colonial style which neither of them really care for anymore. But it is solid, almost impossible to wear out or destroy, and therefore it is thought to be suitable in the family room where it is exposed to everyday use by adults as well as children. This furniture is seen facing a built-in brick fireplace, but one has the impression that the TV – put in an oblique angle – competes with the fireplace about being the center of attention in the room. However, the TV is not only competing for attention. It is in and of itself integrated in the room, the screen being dressed in a wooden frame which carries a photograph of the family's child. Moreover it rests on wooden legs which are carved in colonial style like the rest of the furniture.

Apart from the small TV-sets which seem to be ignored and which can be scattered anywhere, every home also holds one TV which, like the one just described, plays a greater role in the organization of the family room. This TV is bigger, heavier, and in other ways more deeply rooted in the home. The integration of the TV in the center of the family room appears in numerous versions. Some act according to the principle, explained by Mrs. above, of actually hiding the TV behind closed doors. Another approach stems from the family room of a restored farm-house, in a home where primitive farm furniture is preferred. Yet another version was found in a family room deliberately decorated in a modern and contemporary style. In this home, modern equipment is hidden behind the doors of modern furniture. The TV defines the purpose of the space, but no less than in the examples above its presence clashes with the taste of the family room. It has to be covered.

In the homes where I encountered such large TV sets they had an intruding impact on the family rooms, but at the same time the inhabitants were able to mark their own presence by various ways of dressing the TV and integrating it into the room. One could see the screen of the TV encased in a heavy wooden box resembling the furnishings of the room. One might also find that the frame of a painting or poster matched the frame of the TV set, for example, but the combinations are numerous.

II

Fireplaces were often seen beside the TV-set in family rooms, where they both seemed to serve as centripetal elements. But the fireplace also has a space of its own a space from which the TV is excluded, namely the living room. It is often said that both fireplaces and living rooms have died out in modern, open, democratic American homes. It is said that fireplaces are a relic, surviving only as a status symbol among the very wealthy upper-middle classes. But this was not the case in the area where I did my fieldwork. There, fireplaces were observed to be widely distributed. In a fieldwork situation like mine where one meets a mobile population affected by a large world, comparative and contrastive perspectives are by no means limited to the ethnographer. They are essential elements in local self-presentation as well. Some of my informants who had been living in other parts of the United States told me about how a formal part of the home and a corresponding behavior is characteristic of this part of the country. For example, a couple whose former home had been in Texas said that there only the very rich would furnish their home and behave like almost everybody seemed to in this New Jersey suburb.

In one home similar fireplaces are observed in the family room and the living room, but,

> They are not working fireplaces, they are the old-fashioned fireplaces that they used to have in Victorian houses, that had a stove that sat in front of the fireplace and .... — but the people [Mrs. is talking about the people who lived in the house before] had sold the stoves. You have the look of a fireplace, we got the mantels and everything. But it is too expensive to knock down the walls and actually put in a fireplace. It is not a necessity, it is only luxury, we don't need it for heat ... but that is what we always wanted.

While the fireplace itself is not working, the way the fireplace is integrated in the decoration of the living room does work. It serves as a rallying point for a symmetric organization of decorative elements that seem to come with a fireplace in a living room. However, the elements vary greatly from home to home. This fireplace – Mrs. explains – is Victorian, and so is the house. But they have worked at changing its look by putting trimmings along the edge of the ceiling, around the windows and where the walls meet the floor. They prefer "an older type of look." In this way the Victorian fireplace is caught between being too old-fashioned to function and too modern to look right.

Whereas the TV is used but not praised, the fireplace is praised but hardly ever used. As in the quotation above, the importance of the fireplace is often stressed but never really explained. Thus, the day after an interview my informant called me because she wanted to make certain that I understood that for them the fireplace is a very important part of the home. When asked why, her explanation was that before they moved into this house they never had one, so this time they wanted one. A similar kind of argument is put forth by another family. Here Mr. and Mrs. argue that they always had a fireplace, so it was important for them to get at least one in this home as well. In yet another home the heavy stone fireplace, which is built in in the living room and keenly decorated with crafts is stressed as one of the reasons for buying the house. But, "I can't tell you why .... Country style, that's my taste. I have always like the country style"

Fireplaces do not have to be used and hardly ever are, so the warmth they provide must consist in something other than the actual heat of the fireplace. During conversation this warmth was never defined, but it was internalized as a strong element in the emotional arguments about taste, as something you know you like, as something that is part of you but really cannot be explained.

In this way fireplaces in living rooms throw a light on the preferences of taste, which roughly incorporates the situation, possibilities and experiences of the people who refer to the taste expressed by the objects creating their home. Whereas the choice of taste is implicit, the chosen taste is explicitly stressed verbally and visually to explain the process of selecting and combining the elements of the *bricolage*. "I don't know why ... we just had a feeling that we wanted to fix something on our own." — says a member of the family who in the process of restoring and decorating a farmhouse added a new fireplace where previous owners had demolished the original one. Nonetheless, a few moments later Mrs. explains in great detail how the chosen taste guides the selection and unification of the things that make their home. For the restored farm-house the family is hunting down antiques. But not any kind of antiques. The informant explains how they look in the papers for advertisements about garage sales where antiques were sold. Once they found the most beautiful selection of distinguished mahogany furniture. But – they had to tell the lady offering the furniture for sale – this was not what they were looking for. They were in search of "something more primitive for a farmhouse," and then they found what they were looking for in her barn.

The house is a frame within which people create the unity of their home. This unity comes into being by making the furniture match, and by making it express a certain period and style. Thus fireplaces, through the elements of taste, provide a clue to the dialogue between the inhabitants and their objects. This ongoing dialogue permeates the homes where the inhabitants are guided by the idea that things must match, in certain ways they have to merge in the expression of a unity. Since the inhabitants embrace this idea, the objects which have already entered the home place demands on subsequent choices. 2

It is such a dialogue with available means that characterize the creativity of the users who, like the bricoleur, combine heterogeneous elements of things and ideas. A story of how such elements are combined in a home will guide us to the domain of appliances.

III

Mr. and Mrs. are both deeply excited when they relate the story about their move from a huge mansion in a prestigious suburb to a little cottage located in the nearby town where Mrs. grew up. Their children as well as their friends thought that they had lost their money, their sense, or both. The total size of this cottage was exactly the same as that of the living room in their previous home. Their change of residence was influenced by the energy crisis of the 1970s and by intensive studies of the "small is beautiful" movement. They decided that they wanted to cut down. They wanted to concentrate instead of expand. Now their project was to utilize the space of a small cottage without changing its original structures. Within these frames they furnished their home in a simple colonial style and mixed it with colors that are supposed to make one feel good.

This couple chose to build up a certain style – a lifestyle as well as style of decoration. But in order to do that they had to think hard about how to make room for all the things that are considered necessary to make a home. One of their friends remarked that the cottage, especially the compact kitchen, turned out to be very "ship like." When people enter the kitchen, they are surprised to find the refrigerator and the freezer beneath the counter. Likewise they think the dishwasher is an oven because it is situated beneath the hot plates.

The home is made out of a combination of heterogeneous elements, some of which are directly apparent from conversations and observations. The construction is based, for example, on studies of certain life and color philosophies, the choice of a particular style, a memory from Mrs.'s childhood, the small space of the house, and many objects that are paramount to a home. The appliances are objects of this last-mentioned kind. It is not the presence of appliances in the kitchen that surprises people who enter the home, it is rather the uniqueness of their combination. The appliances are objects which, just like the TV – but unlike the fireplace – are used but hardly ever described or praised. When questions were directed towards the appliances, the response would often be confined to remarks like "we have the basics" or "of course we have" followed by random mention of washer, dryer, dishwasher, refrigerator.

This lack of information about things like the appliances does not mean that their presence and the functions they fulfill are indifferent. Quite the contrary, it is because the presence of these remedies is just as natural as that of the TV that it does not have to be articulated. The appliances have been included in a general cultural consciousness whereby they are sunken into deeper and more unconscious levels of the mind. This process is described by Gregory Bateson as an economy of thought, which makes the unconscious take care of matters so familiar that they do not need to be inspected.3 Whereas these unconscious levels are characterized by a lack of contrasts, the experience of something different makes the distinctive nature of local things rise to consciousness. When the appliances are talked about, it is done with reference to changes over time or with reference to experiences from other countries: "I like a nice big refrigerator. I missed my refrigerator when I was in Holland – we had a little one." The appliances sink into the cultural unconscious, and just like the TV and the fireplace they are built into different homes. The residents, indefatigable *bricoleurs*, mark their presence, for example by surrounding the appliances with antiques and country style baskets, or by covering the front of a dishwasher with oak that matches the rest of the kitchen. Again the combinations are innumerable.

The microwave oven is an appliance which is observed on a lot of table tops. It is there but not quite built-in either into the kitchens or the unconscious. The microwaves are reflected on, praised, and feared. In one kitchen the microwave oven is not visible, but when questioned about it, Mrs. says:

We do have a microwave, my husband got me one when they first came out and I said, honey I know you really, really are thoughtful, but I said I don't want a microwave, and he took it back. Our youngest son kept saying you have to get a microwave. And I said I am afraid of radiation leak. I mean, I am really frightened of those things. So my husband compromised, I said look, you can get a microwave, but you have to put it downstairs. So he was able, then, to use the microwave – he got me one for Christmas. Just one month ago I said to my husband – I am scared of that thing, I hate them on counters but you can put it in one of the cabinets – it's gonna be behind closed doors.

This family does have a microwave oven in its home, but it has not been allowed in the kitchen until now. Mr. and Son were persistent in insisting that it has to be there, and so it will. Now it is going to be built in in the kitchen right where Mrs. does her daily work. When is she going to use it? When is she going to use it without even thinking about it?

The microwave oven seems to be in the process of becoming one of the objects that can be taken for granted, an object just like the TV, the fireplace, and the other appliances which are recurrent in every home. But the style or the taste by which these more or less "natural" objects are collected and combined forms a unity which consists of more than the component parts,

190

namely the identity of the home.

IV

The identity which unites the inhabitants in a home is expressed through the material manifestations of taste. But it is also expressed verbally. A family relates how they wonder who constructed the house which they are currently inhabiting. The house is described as an odd mixture of "so much good stuff and so much cheap stuff." But then they add, "anybody would do things differently, they have their own taste." Sometimes one wonders and sometimes one is scandalized at the taste of others, but first and foremost the difference is recognized.

Bourdieu writes: "different things differentiate themselves through what they have in common."[5] So saying, he helps to explain and understand the above mentioned differentiations and identifications. The families distinguish between one another through the combinations of objects in each home. Yet they root the meaning of this distinction in the assumption that everybody expresses an identity through the furnishing of a home.

The couple who diminished the frames of their home was very self-assured and confident about the elements of identity with which they would surround themselves. Other people find it very difficult to have to exhibit an identity. An informant who had married a few years earlier and moved in with her husband and his teenage daughters recalls how she had once spoken about their dwelling as "the *house*." Now, "it is more of a *home*, but that's because it has more of my imprint on it than it did before." Slowly she is starting to leave her own marks on this already established home. Mrs. comments on her considerations and anxieties: "I figured whatever I would pick, I would have to live with, and I never had the opportunity to decorate before. I wanted to do it right. I also figured that I was sort of putting myself on the line, you know, it would be my taste and my idea. And I didn't want myself to look ridiculous. I took a lot of time."

It is difficult. Mrs. is scared of making overwhelming changes in the established order. The teenagers will put her to scorn if she changes anything, though she is also put to scorn for not daring to leave her own mark. "What is wrong with you?," said one of the teenagers, who was outraged at Mrs.'s lack of intervention. There is no getting around having to put things in the home, to choose these things and to combine them. One runs a risk, one has to express one's own taste, ideas, identity, and whatever one does one will be evaluated. There are no alternatives: even when one tries not to, one leaves an expression and an impression.

Thus, objects are woven into an energetic arrangement and production of meaning and identity. Not only elements like TV's, fireplaces and appliances are involved in this process, but also works of art are sprayed with turquoise paint, now that this is the color of the new furniture. Identities are produced through a spreading domestication by which things used are transformed and

191

supplied with the expressions of the inhabitants. Such a domestication, such a domination by the present users, is not confined to the handling of objects in the furnishing of a home. It flows out of the homes into other domains of the culture.

In a process similar to that of furnishing the home, each person and family weaves an identity and a social network through a mobile tactic of combining heterogeneous elements. In countless spheres social actions and expressions are invested with idiosyncratic meaning. A characteristic instance is the mundane situation of the dinner party where each participant manifests his or her personal style and differentiates him/herself within the group through the choice of attire. On the other hand, however, the very expression of a specific dress code provides the norm, the moment of unity, around which this particular social gathering is constituted. The choice of dress code may be looked upon as an act of collective *bricolage*, because the unity it brings about is in fact only momentary; it is stated for and by the specific participants and occasion. The dress code has to be formulated, just as you yourself will have to formulate your choice of drinks. A similar expression of norms and habits also finds its way into in the sacred domain of a church where the printed program tells the congregation how to behave during the service.

On a more general level of suburban American culture, that is in an extended *place* of single family houses – uniform units inhabited by mobile families and filled with uniform objects – it takes the *bricolage*-like combinations of the users to form the basis for the emergence of a cultural *space*. Batesen distinguishes between space and place. A place is the order of positions where elements are distributed beside each other in a relationship of coexistence. Space, on the other hand, occurs as the effects produced by human operations across a place.[5] It is through these compositions that identities are made explicit and currently shared cultural references are negotiated. In the absence of implicit systems of references whereby identity and culture is given or, in the jargon of Bateson, the lack of a comprehensive cultural unconscious — it is the transforming capacity of the users which establishes a common ground. This bricolage makes explicit and modifies contrasting experiences and combines them so that identities occur and shared references arises.

192

References

1. The interpretation of *bricolage* as an aspect of consumption relies on Claude Lévi Strauss, *Den Vilde Tanke*. København: Gydendal, 1969 (1962), and in addition on Michel de Certeau, *The Practice of Everyday Life*. London: University of California, 1988.
2. This explanation of the part played by the taste in the relations between people and their objects is inspired by Martin Hollis. Analytically, he suggests "that social forms can never shape human beings completely, because social forms owe their own shape to the fact that human beings are social agents with ideas about social forms." "Of Masks and Men" in: *The Category of the Person*. Cambridge: Cambridge University Press, 1986, p.132.
3. Gregory Bateson, *Steps to an Ecology of Mind*. New York: Balantine Books, 1972, p.128, 153.
4. Pierre Bourdieu *Distinction. A social critique of the judgement of taste*. London: Routledge & Kegan Paul, 1986, p. 258.
5. Michel de Certeau writes "Space is practiced place." *op. cit.*, p.117, 130)

Black Responses to Consumption:
From Frederick Douglass to Booker T. Washington

Carl Pedersen
Roskilde University Center

In his *Narrative of the Life of Frederick Douglass, an American Slave* (1845), Frederick Douglass depicts his journey from slavery to freedom as a quest for self-realization through physical endurance. He traverses this road to freedom running from South to North by means of his acquisition of literacy and his intimate knowledge of the landscape. Drawing on the Old Testament imagery in slave songs, Douglass refers to the North as a Canaan offering physical and spiritual salvation from the degradation of slavery. However, upon reaching New Bedford, Massachusetts, he discovers that his idea of the Promised Land does not conform to the reality of the North.

> I was quite disappointed at the general appearance of things in New Bedford. The impression which I had received respecting the character and condition of the people of the north, I found to be singularly erroneous. I had very strangely supposed, while in slavery, that few of the comforts, and scarcely any of the luxuries, of life were enjoyed at the north, compared with what were enjoyed by the slaveholders of the south....I had somehow imbibed the opinion that, in the absence of slaves, there could be no wealth, and very little refinement. And upon coming to the north, I expected to meet with a rough, hard-handed, and uncultivated population, living in the most Spartan-like simplicity, knowing nothing of the ease, luxury, pomp, and grandeur of southern slaveholders. Such being my conjectures, any one acquainted with the appearance of New Bedford may very readily infer how palpably I must have seen my mistake....
>
> From the wharves I strolled around and over the town, gazing with wonder and admiration at the splendid churches, beautiful dwellings, and finely-cultivated gardens; evincing an amount of wealth, comfort, taste, and refinement, such as I had never seen in any part of slaveholding Maryland.[1]

Most surprising was the situation of blacks in New Bedford, many of whom, Douglass notes, had made the same journey from the slave South to the free North. He sees blacks living in houses who were better off than the average slaveholder in Maryland. Singling out one example, Douglass records his impressions of a friend, Nathan Johnson, who "lived in a neater house; dined at a better table; took, paid for, and read, more newspapers; better understood the moral, religious, and political character of the nation,— than nine-tenths of the slaveholders in Talbot county Maryland. Yet Mr. Johnson was a working man. His hands were hardened by toil, and not his alone, but those also of Mrs. Johnson."[2] Douglass's astonishment at the sight of a black working man owning his own property is understandable. Growing up in the slave South, Douglass had observed first-hand the incompatibility of labor and the accumulation of wealth. Large segments of the Southern aristocracy enjoyed a leisurely life of conspicuous consumption made possible by slave labor; thus the idea that a prosperous life could be secured by someone whose "hands were hardened by toil" was completely foreign to a fugitive slave like Douglass.

Earlier in the *Narrative*, Douglass provides a counter-image to the North in his description of Colonel Lloyd's garden, a cultivated plot of fruit trees on the plantation where he worked.[3] Slaves were prohibited access to the garden, in a literal sense the "fruits" of their labor. The image of the garden, so dear to early American settlers, has been distorted in the South. The cultivated garden, created by the noble efforts of the American farmer depicted by Crèvecoeur in his *Letters from an American Farmer* (1782) and praised by Thomas Jefferson in his *Notes on the State of Virginia* (1785) has in the South been transformed into a blatant symbol of unlimited power, the absolute and undisguised dominance of master over slave. The possession of land, the mark of the American "new man," remains out of reach for African-Americans. The fence around Colonel Lloyd's garden affords the slaves a view of the abundance produced from cultivated land, while at the same time serving as a constant reminder that they were not meant to partake of its natural riches. In New Bedford, however, Douglass observes a direct link between labor and material prosperity. Following the example of his friend, he obtains employment shortly after coming to New Bedford and comes to know the meaning of free labor.

> I found employment, the third day after my arrival, in stowing a sloop with a load of oil. It was new, dirty, and hard work for me; but I went at it with a glad heart and a willing hand. I was now my own master. It was a happy moment, the rapture of which can be understood only by those who have been slaves. It was the first work, the reward of which was to be entirely my own. There was no Master Hugh standing ready, the moment I earned the money, to rob me of it. I worked that day with a pleasure I had never before experienced.[4]

Douglass's reflections on the disjunction between the Northern work ethic and the Southern slave system echoed the classic Northern perception of the South, which dated from the 1700s and had become increasingly pronounced with the advent of the abolitionist movement in the 1830s. In general, Northerners viewed the Southern planter aristocracy as a parasitic leisure class corrupted by the desire for material comforts acquired through profits from slave labor. This attitude was rooted in the more ambivalent (and problematic) New England Puritan relationship between labor and the accumulation of wealth. The Puritan notion of a wilderness landscape in the North afforded a unique challenge: to transform a hostile environment and establish a community based on the dignity of labor and the zealous preservation of spiritual values. As John Winthrop admonished in his sermon "A Model of Christian Charity" (1630), the possession of wealth was not a sin *per se*, but the rich man had a sacred obligation to use his wealth for the common good. The accumulation of wealth for personal gain threatened the Puritan community by fostering an erosion of spiritual values that might ultimately rend the "city on a hill" asunder. According to this view, the goal of economic self-sufficiency for the Massachusetts Bay Colony was being constantly undermined by the commercial system linking it with the merchant oligarchy. The tension between the temptation of material abundance and the upholding of a spiritual community based on the republican virtues of thrift and industry became a permanent feature of American economic discourse and underlay the critique of consumer society by Thorstein Veblen at the end of the nineteenth century.

In the 1830s, the nascent abolitionist movement further articulated the notion that the North and South were culturally and economically divided by publishing broadsides condemning the inhumanity of the Southern social order and calling for the immediate emancipation of the slaves. By the 1850s, the split between North and South was widely regarded in terms of a conflict between two forms of labor. Southern apologists for slavery like George Fitzhugh rejected Northern labor as nothing more than "wage slavery," while the abolitionist tracts grew increasingly adamant in their demand for an end to the "peculiar institution." However, it was also at this time that the gradual westward expansion by European settlers was being justified by theories purporting the innate superiority of the Anglo-Saxon race. These two developments in antebellum thought were to influence the course of African-American participation in American society in the post-Emancipation era.[5]

A vivid example of the transformation of work and the promotion of Anglo-Saxon racial superiority was the World's Columbian Exposition in Chicago in 1893. The Exposition was touted as a showcase for the achievements of Western civilization set against the backwardness of Africa and Asia since the "discovery" of the New World by Columbus. These achievements were represented to a large extent by commercial interests. As Edward Bellamy observed: "The underlying motive of the whole exhibition, under a sham pretence of patriotism is business, advertising with a view to individual money-making."[6] The exhibitions of American technological innovation and material abundance provided a poignant contrast to the displays of exotic primitivism from underdeveloped nations. Amidst this celebration of Western progress, the voice of the African-American was absent. Prominent blacks had petitioned the managers of the Exposition for permission to set up exhibits on the Fair grounds, but this appeal was rejected. Instead, the managers required that blacks submit proposals for exhibits to screening committees in the various states. Because most of the African-American displays came from Southern states whose screening committees were likely to reject any black proposals, the decision of the board of managers in effect excluded black participation in the Fair.

Two black leaders, Frederick Douglass and Ida Wells, reacted to this decision by raising money to publish a booklet entitled *The Reason Why the Colored American is Not in the World's Columbian Exposition*, intended for foreign visitors. They had originally planned to publish the booklet in English, French, German, and Spanish; however, the several hundred dollars they raised fell far short of the estimated 5,000 dollars needed to print the booklet in several languages, so only a limited edition in English ever appeared.[7]

Perhaps as a conciliatory gesture, the managers did consent to a separate Colored Jubilee Day to celebrate African-American folk culture, as suggested by several blacks from the East Coast. The idea of a Jubilee divided the black leadership. Even Douglass and Wells, who had collaborated on the booklet criticizing black exclusion from the Exposition, disagreed on the merits of celebrating a separate Jubilee. Wells dismissed the idea as a blatant attempt to patronize the black community, while Douglass saw it as an opportunity to proudly display African-American culture. However, in his speech at the Jubilee, Douglass noted that blacks being "outside of the World's Fair is only consistent with the fact that we are excluded from every respectable calling." For Douglass, rejecting black participation at a Fair designed to celebrate American civilization was ironic because a considerable portion of that civilization owed its success to the labor of African-Americans.[8]

Another, younger black leader also appeared in Chicago in August, 1893. Booker T. Washington, the President of Tuskegee Institute in Alabama, had been asked by Henry Demarest Lloyd to attend a Labor Congress in connection with the Exposition. Lloyd, a well-known reformer, whose most famous work *Wealth Against Commonwealth* was published the following year, envisioned the Labor Congress as a forum for discussion of industrial recovery and social reform in the wake of the depression earlier in 1893. Lloyd had also invited perhaps the most famous reformer, Edward Bellamy, to the Congress, but because of illness, Bellamy was unable to attend. However, Washington found himself in the midst of an array of social reformers, such as Single Taxers, Fabians, and Christian Socialists. Evidently, Lloyd's vision of cooperative planning could also include the black community in the South. In his address to the Congress, Lloyd reminded his listeners that blacks were victims of the mortgage system as well as the script system, which forced them to purchase goods at an employer-owned store at exhorbitant prices.[9]

Washington's speech dwelt on the onerous burden of sharecropping, which affected the majority of Southern blacks "not only industrially but morally as well." To replace the detrimental effects of this mortgage system, Washington emphasized the need for manual training. His views became known to Southern white leaders and were instrumental in securing him an invitation to speak at the Atlanta Exposition in 1895, where he gave what has since been regarded as his most important address.[10]

The Chicago World's Fair attempted to link a tribute to the progress of civilization with the promotion of corporate interests encouraging mass consumption. This marriage of progress and consumption precluded the full participation of black Americans, who felt caught between the primitivism of the Dahomean display and the ostentation of the White City. In his speech at the Jubilee, Douglass addressed this issue. "We have come out of Dahomey into this. Measure the Negro. But not by the standard of the splendid civilization of the Caucasian. Bend down and measure him--from the depths out of which he has risen."[11] This statement reflects the dilemma of African-Americans at the end of the nineteenth century. Black leaders like Douglass and Washington accepted the idea of the progress of Western civilization while decrying its social and economic injustices.

However, if African-Americans were to remain on the outside of the corporate America displayed at the Fair, they could, in Lloyd's view, be a part of a social reform movement based on cooperative planning, a movement in opposition to consumer society. Although Washington would probably not have subscribed to this view, his attendence at the Labor Congress is revealing. The epithet most commonly used to describe Washington's policies, "accomodationist," obscures the complexity of his thought. It is important to examine his attitude toward labor, which contains an implicit critique of the degradation of work that accompanied the transition to a consumer society. Washington's emphasis on the dignity of labor evolved from his experience of slavery and exposure to the tenets of New England Puritanism. This combination links him not only to Douglass, who recognized the implications of the black work ethic in a free society, but also to the social reformers from Bellamy to Veblen, who saw in the rise of consumerism the subversion of traditional American values.

Born in 1856, Washington experienced slavery as a young boy. The Burroughs farm in Virginia where he was born was far from being a plantation like Colonel Lloyd's, despite Washington's later efforts to describe his childhood in the context of traditional plantation legend. In cultural terms the Burroughs family had more in common with their slaves than with the owners of large plantations. Indeed, as Louis Harlan notes, the farmers of Franklin County where the Burroughs lived "in many respects lived out the

Jeffersonian agrarian dream. They were many miles from cities and factories, and almost unaffected by the agricultural commercialism of the day."[12]

After the Civil War, Washington became the houseboy of the Ruffners in West Virginia. He recalled in his autobiography that "the lessons I learned in the home of Mrs. Ruffner were as valuable to me as any education I have gotten anywhere since."[13] Viola Ruffner was a transplanted New Englander, and passed on to her houseboy the Puritan virtues of hard work and thrift.[14] Washington's life-long dislike of cities, his praise of yeoman farming and the Puritan work ethic are rooted in the rural black culture of the South and the impact of Mrs. Ruffner's ideas. For him, the Puritan belief in a virtuous society meshed with the community culture of former slaves to form his unique vision of the future of African-Americans in the Southern United States.

Washington's efforts to persuade blacks to stay in the South was a consequence of his interpretation of the changes in Southern society in the post-Emancipation era. In a revealing passage in *The Future of the American Negro* (1900), he drew a scathing portrait of the decadence of the Southern plantation and the dependence of the planter class on their slaves. Contrasting the magnificence of the large estates in the antebellum South with their swift decline after the defeat of the Confederacy, Washington noted that the physical deterioration of the plantation forced the once omnipotent master to realize that his life of leisure had brought about his undoing. According to Washington, the former plantation owner gradually grew aware "to what an extent he and his family had grown to be dependent upon the activity and faithfulness of his slaves; began to appreciate to what an extent slavery had sapped his sinews of strength and independence, how his dependence upon slave labour had deprived him and his offspring of the benefit of technical and industrial training, and, worst of all, had unconsciously led him to see in labour drudgery and degradation instead of beauty, dignity, and civilising power."[15] This negative attitude toward labor, which had fostered the moral degeneration of the slave-owners, stood in contrast to the slave experience. In a lecture given in 1907 entitled "The Economic Development of the Negro Race since Its Emancipation," Washington emphasized the importance of labor to the future of African-Americans. Like Douglass, he distinguished between the degradation of slave labor and the dignity of "free" labor. Responding to parents of Tuskegee students who wanted their children taught "the book" instead of farming, Washington argued "that there was a vast difference between being worked and working. I said to them that being worked meant degradation, that working meant civilization."[16] The value of industrial education lay in its emphasis on the dignity of labor that had been suppressed under slavery, but would in the post-Emancipation era form the foundation of black participation in American society. This work ethic would enable blacks to be the bulwark of a new and strong Southern economy. For this goal to be realized, however, it was essential that African-Americans resist the temptation to seek their fortune in the North and stay close to their cultural roots.

Needless to say, there were strong forces arrayed against any immediate realization of black economic advancement. Ironically, these forces provided the key to Washington's success in rallying the black community to support economic self-sufficiency. The Compromise of 1877, occurring in an atmosphere of rapant materialism and Social Darwinism, spelled the end of Republican support of black aspirations and opened the door to the industrial interests of Northern capitalism. Local Southern state governments were quick to pass a series of "Jim Crow" laws that effectively excluded African-Americans from participation in political and social acitivity. Given this hostile climate, it is not surprising that many blacks chose to leave the South. However much they may have inculcated the notion of wealth as a symbol of success, the road to riches was cordoned off just as surely as Colonel Lloyd's garden. For most blacks, the future appeared to be confined to a choice between sharecropping in the South or menial labor in Northern factories, often as strikebreakers. Washington believed, however, that the North would always be the wrong choice. In his view, blacks were not suited to the urban environment of the North and would readily succumb to all the temptations that had weakened the Anglo-Saxon character. It was rather in economically self-sufficient communities in the South that blacks could escape the impoverishment of sharecropping or factory work.

The perception of the North as detrimental to black aspirations was perhaps most clearly expressed in Paul Laurence Dunbar's novel *The Sport of the Gods* (1902). Written in a naturalistic vein and depicting the fate of blacks transplanted from the rural South to the urban North, Dunbar's novel can be viewed as an African-American pendant to Theodore Dreiser's *Sister Carrie* (1900). The "forces" of urbanism engulf the Hamilton family, who have come to New York after the father, Berry, is convicted of theft and sentenced to ten years in prison. The two children, Joe and Kit, are drawn by the lure of city life and willingly shed their rural identity. Joe sees "the young fellows passing by dressed in their spruce clothes" and longs to be a part of their world. Like Carrie, Kit is drawn to the theater, but soon feels the effect of "the quick poison of the unreal life about her;" in order to gain recognition for her singing talents, she feels obliged to drop the "simple old songs" of her Southern heritage in favor of "coon ditties."[17] Dunbar's sentiments are reflected in the reaction of a local black club to the fate of rural blacks in New York: "'Oh, is there no way to keep these people from rushing away from the small villages and country districts of the South up to the cities, where they cannot battle with the terrible force of a strange and unusual environment? Is there no way to prove to them that woolen-shirted, brown-jeaned simplicity is infinitely better than broad-clothed degradation?"[18] The contrast of the simple working man with the well-dressed city dweller can be found in Washington's work as well and bears an affinity with Veblen's notion of conspicuous consumption. In *The Future of the American Negro*,

Washington argued that the benefits of industrial education would prevent blacks from imitating "the weaker elements of the white man's character;...the high hat, kid gloves, a showy walking cane, and all the rest of it."[19] The development of a leisure class practicing conspicuous consumption was in Veblen's view rooted in the ascendency of what he called the predatory instinct in human nature, a desire for self-serving activity, which had eclipsed the instinct of workmanship and had led to the degradation of labor by businessmen acting in their own self-interest.

Washington's scenario for African-American economic development in the South—the promotion of industrial education and the establishment of all-black business communities—stood in opposition to the declining fortunes of the former plantation owners in the South, and the emerging consumer society in the North. Social and economic separatism would preserve the instinct of workmanship in the black community that was an integral part of African-American culture. In describing the various black communities that had sprung up throughout the South, Washington noted that they permitted "the fundamental racial traits of the Negro, so far as they are peculiar or different from that of the white man, to clearly manifest themselves."[20] Black awareness of the dignity of labor that had been sparked in the North in the antebellum era, and in the black communities in the South in the post-Emancipation era, would prevent the development of a predatory instinct and preserve a group culture.

The tangible results of the black instinct of workmanship after slavery were displayed at a separate "Negro Exhibit" at the Atlanta Cotton States and International Exposition in 1895. The diversity of the exhibit is evident in I. Garland Penn's account:

The exhibit is largely agricultural, such products as negroes (sic) raise on their own farms; of a mechanical character by the engines, boiler, etc., built by negroes; of a business character, such as banks and business houses, either by actual business houses in miniature or represented by photographs; painting and art display of a very creditable character; needlework display, domestic preparations, a horticultural display, etc. In fact, the negroes have something of most every kind and character you can call for.[21]

Penn's description of African-American achievements in the South is vastly different from the displays of technology and corporate power at other Fairs that disturbed white writers like Henry Adams. Blacks were indeed excluded from consumer society, but were in the process of constructing an alternative that in many respects resembled the vision of the older American producer society. Of course, the ever-present factors of racism and economic marginalization frustrated the realization of Washington's goals. Nevertheless, the notion of self-sufficiency has always been a part of African-American thought as both a reaction to social and economic exclusion and an affirmation of black cultural identity. In an age of "the incorporation of America," black self-sufficiency in the South, fueled by the instinct of workmanship, retained many of the features of American life that were elsewhere in the process of disappearing.

References

1. Frederick Douglass, *Narrative of the Life of Frederick Douglass, an American Slave.* Harmondsworth: Penguin, 1982 pp. 147-148.
2. *Ibid.,* p. 149
3. *Ibid.,* p. 59
4. *Ibid.,* p. 150
5. For an account of these developments, see Reginald Horsman, *Race and Manifest Destiny. The Origins of American Racial Anglo-Saxonism.* Cambridge: Harvard University Press, 1981.
6. Edward Bellamy quoted in Alan Trachtenberg, *The Incorporation of America. Culture and Society in the Gilded Age.* New York: Hill and Wang, 1982 p. 215.
7. Elliot M. Rudwick and August Meier, "Black Man in the 'White City': Negroes and the Columbian Exposition, 1893," *Phylon* (1965) pp. 354-61.
8. Douglass quoted in Elliot M. Rudwick and August Meier, *op.cit.,* p. 361.
9. John L. Thomas, *Alternative America. Henry George, Edward Bellamy, Henry Demarest Lloyd and the Adversary Tradition.* Cambridge: Belknap/Harvard, 1983 pp. 282-83 and Louis R. Harlan and Raymond W. Smock, eds., *The Booker T. Washington Papers.* Urbana: University of Illinois Press, 1972, vol. 3, p. 366.
10. *The Booker T. Washington Papers,* vol. 3, pp. 364-66, and Robert W. Rydell, *All the World's a Fair.* Chicago: University of Chicago Press, 1984 p. 83.
11. Douglass quoted in Rydell, *ibid.*
12. Louis R. Harlan, Booker T. Washington. *The Making of a Black Leader 1856-1901.* London: Oxford University Press, 1972, p. 10.
13. Booker T. Washington, *Up From Slavery* in *Three Negro Classics.* New York: Avon Books, 1965, p. 52.
14. Louis R. Harlan, *op. cit.,* pp. 40-44.
15. Booker T. Washington, *The Future of the American Negro.* Boston: Small, Maynard & Company, 1900. p. 43.
16. Booker T. Washington and W.E.B. DuBois, *The Negro in the South. His Economic Progress in Relation to His Moral and Religious Development.* Philadelphia: George W. Jacobs & Company, 1907, p. 49.

17. Paul Laurence Dunbar, *The Sport of the Gods*, excerpted in *The Paul Laurence Dunbar Reader*. New York: Dodd, Mead & Company, 1975, p. 359.
18. *Ibid.*, p. 389.
19. Booker T. Washington, *The Future of the American Negro*, p. 58
20. Booker T. Washington, *The Negro in Business*. Boston, 1907; reprinted New York: AMS Press, 1971, p. 74.
21. Penn's account is in Wayne G. Cooper, *The Cotton States and International Exposition and South Illustrated*. Atlanta: Illustrator Company, 1896.

The Status of African-Americans: Progress and Retrogression

Harvard Sitkoff
University of New Hampshire

The recrudescence of white racism and the discovery (or re-discovery) of the black "underclass" has led to a rash of articles and reports bemoaning the mixed status of African-Americans and belittling the achievements of the civil rights movement. Quite understandably, those most concerned with the current plight of blacks are wary of those who commemorate and celebrate African-American "progress." They rightly want to focus on the inequities that remain rather than those that have been ameliorated. But ignorance of the history of the recent past, as well as the tendency to describe the status of all African-Americans as if they were a homogeneous, undifferentiated entity, compounds the pessimism of Black America and perpetuates a sense of hopelessness that smothers sparks of determination and struggle.

Throughout the first half of this century the vast majority of African-Americans residing in the South had to contend with what Martin Luther King, Jr. called "a degenerating sense of 'nobodiness'" They lived in an air-tight cage of poverty, with a constant fear of white barbarity and violence, their security subject to the whims of those who despised them. They could neither vote nor serve on juries. A host of statutes outlawing everything "interracial" required that blacks be segregated from birth to death. African-Americans could not live where whites lived. They had to attend separate, inferior schools, drink from a "colored" water fountain, relieve themselves in a dirty "colored" restroom, sit in the cramped "colored" sections of buses and theaters. Regardless of age, whites called them "boy" or "girl," never "Mr." or "Mrs."; "WHITES ONLY" signs at city parks and swimming pools, humiliated African-Americans daily, demeaned their spirits, branded them with an indelible mark of inferiority.

Blacks did whatever they could to resist this pervasive system of American apartheid, often covertly, more often futilely. Then an interrelated series of demographic, political, and socioeconomic changes in American society, set in motion by the New Deal and, especially, the Second World War, created the preconditions for a wave of nonviolent black activism to succeed in vanquishing Jim Crow and in guaranteeing to all African-Americans the full and equal rights of citizenship. And for many blacks, much has changed as a consequence of the Supreme Court rulings, national legislation, executive orders, and altered white racial attitudes provoked by the civil rights movement.

A quarter of century ago, Jesse Jackson's sharecropper parents could not vote in South Carolina. Today heir son campaigns for the presidency of the United States, demonstrating his ability to attract white votes as well as to galvanize black voters. Prior to the passage of the Voting Rights Act of 1965 (which effectively reenfranchised Southern Blacks for the first time since Reconstruction), there were but 280 African-American elected officials throughout the United States. Today there are nearly 6500. The number of blacks in Congress has grown from 2 to 24 in these same years, and several with significant seniority, like William Gray, Chairman of the House Democratic Caucus, are posed to assume the positions of House Speaker and Democratic Party Majority Leader in the near future. There are also some 300 cities with African-American mayors today, including such metropolises as Los Angeles and Seattle on the West Coast, Detroit and Cleveland in the industrial heartland, Atlanta, Birmingham, and New Orleans in the South, and Baltimore, Philadelphia, and New York City on the East Coast. And Virginia, the premier exponent of the strategy of massive resistance to desegregation in the 1950s, has just become the first state in this century to elect an African-American as governor. Less than three decades ago, President Lyndon Johnson's decisions to nominate Thurgood Marshall to the Supreme Court and Robert Weaver to the Cabinet occasioned great political controversy and were deemed historic. Today the appointment of General Colin Powell as Chairman of the Joint Chiefs of Staff, the top position in the armed forces, causes no stir and barely makes the news. We have become as accustomed to black political leadership as to black men and women astronauts travelling in space.

Inclusion rather than exclusion has similarly become the norm in countless other aspects of contemporary American society. The dominant athletes in every major American sport are black, and we are now as accustomed to the literary excellence of Toni Morrison and Alice Walker as we are to the physical prowess of Michael Jordan and Florence Griffith-Joyner. A generation of young Americans admires Henry Aaron more than Babe Ruth, and does not consider it unusual to see a black banker or a ballerina, a black electrician or physician. Those Americans addicted to television may well wake up to Bryant Gumbal on the Today Show, share their afternoons with Oprah Winfrey (the highest rated talk show), dine in front of Bill Cosby and his family (the most popular program of the 1980s), and go to bed watching Arsenio Hall, rather than Johnny Carson. And as no segment of the vast and highly influential entertainment industry is without a major black presence, so universities that rarely or never admitted African-Americans today matter-of-factly enroll them, hire black professors, and offer courses in black studies. Most significantly, what the millions of young Americans in college today are taught about race is dramatically different than the lessons learned just a few decades ago., This transformation is encapsulated in the many textbooks used in required surveys of American history. Formerly excluded from the main contours of the American past, except as Sambo-like slaves and childlike freedmen threatening the stability of Southern society, today's textbooks routinely emphasize the horrors and harms of racism and slavery, the long continuity of the black struggle for freedom and equality, the extraordinary achievements of Reconstruction governments, and the many contributions to American life made by African-Americans.

Those best positioned to take advantage of the change wrought by the civil rights movement have also advanced economically. The percentage of black families earning more than $35,000, in real dollars, has increased from 17.7 percent in 1970 to 22.3 percent in 1987; and 10 percent of all black families today (345 thousand families), compared to 5 percent in 1970, have annual incomes of over $50,000. The average annual income of an African-American family in which the husband and wife both work, moreover, is now more than 85 percent of the income of a similar white family.

Nevertheless, there is mounting evidence of stagnation, even retrogression, in critical aspects of Afro-American life. Despite the end of legally mandated and enforced segregation, despite the end of black disenfranchisement, despite the fact that boastful bigotry has become socially unacceptable to most Americans, recent trends point to more rather than less racial separation and inequality. Ominously, the gulf between the races widens, and so does the gap between the growing African-American middle class and the ever larger black "underclass." Many of the victories won in the 1960s were stymied by the benign neglect of the seventies and reversed by the hostile indifference of the eighties.

Progress is not automatic. The Second Reconstruction may well duplicate the First Reconstruction's soaring African-American expectations, followed by white complacency, neglect, and betrayal. Much as the Supreme Court in the late nineteenth century effectively nullified the Fourteenth and Fifteenth Amendments to the Constitution as guarantees of the rights of blacks, the Rehnquist Court today is gutting the gains made by African-Americans in the Second Reconstruction. Mandated busing plans and programs for affirmative action have been crippled; and the Rehnquist Court so emasculated the equal employment provisions of the 1964 Civil Rights Act that the usually moderate Justice Harry Blackman angrily wrote in a 1988 dissent: "One wonders whether the majority still believes that race discrimination — or, more accurately, race discrimination against non-whites — is a problem in our society, or even remembers that it ever was."

Despite the significant victories of individual African-American candidates, blacks as a group are politically isolated and vulnerable. They still constitute less than two percent of the nation's elected officials. Although Selma, Alabama, no longer practices the kind of official violence against blacks attempting to register to vote that so outraged the nation in 1965 and led to passage of the

Voting Rights Act, gerrymandering and redistricting have kept the majority black population of that city and its surrounding counties politically impotent. The Reagan Administration repeatedly capitalized on racial issues to increase its base of white voters, even trying to repeal the Voting Rights Act; and George Bush made a winning issue out of Willie Horton, a black convict who had raped a white woman, with television advertisements mixing images of crime and race that blatantly aroused the racist instincts of white voters. Even the Democrats, struggling to avoid being identified as the party of blacks, did what they could in 1988 to distance Jesse Jackson from the Dukakis campaign.

Increasingly, the victories of the Second Reconstruction seem irrelevant to today's tragedies. What does the right to vote matter to the roughly one-third of the black men in poor neighborhoods who are arrested on drug charges by the age of thirty? Or to a black mother watching her children, as young as eight or nine, working as lookouts for drug dealers, and becoming drug users and dealers themselves in their early teens? Today, more black men are in jail than in college. One out of every twenty black men ends up murdered, a rate seven times greater than for whites. Indeed, murder is the leading cause of death for black men aged 16 to 34.

The immensity of black problems today ranges far beyond crime and drugs, although that is what the media focuses on. There is, for example, a growing polarization of the races on many public issues. Blacks and whites starkly disagree about the fairness of the American judicial system, about whether racially separate schools can ever be truly equal, about the extent of racial prejudice in American society. Recent public opinion polls reveal that although two-thirds of the whites questioned believe that African-Americans have the same opportunities as whites, only 28 percent of the blacks do. While 71 percent of African-Americans thought the government was doing too little to help blacks, only 29 percent of whites thought so. The races are similarly divided on matters of defense spending and foreign policy, and expenditures for social welfare programs versus tax cuts. Symptomatic of these cleavages, since 1968 some two-thirds of the white electorate has voted Republican in presidential contests and 90 percent of the black electorate has voted Democratic.

There is also a geographical or physical gulf between the races. Since the 1960s there has been virtually no progress in residential integration. The Fair Housing Act passed in 1968 is an oxymoron, and desegregated housing remains Black America's Sisyphean rock. On a 1 to 100 scale, in which 100 means total segregation, the sixteen largest metropolitan areas (most with black mayors) have a rating of 80. Demographers have now coined the term "hypersegregation" to describe the phenomenon of race relations without any relations between the races. Typically, Atlanta, a city which prides itself on being racially progressive, is residentially split in half. Despite the tens of thousands of black college graduates who work side by side with whites in the downtown office buildings, Atlanta after 5 P.M. is almost as wholly segregated as it was in the days of Scarlet O'Hara. Although more key activists of the civil rights movement hold public office in Atlanta than in any other city, 90 percent of the whites live north of downtown and 90 percent of the blacks live south of downtown. And the city public school system, officially "desegregated," is more than 90 percent African-American.

Throughout the United States residential segregation is increasing and regaining wide approval. The improving economic status of middle-class African-Americans has not led to spatial mobility. It is simply not true that blacks who make enough money can live where they want to. A host of practices by realtors, bankers, and public officials maintain the color line. And so do the attitudes of the white majority who, fearing an increase in crime and a decrease in the value of their property or the quality of the public schools, oppose racially mixed neighborhoods.

Physical separation, moreover, impedes racial understanding and empathy. It fosters ignorance and suspicions. And it provides a fertile ground for ghettoized African-Americans to diverge even more from the American mainstream in their social practices, patterns of fertility, family life, and basic beliefs. In tandem with the growing distance between the races, black ghetto English has grown progressively more distinct from the standard English of whites. The result is a vicious circle: the more blacks are victims of hypersegregation, the more they appear to conform to the stereotypes that foster hypersegregation; the deeper blacks sink into physical isolation, the less concern for their plight is shown by whites.

So, unlike the response to the publicity about poverty in the 1960s, Americans in the eighties largely ignored the hundreds of thousands, disproportionately black, made homeless by the Reagan Administration's reduction in federal housing programs from more than $32 billion a year to less than $8 billion a year. Turning away from the men, women, and children eating out of trash bins, sleeping and dying on the streets, they maintained that the United States cannot afford to house the homeless, ignoring the fact that the nation spends six times more a year on homeowner's tax deductions, mainly benefitting families earning more than $50,000 a year, than would be necessary to shelter those in need.

Nor is there much public concern about the worsening educational status of blacks. At a time when educational requirements for entry-level jobs are rising rapidly, half of all young African-Americans never finish high school. As a result of the increasing costs of attending college and the decreasing amount of financial assistance and loans, as well as the de-emphasis on affirmative action, the percentage of college-age blacks attending college has dropped from 33.4 percent in 1976 to just 26 percent in 1988. Moreover, only 40 percent of those African-Americans are likely to graduate. Thus, black per capital income today is only 57 percent that of white income — just as it was in 1971. While the unemployment rate of whites has dropped from 5.1 percent in 1972 to 4.7 percent in 1988, the rate for blacks has increased from 10.4 percent to 11.8 percent. Although the poverty rate for whites was cut in half from 1970 to 1988, to about 10 percent, fully one-third of the African-Americans have consistently been designated as living below the poverty level. In absolute numbers, more blacks are poor today than when the War on Poverty was launched in the mid-1960s. And this does not even count many of those who have never had regular jobs or residences, and do not appear in censuses or unemployment surveys, or the many more blacks who live perilously close to the poverty line and can fall below it at any time.

These are the poor rural and inner-city blacks now terned the "underclass." Trapped in a cycle of joblessness, broken homes, illegitimacy, welfare dependency, inadequate health care and nutrition, insufficient education, social disorganization, and, often, crime, drugs, and violence, they are cut off form the jobs that have moved to distant suburbs and from the stable middle-class role models who have left for better neighborhoods. Fully half of all black children today live in poverty. Two-thirds of the African-American babies born last year had unwed mothers, and half of them were teenage mothers. Each day last year some 400 babies were born to unmarried black teenagers. What is the future for these fatherless children, these child mothers? At a time when so much more needs to be done, Americans are doing less, discarding a network of social programs designed to alleviate distress or to assist those willing to work for a better life.

Social Darwinism is back in style and the United States has come to accept the presence of a Third World nation within its borders. Rather than seeking the solution to the problems underlying its existence, the American people have opted for a policy of containment. Much as they did to the Indians living on reservations, they have isolated the black "underclass," made it a nation apart, the other-most America.

Quite obviously, the American Dilemma described by Gunnar Myrdal a half century ago persists. In its treatment of African-Americans the United States has not lived up to its creed. Langston Hughes' dream remains a dream deferred, as does Martin Luther King's. The United States is not yet what it should be. But it is also quite different, and better, in its social practices than it was when Hughes or Myrdal wrote, and when King dreamed of a racially harmonious society. That is as vital to understand as it is to acknowledge what remains to be done. For progress requires struggle, and struggle is born of hope. Those who remember that the Second Reconstruction arose from small and scattered strivings to vanquish what seemed to many to be an impregnable system of racial discrimination and segregation know that there will someday be a Third Reconstruction to complete the unfinished business of American democracy.

The 'Question of Europe:' Henry James and the Debate
Concerning American Culture in the Early Twentieth Century.

Helle Porsdam
Odense University

With the publication in 1921 of Harold Stearn's *Civilization in the United States,* the stage was set for a fierce discussion of American civilization. It was scarcely a surprise to those who knew the work of the contributors — among them, Van Wyck Brooks, Lewis Mumford, H. L. Mencken, George Jean Nathan, and Stearns himself — that they all seemed to agree that America was a cultural wasteland. Mumford considered the city an index of America's material success and (consequent) spiritual failure; to Mencken, the American politician was "incompetent and imbecile," "incurably dishonest," and "the first principles of civilized law-making are quite beyond him"; and to Brooks, the American disbelief in experience, habitual repression of the creative instinct and consequent overstimulation of the acquisitive instinct, had made it impossible for Americans to take advantage of the treasures their own lives had yielded. As a document, *Civilization in the United States* was an almost unanimous indictment of American activity and expression. In his Preface, Stearns commented on the unity of the opinions expressed. This was somewhat surprising, he said, and "significant" inasmuch as these opinions "were unpremeditated and were arrived at, as it were, by accident rather than design."[1] The reason could only be, he suggested, that each contributor had independently reached his conclusion because this conclusion was the only only one possible and available to a concerned observer of American cultural and intellectual life.

As regards the reasons for this cultural failure and possible solutions to it, however, opinions differed. For the former members of 'The Seven Arts' enterprise like Brooks and Waldo Frank, the principal culprit was the Puritan strain in America's past with its overemphasis on expedience and practicality and suppression of any interest in the arts and life of the mind. As America's industrial wealth increased, so its spiritual poverty likewise increased, and it became harder and harder to provide any breathing space for its independent spirits. As early as 1915, Brooks had published the first of a series of examinations of the moral imbalance of the American man. In *America's Coming-*

of-Age, he had drawn attention to a basic division in American cultural life, the two irreconcilable extremes or currents of its character, which had led to the worst forms of cultural illness: the "highbrow," feminine current, "the current of Transcendentalism, originating in the piety of the Puritans, becoming a philosophy in Johnathan Edwards, passing through Emerson, producing the fastidious refinement and aloofness of the chief American writers"; and the "lowbrow," masculine current, the "current of catchpenny opportunism originating in the practical shifts of Puritan life, becoming a philosophy in Franklin, passing through the American humorists, and resulting in the atmosphere of our contemporary business life." American culture had failed to sustain and encourage its artists, and even the most cursory survey of the American past would immediately reinforce the conviction that the Puritan, who had dominated history and was now in command of American life, was responsible for this insufferable state of affairs.[2]

For critics like Paul Elmer More and Irving Babbitt, on the other hand, the most important part of the American past was precisely New England puritanism. For reasons of their own, they claimed, modern critics had vastly misrepresented the Puritans, who represented the presence and the exercise of a moral will in the American tradition. The past for these Humanist critics could not be directly identified with any particular period of time.[3] They were interested in a *kind* of literature, a *kind* of culture more than in any given century. And if these cou..d be found at all, it would be in 18th-century England, before 'romanticism' had arrived and spoiled man's sense of propriety and decorum.

The debate about Puritanism and American culture at large thus hinged upon the matter of the past versus the present, or more precisely the relation of the past to the present. The question was furthermore how and where the researches into present definitions and past causes were to be directed. Whereas the Humanists claimed that culture was to be found in Europe and not in America, the critics represented in Stearns' volume did not unanimously advise Europe as a cure. In fact, they often condemned the tendency among young Americans to flee their problems and thereby waste their talents. In spite of a certain ambivalence on the part of these critics — as Hoffman ironically comments, "Stearns himself could hardly wait for his boat to sail"[4] — it was generally felt that the exodus to Europe in search of culture was the wrong approach. If there was any way out of and possible cure for the present state of affairs — and very few of the contributors to *Civilization in the United States* were able to muster any hope on which to pin a faith — it was to be found in America, in a participation on the part of critics and artists alike in a general examination of the past with the aim of discovering reasons for the country's actual failure.

Whether or not the probing into the American past was considered an enterprise best conducted on American soil by and for Americans, however, the 'question of Europe' was all-pervasive in the works of the critics of the

1910s and '20s. When for example Brooks, pointing back to Emerson and Whitman, called for a "focal center," a "national culture...in which everything admirably characteristic of a people sums itself up," and which could unite the highbrow and the lowbrow tendencies in America, this "focal center" was constantly referred to or defined against the background of Europe. Thus, whereas in Europe, Brooks argued, "the warfare of ideas, of social philosophies, is always an instant, close-pressed warfare in which everyone is engaged," no "warfare of ideas has ever existed" in America where "ideas have always been acutely individual and ethical, where public and social affairs, disjointed, vague, and bare have always met with the yawning indifference that springs from a relative want of pressure behind." It was not that England was not "just as much the wilderness as America," it was just that "while England has at least a handful of trained gardeners, we have nothing but cowboys and flags."[5] Thus, Europe was constantly present in the discussion about American culture; indeed, American culture was often referred to, if not defined as, the *absence* of European culture, the lack of the very elements — history, tradition, ideas transmitted from generation to generation, in short a past — that had made Europe what it was. The word, 'Europe', was used in this connection as a concept, an entity more than as a specific geographic location, and although, as we have just seen, a single European country like England might be singled out for discussion, it was 'Europe' as a concept that was used as a point of departure and reference.

The most important thing about Europe as a concept was that it constituted a contrast, a set of standards against which to 'measure' the American scene. Depending on the circumstances and, of course, on the writer, this contrasting of America with Europe could turn out to the advantage of the former or the latter, or indeed, to the advantage of both. Harold Stearns' preface to *Civilization in the United States* may serve as an illustration. "The most moving and pathetic fact in the social life of America today," he claimed, "is emotional and aesthetic starvation;" Americans "have no heritages or traditions to which to cling except those that have already withered in our hands and turned to dust." In spite of being a "polyglot boarding-house," however, America "is still in the embryonic stage, with rich and with disastrous possibilities of growth."[6] Europe may have the culture, the tradition, the art that we lack in the United States, Stearns seemed to say, but the very absence of these things and the very youth of America make the country malleable and open to creative change.

This very belief in the possibility of shaping or creating an America in its "embryonic stage" is nowhere better expressed than in Brooks' famous and influential essay from 1918, "On Creating a Usable Past." In this essay, Brooks did not confine himself to reflections on a possible future for America; he went as far as to claim that not only the future, but also the past could indeed be created. Accusing contemporary American literary critics of reaffirming the values established by the commercial and moralistic tradition instead of reflecting the creative impulse in American history and literature, he

212

argued that these critics rendered it sterile for the living mind. As the spiritual welfare of America largely depended upon the fate of its creative minds, the time had now come to discard the view of the past promoted by the literary critics as "unuseable" and instead ask the question, "What is important for us? What, out of all the multifarious achievements and impulses and desires of the American literary mind, ought we to elect to remember?" The more personally this question was answered, the better, for the past opened up easily to anyone approaching it with a capacity for personal choices.

> For the spiritual past has no objective reality; it yields only what we are able to look for in it. And what people find in literature corresponds precisely with what they find in life... The present is a void, and the American writer floats in that void because the past that survives in the common mind of the present is a past without living value. But is this the only possible past? If we need another past so badly, is it inconceivable that we might discover one, that we might even invent one?[7]

Whatever the ambivalence towards Europe and European culture inherent in the statements of the critics of the 1910s and '20s, however, it served a distinct purpose. Not only did the search for an *American* as distinct from a European identity create a certain (necessary) distance to the European heritage; it also created a certain nationalistic pride in being American. In this context, Harold Bloom's term, "anxiety of influence" as defined and used in *The Anxiety of Influence*, invariably comes to mind. The ambivalence towards Europe, the simultaneous attraction and repulsion towards the European heritage, combined with the strong wish to assert a distinctly American identity point to a certain cultural anxiety of influence on the part of the young American nation towards its European ancestry.

I.

The ambivalence or the anxiety of influence towards Europe on the part of the American critics of the 1910s and '20s is nowhere more clearly voiced than in their attitude towards American artists or writers who had succumbed to the 'lure' of Europe and had left their native soil. And if, on top of having fled their native environment, these Americans had succeeded in creating a name for themselves, in becoming famous, the ambivalence towards them was only heightened. Being one of the most famous and having by the end of his career successfully proved that an American writer — even while being expatriated — could command the respect of the rest of the world, Henry James is an obvious case in point. Of the "sense of Europe" to which James felt that his "very earliest consciousness waked," his *Autobiography* bears ample evidence. Brought up by "parents homesick, as I conceived, for the ancient order," in a household thriving on "our constant dream of 'educational' relief, of some finer kind of social issue, through Europe," James was aware from a very early age of the existence of two different worlds, the Old and the New. What ensued from this exposure to two different sets of values and styles was an awareness of "otherness," an awareness that resulted "in that early time" in an eagerness "to exchange my lot for that of somebody else, on the assumed certainty of gaining by the bargain." Being at that point in his life "the other," Europe was "in that ecstatic vision...a sublime synthesis, expressed and guaranteed" for him.8

It was precisely this "ecstatic vision" of Europe on Henry James' part that the critics of the 1910s and '20s found hard to stomach. Thus, in *The Golden Day* from 1926, Lewis Mumford accused James of treating Europe as a museum. Instead of wanting to change it, James uncritically gave to Europe his entire loyalty and wished merely to fix it. In his novels, James treated, "in a remote gentlemanly way" the perplexities and delights that "the cartoonists in Life were touching in the eighties: he answered the question, 'How must one behave in Europe?'"9 Likewise, Brooks wrote a book about James, *The Pilgrimage of Henry James* which was an attempt to exorcise the Old World demon of his youth and thereby come to terms with the polarities overshadowing his entire life — "feminine" dependence (highbrow culture) and "masculine" autonomy (lowbrow culture), aesthetic withdrawal and social action.10 Throughout his career, he had kept repeating that an artist's creative powers could flower only in the soil of his native country, surrounded by a supportive community. As a seedbed of literary tradition, this community preserved the writer's "usable past." James' problem was, Brooks claimed, that he had "strayed so far from his natural world that the tree of knowledge had withered and died in his mind," and once that had happened he had become "an artist for whom his own perplexities and the caprices of imagination have taken the place of knowledge and experience of life." Once out of "real-life" material, there was nothing he could do but resort to form. James' `late manner` was thus for Brooks nothing but a protective mechanism.11

Whatever their argument with or against James, Mumford, Brooks and their colleagues all failed to see that James did in fact take part in the whole discussion concerning American culture in which they themselves were so involved. Contrary to what these critics accused him of, James did not for a moment forget his native country and its cultural problems. Situated abroad, he became more aware of being American; his sensitivity to and understanding of his native country was heightened, so to speak. I would argue, in fact, that James' awareness of being American was so intense that America, as a theme and a subject, took precedence in his works over almost any other theme. When James returned to the United States in 1904 after an absence of more than twenty years, one of his aims was to put himself back in touch with his homeland and to write a book about his impressions. The book that came out of these impressions was *The American Scene*, and the question that intrigued and baffled James more than any other was "What meaning, in the presence of such impression, can continue to attach to such a term as the 'American' character? What type, as the result of such a prodigious amalgam, such a hotch-potch of racial ingredients, is to be conceived as shaping itself?"[12] In the attempt James made in *The American Scene* and elsewhere to answer this question, we find a concern with American culture and a search for a national identity that not only parallel but also anticipate those of Mumford, Brooks and the other critics of the 1910s and '20s.

Like his nameless narrator's journey into the visitable past of the Byronic age in "The Aspern Papers," Henry James' journey in *The American Scene* into his own past and that of his native country was more than simply a re-creation of "scenes" or a quest for nostalgia. It was an excursion which was evocative, suggestive and incomplete, inviting the imaginative efforts of the reader to complete its meaning. The exterior forces (or 'reality') of impersonal history merely provided, for James, the frame for the deeper, more personal impression of history that he wanted to explore. Each individual must decide for him- or herself what vignettes of the past are worthy of reflection. Connections and associations are easily established, but James added the element of imagination to this process to allow for a more creative reconstruction of the past. "History is never, in any rich sense, the immediate crudity of what 'happens', but the much finer complexity of what we read into it and think of in connection with it."[13] Thus, James' final answer to his friend who, in connection with "The Aspern Papers," criticized him for inventing unrealistic characters could only be the following,

> What does your contention of non-existent conscious *exposures,* in the midst of all the stupidity and vulgarity and hypocrisy, imply but that we have been, nationally, so to speak, graced with no instance of recorded sensibility fine enough to react against these things? — an admission too distressing. What one would accordingly fain do is to baffle any such calamity, to *create* the record, in default of any other enjoyment of it; to imagine, in a word, the honorable, the producible case.[14]

James' answer was a radical one, and it foreshadowed Brooks' call for a "usable past." If there is a need for a past, one must avail oneself of and select whatever elements one finds useful in order to create one. In exploring in *The American Scene* America and American history, James sought the meaning not only of his country, but also of himself. In this way, the search for an American identity was paralleled by and ultimately culminated in a search for personal identity.

In the simplest sense, the historical process constituted for James the movement of the mind towards some *idea* of history, the need of the aesthetic consciousness to discover forms and shapes in the modern disorder.[15] No work of James' more explicitly deals with the problem of historical consciousness and thus the problem of modernity than does *The American Scene*.16 In the expatriate's return to his native country, the impressions recounted clearly testify to both James' own sense of history and the disappearance of historical value in modern America. Attempting throughout the entire book to find some meaning or purpose in recent American history, James launched a critique of modern America that was explicitly linked to the modern crisis in Western thought as a whole. From the very beginning of his stay in America, James found himself "in presence, everywhere, of the refusal to consent to history," a "perpetual repudiation of the past" in favor of "the hungry, triumphant actual." Ransacking his brain for the sources of this impressiveness, he saw them "of a sudden locked up in that word, 'modern'"; the mystery cleared "in light of the fact that one was perhaps, for that half-hour, more intimately than ever before in touch with the sense of the term...that the attitude affected me as the last revelation of modernity."17

It was the immensity of the scale of things in America that more than anything else impressed James when he first arrived. The "will to grow," "the universal will to move" manifested itself everywhere — it was "a question of scale and space and chance." This "immensity of chance" fascinated him, for "it is rarely given to us to see a great game played as to the very end." Again and again, James came back to the feeling he had of observing an experiment taking place before his very eyes, an experiment as to the outcome of which he had severe doubts,

> It comes back to what we constantly feel...to what the American scene everywhere depends on for half its appeal or its effect; to the fact that the social conditions, the material, pressing and pervasive, make the particular experiment or demonstration, whatever it may pretend to, practically a new and incalculable thing...The thing is happening, or will have to happen, in the American way — the American way which is more different from all other native ways, taking country with country, than any of these latter are different from each other; and the question is of how, each time, the American way will see it through.18

What James described here as the experiment of "the American way," he might as well have described as the experiment of the modern. Along with the general loss of a historical tone, this experiment revealed itself as "the monstrous form of Democracy," a leveling force that threatened to destroy anything <u>un</u>common in its approval of the common. It was as if "a big brush, a brush steeped in crude universal white" had been wielded by this modern democracy, blurring all differences in the name of equality and creating a characteristic American blankness. Purpose and meaning were improvised without any relation to the past or the future. Reflecting the absence of the forms necessary for the creative mind to develop, modern America seemed to James increasingly to adhere to a business ethic and a collectivization of man.

216

This was critical, for as he commented at several points in the book, beauty depends on form and the forms of the present must develop slowly over time from a critical interpretation of the past.[19]

At the heart of the conspicuous consumption and massive production of the post-Civil War era, James found an absence of any social, metaphysical and intellectual principle of order. Modern America displayed a "failure of concurrent and competitive presence's, the failure of any others looming at all on the same scale save that of Business, those in particular of a visible Church, a visible State, a visible Society, a visible Past; those of the many visibilities, in short, that warmly cumber the ground in older societies." The "outward blankness" or "quantity of absence" in America was thus defined or measured by James against the background of "older societies," meaning primarily Europe.[20] Structured around a search on James' part for the center of American life, *The American Scene* is divided according to cities as focal points for regional culture.[21] Everywhere — even in New England where "one lives among English ancientries" — the picture was one of blankness, confusion and ceaseless change. In his climactic description of Washington D.C., James captured that absence and vacancy which more than anything else characterized for him the modern American scene.

Washington already bristles, for the considering eye, with national affirmations...but when you have embraced them all...you'll find yourself wondering what it is you so oddly miss. Numberless things are represented...but something is absent more even than these masses are present — till it at last occurs to you that the existence of a religious faith on the part of the people is not even remotely suggested.

What interested James was not so much religion, and religious belief *per se*; the disappearance of organized religion defined for him the 'negative' as the center of American life. As a "symbolism," the absence of religious faith pointed to the loss of that spirituality and aesthetic quality which were for James the necessary requirements for any cultural and historical consciousness.[22]

II

The American Scene ended on a prophetic note as it foreshadowed the triumph of the superficial and ephemeral in modern America. What it all came back to, James claimed, was to "the general truth of the aesthetic need, in the country, for much greater values, of certain sorts, than the country and its manners, its aspects and arrangements, its past and present, and perhaps even future, really supply." How this need was to be filled and greater values created, James did not explicitly say. The work itself does, however, leave us with the sense that James had much more to say and thus reminds us of what remains: the all-pervasive presence of the critical analyst himself. The real story of *The American Scene* is that of the artist and his creative activity, that process of consciousness coming-to-be, expressed and explained by an investigation of aesthetic form in terms of its historical analogy that is the basic subject of most of James' fiction.

The restless analyst who did his best to understand and make sense of modern America was a curious mixture of detached observer and yearning expatriate. And it was in the latter capacity that James at one and the same time mercilessly defined America's failure to fulfill its promise, yet reaffirmed the potential, the promise itself, that can be renewed by the creative imagination. "Defined in these ways is the complex role that engages James throughout the book: that of suffering and voicing the anxieties generated by American society — voicing the challenge to humane values and the imagination that American society presents — while endorsing, under pressure reinscribing, the myth that envisions redemption and renewal."[23] Even if he did not explicitly say so, that is, James felt that "the aesthetic need" in America for greater values might be "supplied" by the creative artist himself. As we shall see, James' aim was twofold. On the one hand, it had a nationalist bias, revealing itself as a sincere wish on James' part to take his place in a community-in-the-making by joining — if only as an expatriate — in the process of making it. And on the other hand, it was a highly personal and sublime bid to constitute himself as the 'author' of American culture and the modern American novel. Whether nationalist or personal or both, however, James' goal "anticipates the presumption" of the modernist writers "to substitute in a nearly literary manner, their own literary topographies for the unsatisfactory world."[24]

The criticism of, yet at the same time belief in, American culture on James' part resulted in some curious changes of mode throughout *The American Scene*. Thus, after numerous pages of descriptions of "the interesting struggle of the void," the "outward blankness," and the quantity of the "absence of settled standard" in America, the narrative voice suddenly changes — the bleak note of failure and warning so striking in those early pages gives way to a note of hope, even enjoyment. Halfway through the book, James had recognized in that very absence of means and of taste the possibility "to read into" the American scene a meaning and a purpose not immediately apparent. He was, as he phrased it, "at his old trick: he made out, on the spot, in other words, that there was a pale page into which he might read what he liked." The absence in America of fixed and settled standards thus had a potentially positive and hopeful side to it as well. Precisely by being a void, the American world possessed a vastness and a freshness that made development possible on a great scale and at a fast pace — "that is where the American material is elastic, where it affects one, as a whole, in the manner of some huge india-rubber cloth fashioned for 'field' use and warranted to bear inordinate stretching."[25]

Implicit in these statements, moreover, was the belief on James' part that the "'field' use," the "stretching" of the "elastic material" was to be performed by the creative artist himself. Just as little Maisie (*What Maisie Knew*) turned appearances that were in themselves vulgar and empty into "the stuff of poetry and tragedy and art," so James by merely wondering about the trivialities of American life gave them "meanings, aspects, solidities, connexions — connexions with the universal — that they could scarce have hoped for." Maisie, and if we keep up the parallel for a second, James himself, "makes them portentous...so that we get the striking figured symbol." By keenly observing and keeping up his "good faith," that is, the creative artist is able to endow the ordinary with meaning, to form the shapeless, to create, in short, the symbol.[26]

That James, describing Maisie's "play of good faith," would use the word "universal" is, moreover, important in that it points to both the duty and the potential of the artist as James saw him. The prime business of the artist was for James "to gauge an interest out of the vacancy," "to *make* a sense — and to make it most in proportion as the immediate aspects are loose and confused." The moment the artist merely leans back in his chair, sighing that appearances cannot possibly have any sense, he will go to pieces, for "the last thing decently permitted him is to recognize incoherence — to recognize it, that is, as baffling." The role of the artist in modern society thus had a somewhat didactic element to it for James; the reader must be taught by the artist that there is still meaning to be found — or rather made — in what looks to him as a meaningless world. And that it is, indeed, possible for the Jamesian artist to find and pass on this kind of meaning, points to James' belief in the almost sublime potential of the modern artist. In words that recall Emerson and Whitman, James talked about the poet as "the divine, explanatory genius" who knew how "to handle the secret of life." In fact, he went so far as to say at one point, the poet was the direct descendant of God, "the seer and speaker under the descent of the god is 'the poet', whatever his form, and he ceases to be the one only when his form...is unworthy of the god."[27]

If, as James suggested in *The American Scene*, America had failed to materialize the Dream on which it was founded, the remedy or way out of the modern crisis, lay in the ability of the creative imagination to use its "finer wits" to vitalize a meaning in its own artistry. It was in his own impressions and interpretations that the artist might find the basis for a redemptive vision, might turn absence into presence, so to speak. The emphasis James constantly put on the necessity of interpretation, and the priority he gave to the act of present vision and its construction of a past relation and future possibility, thus, in an act of almost existential affirmation, resulted in the survival of the rather presumptuous but impressive Jamesian ego.

The full extent of the ability and power with which James credited the modern artist is revealed, moreover, in the way in which he took it upon himself almost singlehandedly to carve out for the modern novel a respect and a position in literary society which it had not previously enjoyed. As Richard

Brodhead has pointed out, James displayed "the new ethos of the professionalizing movement in classic form" that characterized the history of work in his time.[28] More than just personal ambition, his attempt to master the *art* of the novel, the *craft* of fiction displayed a wish to create, for the sphere of writing, a new structure of ambition: one in which achievement within one's chosen field came to be seen not only as an imperative but also as an end in itself. In claiming that the novel was a craft, and a highly skilled one at that, James constituted for the novel as a genre a place in the category of literature as well as readjusted the claims the novel could make to be taken seriously. As a part of this scheme, he furthermore invented for the novel a whole structure of influence not unlike that of the more traditional high arts. He did so by redefining the novel's history and the relation of one novel to another within that history. This process of constituting for the novel a canon it did not formerly have may be seen as a parallel to the Jamesian notion of a "visitable past": if there is no past available to present needs, one must proceed to create one. In both cases, the finished creation points back to the creator himself; the merit is ultimately his, so to speak.[29]

III

As a genre, the novel suited James' purposes admirably. Being "the most independent, most elastic, most prodigious of literary forms," the novel gave him the liberty for more extravagant maneuvers and speculation than he would have had in any other genre. What the dramatist needed, James repeatedly stated in his prefaces, was freedom to create — whereas "the historian wants more documents than he can really use, the dramatist only wants more liberties than he can really take." Without this freedom, James would argue, the artist would end up imitating or referring to the actual world from which he takes his materials, rather than actively molding it — he would passively give in to the "baffling incoherence" of the modern world instead of attempt to make sense of it. If merely using his artistic skill to imitate the real world, the artist would be guilty of forgetting his prime business, that of "gauging an interest *out* of the vacancy." A work of art based solely on imitation would thus lose its potential power to redeem its materials in the act of creation. "If the life about us for the last thirty years refuses warrant for these examples, then so much the worse for that life. The *constatation* would be so deplorable that instead of making it we must dodge it," as James answered his critical friend who complained about the lack of reality in his fiction.

Central to this potentially redemptive quality of the novel, as James saw it, was the debate he carried on all his life with himself as well as with fellow novelists, the debate concerning the importance of 'romance' and 'realism', respectively, in the novel. *The Art of the Novel* and his critical essays bear ample evidence of the role this debate played for James. Tracing in his preface to "The Aspern Papers," for example, "the germ" of his idea for the short story back to the legend of an ardent Shelleyite searching for original Shelley documents, James commented on the "facts" of this legend that they "were more distinct and more numerous than I mostly *like* facts: like them, that is, as we say of an etcher's progressive subject, in an early 'state'. Nine tenths of the artist's interest in them is that of what he shall add to them and how he shall turn them." Too many "facts" thus would ruin the game for the creative artist by not allowing him those liberties so crucial to his process of creation. To put it in another way, too many facts depreciated the "romance-value" of a potential project. James did not intend with these comments to minimize the importance of exactness. Indeed, the success of a novel depended for James on "the amount of felt life" the writer is able to convey — only in so far as a novel is based on the writer's own experience, is "the result of some direct impression or perception of life" of his own, is it genuine, valid, and sincere. It is, however, not until the writer in the process of creation has converted his experience into art, that this experience gains universal importance. Subject may be prior to form — reality to art — but it is through form, or the creation of form, that the meaning of the subject is revealed.[30]

To make the reader wonder constituted for James a very important goal as a writer, and the medium of romance was the one through which this could be achieved — "since the question for me has ever been but of wondering, and with all achievable adroitness, of causing to wonder, so the whole fairy-tale side of life has used, for a tug at my sensibility, a cord all its own. When we want to wonder, there's no such good ground for it as the wonderful."[31] Reality in itself, as man daily confronts it, and by implication mimetic or imitating art, does not provide mankind with the opportunity to wonder and to hope but merely underscores the sordidness of the modern world. James would thus have agreed with Northrop Frye and his argument in *Anatomy of Criticism* that, being closest to undisplaced myth, the romance is "nearest of all literary forms to the wish-fulfillment dream."[32] For Frye, as for James, it is in the romantic elements of a work of art that the redemptive quality or potential is displayed. For, as James showed in for example "The Real Thing," the real suffers from a rigidity, a lack of flexibility that makes it unfit as material for the artist's palette. Thus, in that story, it is the two upstarts who 'win' in the end, as the elderly couple, the "real thing," lack every kind of suggestive quality and consequently leave the artist's imagination untouched.

In the ghost-story, James found a sub-category of romance that gave him ample opportunity for giving the imagination "absolute freedom of hand." Constituting "the most possible form of the fairy-tale," as he "confessed" in the preface to "The Altar of the Dead," the ghost-story presented him with a "clear field of experience, as I call it, over which we are thus led to roam; an annexed but independent world in which nothing is right save as we rightly imagine it." In the ghost-story, things cease to be merely themselves, gestures cease to be merely tokens of social intercourse whose meaning is assigned by a social code; they become, instead, the vehicles of metaphors whose tenor suggests another kind of reality. Any kind of meaning — ordinary or transcendent — may be read into the opaque whiteness or indistinctiveness of a ghost.

James' ghosts were rarely benign. In fact, as he commented in his preface to "The Turn of the Screw," they were not "ghosts" at all, "as we now know the ghost, but goblins, elves, imps, demons as loosely constructed as those of the old trial for witchcraft," and their function was to cause "the situation to reek with the air of Evil." By thus introducing into the medium of pure romance elements as far removed from the romantic as possible — this being, as he said, exactly his "central idea" — James turned the old gothic romance into a modern psychological romance or drama. And in the process, I would argue, he ran the risk of undermining the very function of romance, as he saw and defined it in his prefaces. The air of foreboding, even doom that hovers over his ghost-stories seemed to question or jeopardize the redemptive quality of romance — the "bad dead" that he brought "back to life for a second round of badness" were at odds with or contradicted the visionary elements of romance, so to speak.[33] Like the ghosts of the gothic romance, James' ghosts come back to haunt the living, as alter egos often raising the question of what might have been — e.g. "The Jolly Corner" — or as encounters with a character's failure to realize himself and the appalling emptiness of his experience — e.g. "The Beast in the Jungle"; but they do so in an essentially 'daemonic way' that is associated with the fear of mortality and the crushing sense of being isolated in our own doomed individuality that results. What I want to suggest here is that James, in his use of the ghost-story as a subcategory of romance, displayed the ambivalence and dilemma of modern man: the realization, on the one hand, that living in a meaningless universe man has to find whatever meaning he can for himself in his own consciousness; and the fear, on the other, to take on the responsibility of that attempted sublimity and the resulting life-denying resentment of time and becoming. In this way, James' ghosts and their "portentous evil" may be said to show signs of the "dark sublime" in American literature that Klaus Poenicke has identified.[34]

222

IV

The act of expatriation was a response on James' part to the failure he originally perceived the American experiment to be. Rather than the cause of such alienation, that is, his expatriation was the product of the cultural dissociation he felt towards his native country. His discovery of a relation to the Old World had come about as a result of his search for cultural identity, and what emerged out of this complex relationship between expatriation and the question of American nationality was the Jamesian 'international theme.' Attempting to give historical actuality to the international connection, James embraced the psychology of nationalism as the more general need of the modern for identity, significance, and relation to others. The question of America became for James the question of modernity, and it could not be fully understood without its contrary and cultural ancestor, Europe. "James' international theme is the psychic and linguistic *problem of modernity*, which involves a theory of artistic expression that goes well beyond the limits of any historical period," as John Carlos Rowe aptly puts it.[35] In his *Autobiography*, James explicitly set up the contrast of Europe and America as that of the ancient and the modern, a contrast that could be successfully handled only if he made a serious attempt to absorb himself in and thus come to a deeper understanding of the ancient:

> I saw my parents homesick, as I conceived, for the ancient order and distressed and inconvenienced by many of the more immediate features of the modern, as the modern pressed upon us, and since their theory of our better living was from an early time that we should renew the quest of the ancient, on the very first possibility I simply grew greater in the faith that somehow to manage that would constitute success in life. I never found myself deterred from this fond view, which was implied in every question I asked, every answer I got, and every plan I formed.[36]

In the international theme James found the perfect vehicle for renewing that "quest of the ancient" which constituted a necessary first step for any insight into and discussion about the modern — and what could be more fitting as a metaphor of modern alienation and rootlessness than precisely the international theme.

James' attitude towards Europe was by no means unambiguous. As a concept of the ancient, Europe possessed a "positively pleasant 'tone'" due to the fact that "it has had in its past some strange phases and misadventure," possessed a rich past, that is, compared to which the American scene looked a mere blank. At the same time, however, James saw this rich European past as a burden, "the consequence of too much history," in contrast to which the very blankness of America held up a promise of newness and freshness.[37] In this way, the European past betrayed a sense of narrowness and rigidity that could be downright suffocating and consequently useful only in negative terms. In his unfinished novel, *The Sense of the Past*, James had his main character go through precisely such a stifling European experience. Unconsciously looking for and finding in the past the link with the present, Ralph's encounter with the European past gives him only anguish and unease. Being compelled to project himself at each step onto a virtual future, he ends by choosing the way of modifying the past. Yet modifying the ordered development of the past amounts to a refusal of the past as such, to a disowning of his early enthusiasm. Furthermore, he modifies the past in order to *escape* from it. In this late novel, that is, Europe and the past are utterly defeated and explicitly denounced.

Like so many other of his countrymen in James' novels, Ralph originally came to Europe in search of knowledge. As James commented in *The Art of the Novel*, "the most general appearance of the American (of those days) in Europe" was "that of being incredibly unaware of life," and the only way in which he could overcome this "state of innocence" was to go to Europe.[38] What supplanted innocence as purity was necessarily consciousness; at root the knowledge of good and evil. This, James' American characters gained by crossing the Atlantic — the price being a "death of childhood" not unlike the one Maisie suffered upon gaining knowledge. The fall from innocence caused by the encounter with Europe was thus a violent one and may be seen as a general initiation into the problem of modernity. In this connection, it is interesting to note how James linked his own mysterious "wound" to the Civil War, seeing his inability to participate as his personal lack. The feeling of guilt that ensued, guilt of <u>not</u> participating in this major historic event in America became at once the cause and the effect of his expatriation — the link between a physical but mainly psychological wound and expatriation is a telling one.[39]

In a curious paragraph in *The American Scene*, James summed up the story of his having become an expatriate. It was to Europe, he explained, that he had in his youth looked for "some likelihood of impressions more numerous and various and of a higher intensity than he might gather on the native scene; and it was doubtless in conformity with some such desire more finely and more frequently to vibrate that he had originally begun to consult the European oracle." This had led, in the event, to his settling down in Europe. As Europe had become increasingly familiar, however, it had lost for him "its primal note of mystery" — the European complexity that had originally fascinated James came to present itself to him, that is, as "the very stuff, the common texture, of the real world." Romance and mystery would consequently have to be found elsewhere and in a curious inversion of logic, James found himself turning to the native, the forsaken scene for an appeal to his faculty of wonder. It was, in fact, very simple, he concluded: "Europe had been romantic years before, because she was different from America; wherefore America would now be romantic because she was different from Europe."[40] The dramatic change James' view of Europe had undergone over the years is very interesting, pointing as it does to the major distinction in his late fiction between Europe as 'reality' and America as 'romance'. Burdened as Europe was by its past and built as it was on historical contingencies, it had been reduced to so many "facts," stifling the creative imagination which had, consequently, to seek its nourishment in the aura of romance and freshness that surrounded young America.

Implicit in the Jamesian notion of romantic America was a belief that his native country — as opposed to Europe — was freed from the burden of history. Indeed, one may argue, it was this very belief in a redemptive America that gave rise to James' sublime bid to constitute himself as the 'author' of American culture and the modern American novel. What this survival of the all-pervasive Jamesian ego revealed, one may furthermore argue, was the illusion of modernity, the illusion of a decisive absolute discontinuity in history, a fundamental change in direction. Whether consciously or subconsciously on James' part, however, this illusion surfaced from time to time *as* an illusion — to this, his ambiguity towards Europe and his 'international theme' as well as towards his ghost-stories bear evidence. Somehow, the past simply refused to be repudiated — it insisted on returning.

References

For Henry James, Europe came to be seen as an alternative to, perhaps even a repudiation of, the emerging culture of consumption in America. For a different approach to James' role in the culture of consumption, see e.g. Jean-Christophe Agnew, "The Consuming Vision of Henry James," in Richard W. Fox and T.J. Jackson Lears, *The Culture of Consumption*. As several critics have pointed out, James' statements about himself and his own fiction are often to be taken with a grain of salt; in this essay, I will, however, risk on a couple of occasions to rely on quotes from James' *Autobiography* and *The Art of the Novel*.

1. Harold Stearns, *Civilization in the United States*. New York: Harcourt, Brace and Company, 1922, pp. 23, vi.
2. Van Wyck Brooks, *America's Coming of Age*. New York: B.W. Huebsch, 1924, p. 9.
3. See Frederick J. Hoffman, *The Twenties, American Writing in the Postwar Decade*. New York: Viking Press, 1955, pp. 139-45.
4. *Ibid.*, p. 13.
5. Brooks, *op. cit.*, p. 119.
6. Stearns, *op. cit.*, p. vi.
7. Van Wyck Brooks, "On Creating a Usable Past," *The Early Years*. New York: Harper and Row, pp. 220-23.
8. Henry James, *Autobiography*. Princeton, New Jersey: Princeton University Press, 1983, pp. 22, 110, 101, 161.
9. Lewis Mumford, *The Golden Day*. New York: W.W. Norton and Company Inc., 1926, pp. 207-08.
10. See T. Jackson Lears, *No Place of Grace: Antimodernism and the Transformation of American Culture, 1880-1920*. New York: Pantheon Books, 1981, pp. 251-60.
11. Van Wyck Brooks, *The Pilgrimage of Henry James*. New York: Octagon Books, 1972, pp. 141, 123, 104.
12. Henry James, *The American Scene*. Bloomington: Indiana University Press, 1968, pp. 120-21.
13. *Ibid.*, p. 182.
14. Henry James, *The Art of the Novel*. Boston: Northeastern University Press, 1984, p. 222.
15. For an excellent and extensive treatment of James' view of history and the historical process, see John Carlos Rowe, *Henry Adams and Henry James. The Emergence of a Modern Consciousness*. Ithaca and London: Cornell University Press, 1976, Chapter 5.
16. When I use the term, 'modernity', here, I am thinking of the 'modernity' defined by Paul de Man and developed by Harold Bloom's 'anxiety of influence': "As soon as modernism becomes conscious of its own

strategies...it discovers itself to be a generative power that not only engenders history, but is part of a generative scheme that extends back far into the past." Paul de Man, *Blindness and Insight. Essays in the Rhetoric of Contemporary Criticism*. New Haven and London: Yale University Press, 1979, p. 150.

17. James, *The American Scene*, pp. 21, 55, 183.
18. *Ibid.*, pp. 54, 84, 55, 357.
19. *Ibid.*, pp. 288-94.
20. *Ibid.*, pp. 135,43.
21. Rowe, *op. cit.,* p. 154.
22. James, *The American Scene*, pp. 24, 380.
23. Lawrence Holland, *The Expense of Vision*. Baltimore and London: Johns Hopkins University Press, 1982, p. 420.
24. John Carlos Rowe, *The Theoretical Dimensions of Henry James*. Madison, Wisconsin: The University of Wisconsin Press, 1984, p. 154.
25. James, *The American Scene*, pp. 162, 44, 384, 321.
26. James, *The Art of the Novel*, p. 147.
27. James, *The American Scene*, pp. 13, 273, 123, 340.
28. Richard Brodhead, *The School of Hawthorne*. New York and Oxford: Oxford University Press, 1986, p. 112.
29. See Brodhead, pp. 113-116.
30. James, *The Art of the Novel*, pp. 326, 162, 222, 163, 161.
31. *Ibid.*, p. 254.
32. Northrop Frye, *Anatomy of Criticism*. Princeton, New Jersey: Princeton University Press, 1957, p. 186.
33. James, *The Art of the Novel*, pp. 170, 254, 171, 175, 176.
34. Klaus Poenicke, *Dark Sublime: Raum und Selbst in der amerikanischen Romantik*. Heidelberg: Carl Winter Universitätsverlag, 1972.
35. Rowe, *The Theoretical Dimensions of Henry James*, p. 47.
36. James, *Autobiography*, p. 50.
37. *Ibid.*, p. 175.
38. James, *The Art of the Novel*, p. 187.
39. See Rowe, *The Theoretical Dimensions of Henry James*, p. 55. If James' attitude towards Europe was ambivalent, so was by implication his attitude towards his 'international theme'. In *The Art of the Novel* he kept coming back to this theme, but in doing so he assigned it varying degrees of importance. The impression one gets from James' remarks is that he was somehow reluctant to get into a thorough discussion of the issue. Whether this reluctance was due to the mere immensity of the task or to a fear of getting lost in the intricacies of the topic is hard to tell. The fact remains, however, that there was "really too much to say," much more "than I can touch on by the way."
40. *The American Scene*, pp. 365-366.

Flatness and Depth:
Two Dimensions of the Critique of American Culture in Europe

Rob Kroes
University of Amsterdam

For as long as Americans have tried to chart their own national destiny and identity as distinct from the Old World, Europeans have been engaged in a similar pursuit. On both sides of the Atlantic, inquisitive minds were one in their perception and awareness of difference, in their intimation that America was not a mere offshoot of Europe, not a mere replica of its society and culture, but that, in one way or other, it represented a break with European precedent. America, in the eyes of both Americans and Europeans, was seen as different from Europe, not in the sense that European nations differ from each other, but as different in a different way. It was a difference of a new order, as if America had ventured onto a new plane of historical development. This basic awareness could be expressed in various ways, depending on the dominant rhetoric and mental perspective of an age. It could be cast in terms of biblical prophecy and providential history, as in early Puritan thought, or in terms of the time-honored myth of the *translatio imperii*, the westward course of empire, by theologians like Bishop Berkeley or those of a more secular-humanist cast of mind, like Crèvecoeur, the European aristocrat posing as American farmer. It could also be rendered in language that was more radically secular, reflecting views of history as continuing progress, as, for example, in Tocqueville's analysis of democracy in America. In all such views America was perceived as having ventured out ahead of Europe, leaving it to stew in its internal broils, or at best holding out a promise of things to come to Europe later.

But this was never the only way one could conceive of America's special place. Even when people accepted the view that America was *sui generis*, on a plane of history different than Europe's, it need not necessarily be on a higher plane. Many are the views that, at one time or other, have belabored the point of America being a withered transplant of Europe, a nation and a culture that had lapsed to a more barren stage of development. From the more facetious European views of Buffon, De Pauw and others, to the long litanies of cultural absences by Americans such as Hawthorne or James, we find illustrations of this more negative view of the European-American relation.

There is one peculiar fusion of the two perspectives which is of special relevance to my argument. In this view, one could conceive of America as the harbinger of future trends in store for Europe, yet at the same time see them in a negative light. It is a perspective that casts America as the corrupter of European values and cultural standards, as an erosive force that works to flatten the intricate contours of Europe's cultural landscape. The *locus classicus* of this view is Tocqueville's analysis of cultural life under conditions of social equality. He develops the argument in the second part of his study on democracy in America, the gloomier part, in which America is a mere illustrative case in his far more general reflections on the sociology of an egalitarian society. If liberty and its preservation — that old quandary of political philosophy — is arguably the central theme of the first part of his work (which, parenthetically, came out as a self-contained single volume in 1835, followed only a full five years later by the second volume), equality is the central concern of the second part. There, remarkably foreshadowing much later work in the area of the cultural and political critique of mass democracy, we find his famous dissections of individualism as a form of hide-bound conformism and of citizen apathy towards the political sphere. Equality, as almost a Durkheimian state of anomie, is the driving force behind this flattening of the landscape. As Tocqueville put it, "le désir de l'égalité devient toujours plus insatiable à mesure que l'égalité est plus grande." (The greater the extent of equality, the more insatiable the taste for it becomes.) The bounds of human aspiration have not just changed location, they have changed in form and nature. "Lorsque les hommes sont à peu près semblables et suivent une même route, il est bien difficile qu'aucun d'entre eux marche vite et perce à travers la foule uniforme qui l'environne et le presse." (When people have become roughly similar and follow the same route, it is hard for any single one among them to walk fast and to leave behind the uniform crowd that surrounds and presses him on all sides.) Not only is there a collective force working against individual excellence, the very idea of excellence has shrunk to a narrow sphere of marginal differentiation.

Quelques démocratiques que soient l'état social et la constitution politique d'un peuple, on peut donc compter que chacun de ses citoyens apercevra toujours près de soi plusieurs points qui le dominent, et l'on peut prévoir qu'il tournera obstinément ses regards de ce seul coté." (No matter how democratic the social state and the political constitution of a people, one can be sure that every single citizen will always see near him some points that rise above him. One may expect that he will fix his gaze on precisely those points, with a view — one may add — to either flattening them or to becoming level with them.)

The quest for distinction, ardent and unending as it may be, has not only lowered its view, it has also become utterly self-defeating. Not only does it prevent men from rising above the multitude, more seriously it prevents them from striving to rise above themselves. They have become thoroughly socialized animals, meekly taking their cues from the collectivity that envelops them. In matters of cultural taste and cultural standards too this erosive flattening is at work. As Tocqueville argues, in the production of literary works time-honored rules of construction, yes, form itself will be neglected. A sense of literary tradition, of the history of an art, no longer makes itself felt in the present. History — time — has contracted into an ephemeral and ever-changing Here and Now. The imaginative effect to stun the reading public will take the place of profundity, of depth. The levelling works on both ends, eroding heights as much as filling in depths, leaving vacant horizontal space for the insatiable levelling appetite further to consume itself.

In his critique of America, seen as the ideal type of an egalitarian democracy, Tocqueville ushered in a repertoire of metaphors that would recur over and over again in later critical writings on mass consumption societies. In their evocation of pairs of logical opposites — flatness versus height or depth, constraint versus boundlessness, time versus the single moment, the group versus the individual — the underlying antithesis is always between the ways of Europe and those of America, or, in more historical terms, between societies in an aristocratic mould and the emerging type of the democratic society. It would not be until the traumatic advent of mass democracy in Europe, in the turmoil of the immediate post-World War I period, that this rhetorical repertoire would gain currency among a generation of conservative critics of culture. Once again America provided them with the material for their case. Once again they looked toward America with the ominous sense of watching Europe's future. People like Oswald Spengler in Germany, Georges Duhamel in France, Johan Huizinga in the Netherlands are among the better known examples of this era of cultural pessimism in Europe. Ironically, one name that is usually mentioned in this connection, the Spaniard Ortega y Gasset, had no use for America in his critique of cultural trends in Europe. To him, America did not foreshadow Europe's future. America, to him, had only just entered history and Europe could learn nothing from its experience. America was still at a primitive stage, albeit in the camouflage of the latest inventions. In a "Preface to French Readers," which in 1937 he added to a reprint of his *The Revolt of the Masses*, first published in 1929, he felt the satisfaction of having been proved right by history. Against all those that in the twenties, from a stagnant Europe had looked hopefully toward an America wallowing in prosperity, he had maintained that America, far from holding out the prospect of the future, was truly a distant past, a primitivism. But he was an exception among all those that, either hopefully or in ominous foreboding, watched the American example. Let us analyze a little more in depth what those others had to say about America.

Why I reject "America."(Waarom ik "Amerika" afwijs).[1] Such was the provocative title of a piece, published in 1928, by a young author, Menno Ter Braak, 26 years old, and due to become a leading force in Dutch intellectual life during the thirties. Despite the occasional reference to its title, the piece apparently is little-read, or at any rate misread. For the America which is so curtly dismissed is really an America in quotation marks, "America," a construct of the mind, a composite image based on the perception of dismal trends which are then linked to America as the country and the culture characteristically, but not uniquely, displaying them. Nor, on the other hand, is it uniquely for outsiders to be struck by them and reject them. Indeed, as Ter Braak himself admits, anyone sharing his particular sensibility and intellectual detachment he is willing to acknowledge as a European "even if he happens to live in Main Street." It is an attitude for which he offers us the striking parable of a young newspaper vendor whom he saw one day standing on the balcony of one of those pre-war Amsterdam streetcars, surrounded by the pandemonium of traffic noise, yet enclosed in a private sphere of silence. Amid the pointless energy and meaningless noise the boy stood immersed in the reading of a musical score, deciphering the secret code which admitted entrance to a hidden inner world. This immersion, this loyal devotion to the probing of meaning and sense, to a heritage of signs and significance are, to Ter Braak, the ingredients of Europeanism. It constitutes, to him, the quintessentially European reflex of survival against the onslaught of a world increasingly organized around the tenets of rationality, utility, mechanization, instrumentality, yet utterly devoid of meaning, and prey to the forces of entropy. The European reaction is one that pays tribute to what is useless, unproductive, defending a quasi-monastic sphere of silence and reflexiveness amidst the whirl of secular motion.

This reflex of survival through self-assertion was of course a current mood in Europe during the interbellum, a Europe in ruins not only materially but spiritually as well. Amid the aimless drift of society's disorganization and the cacophony of demands accompanying the advent of the masses on to the political agora, Americanism as a concept had come to serve the purpose of focussing the diagnosis of Europe's plight. The impulse toward reassertion — toward the concentrated retrieval of meaning from the fragmented score of European history — was therefore mainly cultural and conservative, much as it was an act of protest and defiance at the same time. Many are the names of the conservative apologists we tend to associate with this mood. There is Huizinga, the Dutch historian, who, upon his return from his only visit to the United States at about the time that Ter Braak wrote his apologia, expressed himself thus: "Among us Europeans who were travelling together in America ... there rose up repeatedly this pharisaical feeling: we all have something that you lack; we admire your strength but we do not envy you. Your instrument of civilization and progress, your big cities and your perfect organization, only make us nostalgic for what is old and quiet, and sometimes your life seems hardly to be worth living, not to speak of your future" [2] — a statement in which we hear resonating the ominous foreboding that "your future" might well read as "our future". For indeed, what was only implied here would come out more clearly in Huizinga's more pessimistic writings of the late thirties and early forties, when America became a mere piece of evidence in his case against contemporary history losing form. Much as the attitude involved is one of a rejection of "America" and Americanism, what should strike a detached observer is the uncanny resemblance with critical positions which Americans had reached independently. Henry Adams of course is the perfect example, a prefiguration of Ter Braak's "man on the balcony," reading the disparate signs of aimlessness, drift and entropy in a desperate search for a "useless" and highly private transcendence. But of course his urgent quest, his cultural soul-searching was much more common in America, was much more of a constant in the American psyche than Europeans may have been willing to admit. Cultural exhortation and self-reflexion, under genteel or not-so-genteel auspices, were then as they are now a recurrent feature of the American cultural scene. During one such episode, briefly centered around the cultural magazine *The Seven Arts*, James Oppenheim, its editor, pointed out that "for some time we have seen our own shallowness, our complacency, our commercialism, our thin self-indulgent kindliness, our lack of purpose, our fads and advertising and empty politics."[3] In this brief period, on the eve of America's intervention in World War I, there was an acute awareness of America's barren cultural landscape, especially when looked at through European eyes. Van Wyck Brooks, one of the leading spokesmen for this group of Young Turks, pointed out that "for two generations the most sensitive minds in Europe — Renan, Ruskin, Nietzsche, to name none more recent — have summed up their mistrust of the future in that one word" — Americanism. "And it is because, altogether externalized ourselves, we have typified the universally externalizing influences of modern industrialism."[4] Here, in the words of an American cultural critic, we have a crisp, early version of Ter Braak's and Huizinga's later case against Americanism, against an America in quotation marks. American culture no more than "typified" what universal forces of industrialism threatened to bring elsewhere.

One further example may serve to illustrate the sometimes verbal parallels between European and American cultural comment. In a piece written in honor of Alfred Stieglitz, entitled "The Metropolitan Milieu," Lewis Mumford spoke of the mechanical philosophy and the new routine of industry and the dilemmas this posed to the artist whose calling it was "to become a force in his own right once more, as confident of his mission as the scientist or the engineer," without succumbing however to the lure of senseless conquest as conceived by the scientist or engineer. "In a world where practical success canceled every other aspiration, this meant a redoubled interest in the goods and methods that challenged the canons of pecuniary success — contemplation and idle reverie," — it is almost as if we hear Ter Braak — "high craftsmanship and patient manipulation, ... an emphasis on the ecstasy of being rather than a concentration on the pragmatic strain of 'getting there'."[5]

Yet, in spite of these similarities, the European cultural critics may seem to argue a different case and to act on different existential cues: theirs is a highly defensive position in the face of a threat which is exteriorized, perceived as coming from outside, much as in fact it was immanent to the drift of European culture. What we see occurring is in fact the retreat toward cultural bastions in the face of an experience of a loss of power and historical position; it is the psychological equivalent of the defense of a national currency through protectionism. It manipulates the terms of psychological trade. A clear example is Spengler's statement in his *Jahre der Entscheidung*:

> "Das Leben (in Amerika) ist ausschliesslich wirtschaftlich gestaltet und entbehrt der Tiefe, um so mehr als ihm das Element der echten geschichtlichen Tragik, das grosse Schicksal fehlt, das die Seele der abendländischen Völker durch Jahrhunderte vertieft und erzogen hat ...".[6]
> (Life in America revolves solely around its economy and is lacking in depth, the more so as the element of true historical tragedy, of true fate, is absent, which has deepened and educated the souls of the European nations ...)

Huizinga made much the same point in his 1941 essay on the formlessness of American history, yet Spengler's choice of words is more revealing. In his elevation of such cultural staples as "depth" and "soul," he typifies the perennial response to an experience of inferiority and backwardness of one society toward more potent rivals. Such was the reaction, as Norbert Elias has pointed out in his magisterial study of the process of civilization, on the part of an emerging German bourgeoisie vis-a-vis the pervasive radiance of French *civilisation*. Against French "civilisation" as a mere skin-deep veneer it elevated German "Kultur" as more deep-felt, warm and authentic. It was a proclamation of emancipation through the declaration of cultural superiority. A similar stress on feeling, soul and depth vis-a-vis the cold rationality of an imperialist civilization can be seen in an essay entitled "Ariel," written in 1900 by the Uruguayan author José Enrique Rodó. He opposed the "alma" of the weak Spanish-American countries to the utilitarianism of the United States. Once again cultural sublimation was the answer in this so-called Arielista ideology, which inspired several generations of Latin-American intellectuals.

Americanism, then, is the twentieth-century equivalent of French eighteenth-century "civilisation" as perceived by those who rose up in defense against it. It serves as the negative mirror image in the quest for a national identity through cultural self-assertion. Americanism in that sense is therefore a component of the wider structure of anti-Americanism, paradoxical as this may sound.

If, to all these cultural critics, American and European alike, America had surfaced as the nation that had advanced farthest on the road toward a culture of mass consumption, it had surfaced in a highly metaphorical sense. Not only had it reached surface, it had become mere surface. It had produced a national culture that was quintessentially superficial, a surface phenomenon whose main cultural vectors were all horizontal. In its conformism, in its peer group emulation, in its consuming quest for ever-changing thrills and satisfactions, it presented a picture of all drift and no mastery. In the great Tocquevillean tradition, Duhamel, in his *Scènes de la vie future*, described the Americans as slaves, enslaved to the social dictates of a consumption society, in spite of their hallowed rhetoric of freedom and liberty. Film, that new form of mass entertainment, "le plus puissant instrument de conformisme moral, esthétique et politique" (that most potent instrument of moral, esthetical and political conformism), to Duhamel, hurled itself as a wave of destruction from America across the intellectual landscape of France. Yes, film had the power to entertain, even at times to move the audience, but never, like any form of true art, did it incite the individual consumer "de se surpasser" — to rise above himself. Never did American culture challenge the individual to pause and reflect, to find coherence and meaning, to consummate rather than merely to consume.

In a similar vein, in 1927, the young Flemish poet and novelist Marnix Gijzen, born in 1899, prefaced a collection of travel reports that he had sent from America to the Belgian newspaper *De Standaard*: "Practically all of us are subject to the levelling influence of the American film *de quatrième zone*. In its efforts to accommodate every conceivable audience, its inner meaning has vanished ... . Yet it influences our thoughts and behavior. By its systematic neglect of everything problematic, it creates an atmosphere of intellectual indifference and constitutes a dissolving factor of our entrenched folk life." Film was not the sole carrier of pernicious influence in Gijzen's view. "The cheap car and the mobility it brings are gradually changing our society in ways that we cannot always perceive clearly, but whose advanced development I had the chance to study closely in America. The car as an object of everyday use rather than a mere luxury item is a common American notion: . . . It is the main supporting element of the nomadic way of life, the extreme mobility that characterizes America. . . .The time which it helps to save on the one hand, tends to get lost in mere agitated motion on the other. The car helps to make life 'superficial', it exteriorizes it to a large degree. . . . Problems are in store for us which, without the lessons from America, we are unable to foresee."[7] Again we recognize the context of perception and the metaphors used for its description. Again, America is seen as a country and a culture way ahead of Europe down the road to cultural decay and social dissolution. The metaphors are once again those of the surface, of horizontal movement, of loss of depth and meaning. Whatever the precise charge levelled against American culture, it was always in one way or other a variation on the charge of a vertical dimension missing. Whether America was seen as cold, instrumental, efficient, conformist, endlessly energetic, they were all the qualities of a collective mind remaining on the surface of life, never probing the depths of its soul, nor trying to transcend its concern with the Here and Now. If, to Tocqueville, egalitarianism was the central explanation of this life on the surface, to many twentieth century cultural critics, consumerism was the main culprit. Yet the relationship between the two had already been suggested by Tocqueville and would later be taken up again and further developed in the work of Thorstein Veblen and, half a century later, in David Riesman's *The Lonely Crowd*, and W. Lloyd Warner's sociology of status and taste. If competition was the driving force in the world of production, the narcissism of marginal differentiation would become the engine of a frenzied consumerism. The role that etiquette had played in Europe's hierarchical societies for the maintenance of its status boundaries, was now played by the ever-shifting rulebook of taste, defining the fine distinctions between taste communities, or, as Daniel Boorstin called them, consumption communities.

Thus, one central theme in Tocqueville's work — his analysis of individualism and conformism — can be seen as crucially informing the later sociology of our contemporary consumption society. The shift that he noticed, away from an independent, self-reliant individual towards the obsequious social animal inhabiting an egalitarian social world, would recur in Riesman's felicitously named pair of the inner-directed and the other-directed man. Riesman, though, was relatively detached in his analysis of this shift from one historical type to the other. He had a keen eye for the roguish, if not picaresque aspects of life in an other-directed society. The social games of one-upmanship that he explored in a number of areas of life were still cast in a mould of rational strategies and tactics.

That would change in the work of contemporary critics whose inspiration was more in a Marxist or Freudian than a Tocquevillean vein. With their keen eye for the erosive impact of capitalism on such central concepts of a liberal world view as self-interest, individual need, and more generally the rationality of individual behavior, theirs was essentially an exploration of the massive false consciousness of consumerism, or, as Marcuse would have it, of the repressive tolerance of capitalism. A telling illustration of this view, again from France, is Simone de Beauvoir's travelogue, *L'Amérique au jour le jour* (America from Day to Day).8 Travelling in America in the early post-war years, she finds herself torn between exhilaration and rejection. At times, amidst profusions of rapture brought about by the pace and variety of American life, a censorial voice takes over that is reminiscent of both Tocqueville and Marx:

> . . . dans cette profusion de robes, de blouses, de jupes, de manteaux une Française aurait peine à faire un choix qui ne choquât pas son goût. Et puis on s'aperçoit bientôt que sous les papiers multicolores qui les enrobent, tous les chocolats ont le même goût de cacahuète, tous les best-sellers racontent la même histoire. Et pourquoi choisir un dentifrice plutôt qu'un autre? Il y a dans cette profusion inutile un arrière-goût de mystification. Voici mille possibilités ouvertes: mais c'est la même. Mille choix permis: mais tous équivalents. Ainsi le citoyen américain pourra consommer sa

liberté à l'intérieur de la vie qui lui est imposée sans s'apercevoir que cette vie même n'est pas libre."

(...in this profusion of ladies' garments, a French woman would be hard put to make a choice and not offend her taste. And then one begins to notice that underneath their multi-colored wrappers, all chocolates have the same taste of peanut, all bestsellers tell the same story. And why choose one toothpaste rather than another? There is an after-taste of mystification in all this useless profusion. A thousand possibilities are open: yet they're all the same. A thousand choices allowed: all equivalent. Thus the American citizen will be able to consume his liberty inside the life that is imposed on him without so much as noticing that such a life itself is not free.)

We recognize the repertoire: taste in its refined European sense versus its spurious imitation in America, European elitism versus crude American egalitarianism, hierarchy versus flatness, but above all the European recognition of the aspect of captivity in American liberty.

Similar views inspired the rhetoric of the liberationist counter-culture of the late '60s, both in America and in Europe. The short-lived vogue of the Frankfurt School in Germany, and of Marxist sociologists like Baudrillard in France, further sustained this international critical consensus. Again, if capitalism was the main target in theory, America as the epitome of all that was wrong with capitalism was the main target in a rhetoric of anti-Americanism, in both the American and the European varieties of the counter-culture.

But it was never the whole story. There was always a repressed pleasure principle in the most rabid anti-American intellectual, ready to indulge in the temptations of American culture. If American B-movies underwent a critical re-appraisal, it happened at the hands of young French film critics writing for the *Cahiers du Cinéma* in the late '50s and early '60s. If one of them, a documentary filmmaker, François Reichenbach, produced a critical film document on America — *L'Amérique insolite* — it was at the same time a document of the film maker's fascination, if not infatuation with that strange New World.

The demise of Marxism, the decline of that other infatuation of intellectuals, particularly in France, with the rigors of a rejectionist ideology, has allowed them more freely to indulge their fascination with American culture. It is interesting in this respect to follow the intellectual trajectory of a man like Jean Baudrillard, away from a critical position which was *de rigueur* in the late '60s, toward an unreserved infatuation with American life. If, to a visiting European intellectual, America still offers a shocking sense of alienation, he now appraises it as a fountain of youth, a sacred fount. To Baudrillard, Europe has now become mired in its heritage of intellectual rituals, caught in rigid conceptual frames, decadent, incapable of an unmediated, direct confrontation with reality. America, to him, offers the

236

liberation from that conceptual imprisonment. "What we lack is the inspiration and courage for what one might call the zero degree of culture, for the power of non-culture. ... We will always remain nostalgic utopians, torn between the ideal and our reluctance to realize it. We declare everything to be possible, while never proclaiming its realization. Precisely the latter is what America claims to have achieved." "It is us who think that everything culminates in its transcendence and that nothing exists without first having been thought through as concept. Not only do they (the Americans) hardly care for that at all, they rather see the relationship in reverse. They don't care to conceptualize reality, but to realize the concept and to implement the ideas."9

We cannot but hear old echoes resounding in this statement. Baudrillard, after all, is not the first to hold that America has had the audacity to implement what had been thought out and dreamed of in Europe. It has shed off the old Europe, burdened by history, caught up in unreal structures of thought. Thus, America could have become the authentic expression of modernity, while Europe, in Baudrillard's words, will never be more than its dubbed or subtitled version. But there is more to Baudrillard's argument than this. In a sense, he seems to return to the '60s, hankering for the libertarian rapture, the sense of instant gratification unmediated by the intellect, which to so many at the time was the appeal of the counter-culture. Much as he was on the Left himself, as an ideologue he had missed out on the excitement of the moment. It took the disenchantment of the French Left during the '70s, their sense of ideological bankruptcy, for Baudrillard to become susceptible to the lure of American culture.

And once again, before our eyes, a romance unfolds, a game of cultural adultery, which so many French intellectuals have indulged in. They have a keen eye for all that is banal and vulgar in America, yet at the same time more than anyone else they are tempted by the vital élan, the shameless authenticity of American culture. These romances always have one basic plot. It is always a case of a tired, elderly European turning towards America in the hope of regeneration, if not rejuvenation. America is unspoiled, primitive, youthful. It is unaware of itself. It is just there. It is Eden before the fall. Europeans have tasted the forbidden fruit — they are obsessed by knowledge and reflection — yet hope to lose themselves in America. Baudrillard is in a sense a twentieth century Crèvecoeur, reaffirming America's regenerative potential.

In Baudrillard's book, and similarly in Umberto Eco's *Travels in Hyperreality*, a remarkable twist is given to every argument in the book of so many critics of America mass culture. Where critics from Henry Adams on have deplored America's forsaking its historical spirituality, where they have seen the signs of a fall from grace precisely in the mindless entropy of consumerism, Baudrillard and Eco testify to a sense of exhilaration. Cities, traffic, highways, they are all as meaningless as America's deserts, but their impact is equally liberating. It is all utterly devoid of significance. It is just there, but in a rather complex way. Both Baudrillard and Eco speak of hyperreality. Reality has spawned its own replicas. Surrounded by phantom images of itself, one can no longer tell which is the real thing. America is just like Disneyland. Whether it is vulgar or sublime matters no longer. Those are European categories which one had better leave behind. One should undergo America as it presents itself, the only truly primitive society of our age, a utopia become reality.

Eco at one point refers to America as the Last Beach of European culture.[10] It will all still be there, when the real heritage will have crumbled to dust in its countries of origin. For America to fulfill this salvage mission, it has to treat Europe's culture in a highly modernist fashion, treating all of it as one large *objet trouvé*, recasting, duplicating, multiplying, cross-breeding, mass-marketing it. On the whole, Eco's tone and choice of words is slightly more critical, quoting Louis Marin on Disneyland as degenerate utopia. In this world of the Fake, "what is falsified is our will to buy, which we take as real, and in this sense Disneyland is really the quintessence of consumer ideology." Baudrillard is well beyond such criticism and seems to revel in alienation. Freely floating through America's universe, an escapee from European gravity, he offers a reader's guide to America's phantom images. With great metaphorical virtuosity he moves from image to image. At one point he calls America "a special effect". It leaves the reader slightly puzzled. Who is behind the effect? The French book cover doesn't help. It gives us two names: "Amérique" and "Jean Baudrillard." Is it Baudrillard who allows us to perceive America in its many phantom images, or is it the other way around? I tend toward the latter option. America becomes one wide projection screen for Baudrillard's fantasies of self-liberation. In one ongoing stream of aphoristic, often highly imaginative, but totally noncommittal snippets, he takes us on his psychological journey. But strangely, he still seems entrapped in habits he tells us to believe he has quit. With all his metaphors and associations he is still busy weaving America into an argument and a structure of concepts. He is still quintessentially the European, involving America into a world of preoccupations that are typically those of a European intellectual. Enjoying life "on the surface," sucked along in the slipstream of American life, Baudrillard too testifies to the European sense, expressed by Huizinga and others, that "we have something that you lack." But the point that Baudrillard belabors to argue is precisely that Europeans cannot be too sure they should cherish that "something."

238

References

1. Menno Ter Braak, "Waarom ik 'Amerika' afwijs", *De Vrije Bladen*, V, 3, 1928; repr. in: *Verzameld Werk*, I, pp. 255-65.
2. Johan Huizinga, *Amerika levend en denkend — Losse opmerkingen*. Haarlem: H.D. Tjeenk Willink & Zoon, 1926; p. 162. The translation is by Herbert H. Rowen; cf. Johan Huizinga, *America: A Dutch Historian's Vision, From Afar and Near,* New York: Harper and Row, 1972, p. 312.
3. *The Seven Arts,* June 1917, pp. 199 ff.
4. *The Seven Arts,* March 1917, pp. 535 ff.
5. Lewis Mumford, "The Metropolitan Milieu", in: Waldo Frank a.o., eds., *America & Alfred Stieglitz: A Collective Portrait,* (1934), Millerton, N.Y.: Aperture, Inc. 1975, p. 32.
6. Oswald Spengler, *Jahre der Entscheidung.* München: Beck, 1933; p.48.
7. Marnix Gijzen, *Ontdek Amerika* (Discover America), Brussels: Standaard Boekhandel, 1927; pp. 8,9.
8. Simone de Beauvoir, *L'Amérique au jour le jour.* Paris: Gallimard, 1954; p. 27.
9. Jean Baudrillard, *Amérique.* Paris: Grasset, 1986.
10. Umberto Eco, *Travels in Hyperreality.* London: Picador, 1987; pp. 37, 43.